KU-266-233

TIME-LIMITED DYNAMIC
PSYCHOTHERAPY

TIME-LIMITED DYNAMIC PSYCHOTHERAPY

A Guide to Clinical Practice

HANNA LEVENSON

BASIC BOOKS

A Member of The Perseus Books Group

Copyright © 1995 by Hanna Levenson.
Published by Basic Books, A Member of the Perseus Books Group

All rights reserved. Printed in the United States of America. No part of this book may be reproduced in any manner whatsoever without written permission except in the case of brief quotations embodied in critical articles and reviews. For information, address Basic Books, 387 Park Avenue South, New York, NY 10016-8810.

Library of Congress Cataloging-in-Publication Data
Levenson, Hanna, 1945–
    Time-limited dynamic psychotherapy : a guide to clinical practice / Hanna Levenson.
        p. cm.
    Includes bibliographical references and index.
    ISBN-10: 0-465-08651-9   ISBN-13: 978-0-465-08651-1
    1. Brief psychotherapy. 2. Psychodynamic psychotherapy. 3. Brief psychotherapy—Case studies. 4. Psychodynamic psychotherapy—Case studies. I. Title.
    [DNLM: 1. Psychotherapy, Brief—methods. WM 420.5.P5 L657E 1995]
    RC480.55.L48 1995
    616.89′ 14—dc20
    DNLM/DLC
    for Library of Congress   95-13934
                                                                            CIP

LEEDS METROPOLITAN
UNIVERSITY
LIBRARY
1705403610
HI-D
CC- 111141
14. 4. 10
616· 8914 LEV

To Shirley and Lou, my parents, with love
F.U.D.

Contents

Foreword

BRIEF, SHORT-TERM, or time-limited psychotherapy is rapidly becoming the wave of the future. There are several major reasons for this development: First and foremost are the rising health care costs that have prompted the cries for "containment." Second, as a result of numerous empirical studies that have demonstrated the utility of psychotherapy as a treatment modality, a growing number of people are availing themselves of the services provided by the major mental health professions (psychiatry, clinical psychology, and psychiatric social work). Third, consumers are increasingly relying on third-party payers, primarily insurance companies and the government, to finance at least part of the cost of psychotherapy. Fourth, the number of therapists, primarily in clinical psychology and psychiatric social work, has steadily grown in recent years. These factors, among others, have helped lessen the stigma of being labeled a "psychiatric patient."

There can no longer be any serious doubt that, in an important sense, the "safety and efficacy" of psychotherapy have been demonstrated, although considerable controversy persists concerning the effectiveness of particular forms of psychotherapy for specific conditions, its value in relation to psychopharmacology, and the extent to which insurance companies and, more recently, managed care companies are willing to foot the bill for these treatments that have yet to be standardized or stringently defined. In short, Freud's prophecy that modified forms of psychoanalysis would spread and become widely available has come true, although many forms of psychotherapy practiced today have only a remote resemblance to orthodox psychoanalysis. Psychoanalysis itself has undergone a steady decline and has been replaced by a wide array of different forms of psychotherapy.

Gone, too, are the days when a course of psychotherapy of whatever kind might take many months or even years. The search for shorter forms of psychological treatment has been gathering momentum. Most of these treatments are provided on an outpatient basis, and are often complemented by psychoactive drugs. One telling example is the contemporary treatment of various forms of depression in which psychotherapy is typically combined with antidepressant medications. Then, too, the expectations of patients as well as those of therapists have become sharply curtailed; the search for "radical cures" has given way to much less ambitious interventions. The goal is no longer the greatest amount of change, no matter the therapy's cost and length, but rather the greatest amount of change that can be achieved relative to the available resources. All interested parties—consumers, therapists, third-party payers—have become thoroughly pragmatic.

After some modest attempts to shorten psychoanalysis in the early 1920s, the short-term field lay fallow until Franz Alexander and Theodore French (1946) did important pioneering work, which, however, was generally met with hostility and rejection by the psychoanalytic establishment. Beginning in the 1960s, Michael Balint and David Malan, among others, made serious efforts to develop forms of time-limited therapy based on psychodynamic principles. These attempts grew impressively in the following decades, which also saw the emergence of cognitive–behavioral methods which, together with psychodynamic psychotherapy, account for the bulk of short-term therapies being practiced today.

Coupled with the introduction of short-term or time-limited treatment was the development of so-called treatment manuals, treatises that describe in more or less specific terms the treatment methods guiding practitioners in their work. Prominent examples of treatment manuals are the books by Gerald Klerman and associates (1984), Lester Luborsky (1984), and myself and Jeffrey Binder (1984). Existing manuals, however, are still insufficiently specific, detailed, and comprehensive. Furthermore, the vast majority of therapists who began to practice short-term or time-limited forms of psychotherapy had received no specific training in these modalities. This present volume is a significant step toward overcoming that deficiency.

Dr. Hanna Levenson, a thoroughly trained and highly experienced psychotherapist in the psychodynamic and interpersonal tradition, has for 15 years devoted intensive effort to the training of young therapists (notably psychiatric residents and graduate students in clinical psychology). In addition, she has considerable experience consulting with seasoned clinicians seeking to enhance their brief-therapy skills; therefore, she understands where students at all professional levels get stuck.

Following the approach presented by Strupp and Binder (1984), Dr. Levenson has developed her own training program, which is set forth and well illustrated in this book. She starts with the realization that time-limited dynamic psychotherapy is not an abbreviated form of open-ended therapy; rather, it has its own requirements and makes considerable demands on the learner. Her approach is clear, concise, and thoroughly down-to-earth; yet it is highly sensitive and sophisticated.

In particular, the learner becomes an active participant who is presented with clinical material taken from videotapes of actual therapeutic sessions. The professional literature has offered very few examples of specific patient–therapist interactions, although as the field has come to realize, they are absolutely essential in the learning process. Students, to be sure, must acquire a knowledge base of therapeutic principles but, even more important, they must become active participants in the difficult tasks facing the practicing therapist in every therapeutic session. In Dr. Levenson's book the rich clinical material provides a "how to do it" focus and creates a bridge from the theory to the reality of practice. Furthermore, Dr. Levenson provides the reader with transcripts of supervisor–trainee discussions of the clinical cases. The result is a vast improvement over the typical text on supervision, in which the trainee is presented only with summaries of therapeutic transactions.

Dr. Levenson emerges as a master teacher who challenges her seminar students as well as the readers of this book to deal more effectively and creatively with the obstacles with which every therapist is familiar. In the final analysis, of course, psychotherapeutic skills cannot be solely acquired from a book; the student must learn to cope with highly specific practical situations that must be taught and mastered *in vivo*. Dr. Levenson's book places the student *in vivo* and thus contributes materially to the enhancement of the reader's theoretical and practical understanding. I venture to predict that the book will be a major contribution to the continuing effort to master the art of time-limited dynamic psychotherapy.

—Hans H. Strupp, Ph.D.
Distinguished Professor of Psychology, Emeritus
Vanderbilt University

Acknowledgments

FIRST AND FOREMOST I wish to express my gratitude to the hundreds of patients who allowed their sessions to be videotaped and studied for teaching and training purposes. The strength and spirit of these patients in the face of sometimes seemingly overwhelming obstacles were a constant inspiration to me.

My work with over 300 students during the past 15 years forms the foundation and direction of this book. I wish I could name them all. With their collaborative and earnest feedback in didactic and case seminars, I learned what I was teaching and how to do it better. These students impressed me with their willingness to share their struggles with understanding the process of human interaction and change. Their enthusiasm and growth reciprocally and dynamically expanded my own. Special thanks go to the following trainees for feedback on specific sections of the book: Ed Bein, Vera Dujovne, Lisa Kuhlman, Avvy Mar, Jeremy Ogel, Don Schwarcz, Laura Seitel, Jonne Van Meer, Dan Wolverton, and Sharon Wood, and to students in Julia Shiang's psychotherapy class at the Pacific Graduate School of Psychology for their critiques of earlier versions.

My sincere appreciation goes to my former trainees, now colleagues, who worked closely with me in the early years of the Brief Therapy Training Program at the California Pacific Medical Center and VA Medical Centers in San Francisco and Palo Alto: Anita Barzman, Jeanne Burns, Kay Bolter, Denise Capra-Young, Michael Dressler, Rick Ferm, Darrah Garvin, Nancy Glenn, and Pamela Reaves.

Ten years ago, stimulated by the work of Hans Strupp and his psychotherapy research team, I invited myself to visit Vanderbilt University in Nashville, where the second phase of their NIMH study on training in time-limited dynamic psychotherapy was under way. Since then, the influence of the ideas and personal support of Hans

Strupp, Jeffrey Binder, Stephen Butler, and William Henry have been immeasurable. In particular, Dr. Strupp's work on the role of the therapist's contribution to the treatment process has greatly influenced my own thinking. I also wish to express my appreciation to the research team for permission to include the Vanderbilt Therapeutic Strategies Scale and its manual in the appendixes.

I am indebted to those colleagues who read portions of the book in process and provided invaluable feedback and sustaining encouragement: Linda Alperstein, Avis Begoun, Jeffrey Binder, Kathryn DeWitt, Bram Fridhandler, Marc Jacobs, Stanley Messer, Jacqueline Persons, Judy Pickles, Saul Rosenberg, Julia Shiang, David Silven, Susan Steinberg, Mark Zaslav, and Joan Zweben.

Special thanks go to Jackie Persons, who, after repeatedly listening to my reasons for not having the time to write this book, responded with "Just do it!"

I also would like to acknowledge my various "bosses" who were graciously tolerant of my need to devote time to this project: Jacqueline Becker, Robert Hales, Russell Lemle, and Gene Zukowsky.

I am appreciative of Jo Ann Miller, senior editor at Basic Books, for her enthusiastic interest in publishing this book, and Stephen Francoeur for his enduring efforts in making it happen.

Writing this book would not have been possible without the understanding and support of my family. Larry's unflagging enthusiasm nourished me during the years this project took; Zachary and Adam good-naturedly accepted my unavailability more times than I would like to admit and graciously did not ask "Is it done yet?"; and Moe, our dog, provided loyal companionship at my feet during many long hours at the computer.

TIME-LIMITED DYNAMIC
PSYCHOTHERAPY

CHAPTER 1

Introduction

WHEN I BEGIN teaching my seminars in time-limited dynamic psychotherapy, my first question to the participants is, "Why have you decided to take this training?" (The parallel question for the reader would be, "Why are you interested in reading this book?") The most common response is that they feel ill prepared to work in situations where short-term treatments are required. This concern is heightened for many of them who are already working in such settings. In addition, many with psychodynamic training doubt that it is possible to do therapy that is both brief and deep. They are loath to abandon their conceptual framework and clinical wisdom in order to adapt to economic necessity.

Some decide to attend because they specifically want to learn how to work with difficult clients in a brief therapy. Therapists who have even limited experience are well acquainted with patients such as these: patients who are so infuriating, you feel like strangling them; who are so threatening, you are relieved when they do not show up for a session; who are so confusing, you become disoriented; who are so boring, you become impatient; who are so overwhelming, you feel inept; who are so passive, you want to shake them into action; who are so amusing, you let yourself be entertained; who are so appreciative, you bask in their admiration. How are we to treat these patients in a time-effective manner?

Some participants decide to take the brief-therapy training because of its focus on formulation: how to formulate quickly and explicitly, and how to use the formulation as a blueprint for the entire therapy.

And still others attend to learn from the videotapes I show of actual therapy sessions. They are interested in delving into rich clinical material which provides a "how to do it" focus and creates a bridge from the theory to the reality of practice. Videotape provides a vivid account of what actually occurs in therapy, unlike a therapist's summary, which often glosses over critical details and portrays the therapy as more coherent and cogent than it ever was. In addition, the realistic context provided by videotape can be used to facilitate an active wrestling with relevant material, which counteracts the negative effects of inert knowledge (Schacht, 1991).

The goal of this book is to present a well-established model of brief psychodynamic psychotherapy—time-limited dynamic psychotherapy (TLDP; Strupp & Binder, 1984)—which I have found particularly useful in treating difficult patients. My plan is to combine ample didactic material with actual clinical cases to permit the reader to try out components of TLDP with patients tomorrow.

TLDP grew out of an empirically based approach designed to foster helpful formulations and appropriate interventions. Furthermore, TLDP is "user-friendly"; it is readily accessible to therapists because it relies on observable data of clinical relevance and is flexible enough that therapists can adapt it to their own therapeutic style. While the framework of TLDP is psychodynamic, it incorporates current developments in interpersonal, object-relations, and self-psychology theories, as well as cognitive–behavioral and systems approaches.

This book is an outgrowth of my years teaching clinicians to use the rationale and strategies of TLDP. It is intended as a guide to clinical practice for experienced professionals who are expanding their repertoires into briefer forms of intervention; for recently licensed therapists; and for professionals-in-training such as graduate students, psychiatric residents, or psychology or social work interns. The goal is to provide practical assistance to therapists who wish to be more efficient and effective with hard-to-treat patients.

My approach is active, experiential, and integrative—something like driver training. When we learned to drive we had to get behind the wheel, with a licensed driver/teacher (ideally, an empathic, experienced one) next to us. We could not be given the right way to do things at all times (e.g., turn a corner, brake, park), because each situation was different depending on its context (e.g., road conditions, speed, type of vehicle). Since it is impossible to anticipate each and every situation a driver will encounter, what must be taught is a generalized approach to recognizing, evaluating, and performing competently behind the wheel. Ultimately we learn from our experience in the driver's seat. I do not mean to deny the "psychotherapy as art" aspects of clinical work by comparing it to driver's education, nor do I wish to demean the human interactive aspects by alluding to skills operated on an inanimate machine. Rather, I believe that doing psychotherapy successfully means experientially and contextually integrating a set of skills, any one of which by itself is relatively meaningless, and making decisions about when and how to use these skills, in order to get to a destination.

When I teach, I encourage trainees to get in the driver's seat. My preferred format for training is to present videotapes of actual therapy sessions to small groups of trainees* over an extended period of time (usually 6 months). The trainees in these seminars are asked, as they watch videotapes of these sessions in a stop-frame approach, to say what is going on in the vignettes, to distinguish between relevant and irrelevant material, to propose interventions the therapist might use, to justify their choices, and to anticipate the moment-to-moment behavior of the patients. Trainees are expected to take the wheel and begin navigating the clinical terrain. The more experienced of them are able to perceive the surroundings and appreciate the power and responsiveness of the vehicle. The neophyte tries to stay on the road and avoid a major accident. The learning approach I am advocating is consistent with the teaching format of "anchored instruction" where the knowledge to be learned is specifically tied to a particular problem using active involvement of the learner in a context that is highly similar to actual conditions (Binder, 1993; Bransford, Franks, Vye, & Sherwood, 1989; Schacht, 1991).

THE PLAN OF THE BOOK

The format of this book parallels these training seminars. The following chapters contain actual dialogues between the trainees and myself as we attempt to deal with the videotaped clinical cases. Although the classroom vignettes are composites, the questions and issues the trainees bring up in these chapters are real questions and issues that actual trainees in seminars were finding problematic. These interchanges are presented in transcript form, with the *ums* and *ahs* omitted for ease of reading.

Many clinical books and courses present material linearly and didactically in isolation (e.g., separate chapters on interpretation, resistance, therapeutic alliance). In clinical practice, however, everything seems to happen at once (because it usually does). The student driver must deal with braking, steering, and accelerating all in the same first lesson, because each skill intricately and integrally depends on the others. Therefore, the issues that are covered in any one chapter are not artificially broken down into discrete topics. Rather, they are dealt with based on the trainees' concern with clinically relevant material as it emerges in a particular session. Nonetheless, this book

---

*In this book I will use the word *trainee* when I am referring to anyone who is learning to apply briefer forms of intervention regardless of his or her clinical experience.

was intended to be read in sequence. The material presented builds on the learner's knowledge, much as one learns to steer the car before one learns how to parallel park.

The clinical cases discussed in the chapters are based on actual patients treated by myself or trainees. Verbatim transcripts from videotaped sessions are presented, with the exception of adding or deleting specific material to protect the patients' identities. At any one time, the reader can identify with the students in the seminar, the therapists or patients on videotape, and/or the teacher in the classroom, depending on one's experience, expertise, and/or inclination.

I believe the goals of professional training are similar to the goals of therapy: to have people actively make discoveries and find solutions of relevance to them in a collaborative, supportive, and challenging atmosphere. I try to do this in my classes, and I've tried to do the same in this book.

In chapter 2, I delineate the qualities that define brief dynamic psychotherapy and review some of the literature on training in short-term psychotherapy, the relationship between the duration of therapy and outcome, and therapist values and attitudes toward brief therapy. The purpose of this chapter is to provide a context for the more TLDP-specific material to follow.

In chapter 3, I outline the basic premises and goals of TLDP, setting the stage for the clinical/teaching vignettes comprising the remainder of the book.

Chapter 4 shows how I help the trainees develop a dynamic focus from material presented in an initial session with a very unfocused, externalizing patient, Ms. Ludlow.

Chapter 5 deals with how the trainees assess Ms. Ludlow's suitability for TLDP. It also explores the manner in which both Ms. Ludlow and her therapist, Dr. Ellison, reenact a cyclical maladaptive pattern.

Chapter 6 examines the ramifications of Dr. Ellison's countertransferential reactions to her demanding patient.

In chapter 7, I explore with the trainees those qualities of the therapist and the therapeutic interaction that promote a beneficial therapeutic process. Dr. David's approach with a well-defended and distancing patient serves to illustrate.

Chapters 8 through 12 cover the areas of TLDP technique with a resistant, depressed, somatically preoccupied elderly man. The trainees learn how to use the dynamic focus as a blueprint for the entire therapy as they follow my work with the patient from the opening minutes of the first session through the last minutes of the last session.

The last chapter, chapter 13, presents a model of TLDP treatment for any type of specific presenting problem when those symptoms are superimposed on an underlying dysfunctional personality style. Two patients with medical problems are presented, one infected with HIV and the other chronically incapacitated by diabetes.

The appendixes contain the Vanderbilt Therapeutic Strategies Scale and accompanying manual. These can be used for assessing the degree to which a therapist is adhering to TLDP principles and strategies as outlined in this book, and as such are an additional learning tool for the reader.

CHAPTER 2

General Issues in Brief Dynamic Psychotherapy

EVERYONE DOES "BRIEF" THERAPY

A T THE OUTSET of my seminars in time-limited dynamic psychotherapy, after I ask the participants why they have decided to take such training, I inquire how many of them do brief therapy, either in private practice or in an agency or institutional setting. After a show of hands, I confess it is a trick question: They all do brief therapy whether they intend to or not.

The reason is that most patients choose to stay in therapy only a short time. A number of studies with a variety of patients, across a range of settings with diverse agendas, have established that regardless of the type of outpatient treatment, the great majority of patients are seen for only 6 to 12 sessions (Garfield, 1989; Phillips, 1987; Reder & Tyson, 1980; Straker, 1968). In fact, theoretical attrition curves predict (Phillips, 1985) and empirical evidence confirms (Rau, 1989) that 60% to 75% of all outpatients drop out of treatment before the eighth session. These findings hold even for psychodynamic treatments that are intended to be long-term (Pekarik & Wierzbicki, 1986). These consumer-defined brief therapies, or what Steven Stern (1993) calls "naturally occurring brief therapies," are quite different from therapies that are planned from the start to make the most of limited time. Brief therapy *by default*, which has been the norm, can be contrasted with brief therapy *by design* (Budman & Gurman, 1988).

Gene Pekarik and Michael Wierzbicki (1986) found that clients at a non-profit mental health clinic expected to come for a relatively few therapy sessions (approximately half said five or fewer sessions), and in fact, these patients' expectations predicted their actual attendance patterns. The therapists, on the other hand, preferred to see the patients for a longer period of time.

The attendance curve in figure 2.1 graphically shows the dramatic drop in the number of patients from the second to the eighth session. This means that most mental health professionals are conducting therapies that are quite abbreviated—however unintentionally. We tend to forget that long before third-party payers began setting limits on treatment, patients themselves did.

These statistics illustrate that an extremely large number of people seek brief interventions. In figure 2.1, the attendance curve is almost a mirror of the improvement curve, the rate at which patients benefit from treatment (Howard, Kopta, Krause, & Orlinsky, 1986). In combination, the two curves suggest that patients are choosing to leave therapy during the time they are experiencing the greatest rate of clinical improvement.

People who are coming for therapy are in emotional pain and they want to have this pain alleviated as soon as possible. Most of them are not fascinated by their psyches, nor are they pursuing mental health perfection. Sometimes patients experience their needs for immediate relief as being at

Figure 2.1

Improvement and attendance curves as a function of the number of sessions

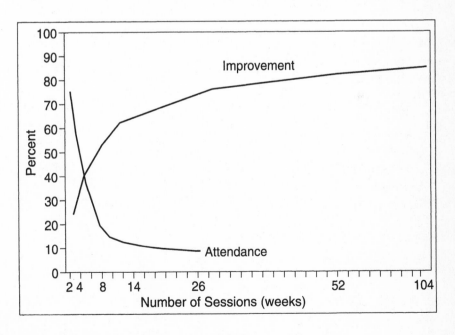

(From MacKenzie, 1991; reprinted by permission.)

variance with their therapists' goals for "problem resolution." Oftentimes, too, patients in open-ended therapies feel that they lose a sense of purpose or goal. "Where are we going?" is a frequently asked question. Some intriguing evidence suggests that offering patients time-limited but focused therapies can actually decrease the dropout rate.

William Sledge and colleagues (1990) found that "premature terminations" at a large, urban, university-affiliated community mental health center were dramatically reduced when patients were seen in time-limited therapy. Patients who received 12 sessions had approximately half the dropout rate of those receiving therapy expected to last 3 to 4 months or an unspecified duration. These findings could not be accounted for by patient demographic or diagnostic variables or by therapist characteristics. The authors proposed that having a specific ending date could have reduced patients' fears about dependency and tendencies to enact conflicts about termination. When patients have a structure of a beginning, middle, and end of the therapy, they may be more willing to complete the treatment. In addition, the investigators recognized that the clear focus in the time-limited therapy, the greater therapist activity, and the emphasis on a positive therapeutic alliance could have also contributed to the dramatically lower dropout rate. These are some of the qualities that have been used to describe planned brief dynamic therapy in general. The next section will examine these parameters in more detail.

QUALITIES THAT DEFINE BRIEF DYNAMIC PSYCHOTHERAPY

In a content analysis of books and articles addressing essential features that distinguish brief therapy from other types of therapy (Levenson & Butler, 1994), I found a number of fundamental qualities repeatedly mentioned in the literature. These qualities can be organized into two main categories: those relevant to the brief features per se, and those germane to the psychodynamic aspects. Below these qualities are rank-ordered (within each category) in terms of the frequency with which they are mentioned in publications. These characteristics provide a consensual, operational definition of short-term dynamic psychotherapy.

Brief Qualities
    Limited focus (and limited goals)
    Limited time
    Selection criteria
    Therapist activity

Therapeutic alliance
Rapid assessment/prompt intervention
Planned termination
Optimism
Contract
Psychodynamic Qualities
  Analytic concepts
  Analytic techniques

(Levenson & Butler, 1994; reprinted by permission.)

LIMITED THERAPEUTIC FOCUS

The major quality distinguishing brief dynamic psychotherapy approaches from long-term, open-ended psychotherapy or psychoanalysis is the limited focus of treatment. All brief therapies need a central theme, topic, or problem to keep the therapist on target—a necessity when time is of the essence. As Yogi Berra once said, "If you don't know where you're going, you will wind up somewhere else."

Of the various ways of conceiving a focus in brief dynamic therapy, the more popular ones include the core conflictual relationship theme (Luborsky, 1984; Luborsky & Crits-Christoph, 1990); role–relationship models (M. Horowitz, 1988); unresolved Oedipal conflicts (Sifneos, 1979/1987); plan formulation method (Weiss, 1993; Weiss, Sampson, & the Mount Zion Psychotherapy Research Group, 1986); individuation/separation (Mann, 1973); and the topic of this book, the cyclical maladaptive pattern (Strupp & Binder, 1984).

The therapeutic theme serves as a compass to prevent therapists from being dashed on the rocks of superficiality or going adrift in a sea of diffuseness. In keeping with the nautical metaphor, "the psychodynamic understanding of a patient serves as a stabilizing force in conducting any form of therapy; its general effect is conservative, discouraging a change in tack with every slight shift in the wind" (Perry, Cooper, & Michels, 1987, p. 543). Both the therapist and the patient need to embrace the idea of a restricted range in order to work briefly. This idea may be difficult for both parties if they have problems accepting limitations (Bauer & Kobos, 1987).

The use of rather explicit methodologies for generating central themes is a major thrust of modern formulation technique in brief psychotherapy. The development of more formalized, systematic methods for defining therapeutic foci initially grew out of researchers' needs to define concepts more reliably and teachers' needs to train therapists more effectively. Now there is increasing evidence that therapies have better outcomes when clinicians make use of such methods to inform their technique (see Crits-Christoph, Cooper, & Luborsky, 1988; Hartmann, 1994; Silberschatz, Fetter, & Curtis, 1986).

TIME LIMITS AND TIME MANAGEMENT

Time seems like the obvious variable that defines brief therapy. Given the influence of managed care, one can take the jaded and inaccurate position that limits on therapeutic time are driven only by administrative and economic concerns. Conceptually, however, the rationing of time can be used to accelerate or influence the therapeutic work, either by heightening the existential issues, by instilling hope, or by encouraging therapist activity and adherence to a focus. Pragmatically, it also makes use of the fact that most patients themselves choose to remain in therapy for only a brief period of time.

Traditionally, 25 sessions has been taken as the upper limit of brief dynamic therapy (Koss & Shiang, 1994), but the range may be as few as 1 (e.g., Bloom, 1992; Talmon, 1990) or as many as 40 (Sifneos, 1979/1987). Many health maintenance organizations (HMOs) have a limit of 20 sessions per year (with the actual number often closer to six); other plans and institutions impose various time limits, with most falling between 6 and 20 visits.

Recently, however, researchers, theoreticians, and clinicians have been moving away from a simplistic conceptualization of brief therapy merely in terms of the number of sessions. Instead, they are emphasizing time-attentive models (Burlingame & Fuhriman, 1987), which address how to make every session count regardless of the duration of treatment. With this more sophisticated approach, the emphasis is on the therapist's and patient's *time-limited attitude* (Binder, Henry, & Strupp, 1987), and terms such as *time-effective, time-sensitive* (Budman & Gurman, 1988), and *cost-effective* seem more appropriate.

SELECTION CRITERIA

The topic of selection criteria is perhaps the most controversial one in the field of brief psychodynamic psychotherapy. Probably we can point the finger at Freud for having started this debate when he suggested that treatment might be shortened for the healthier patient (Freud, 1904/1953). Working from this idea, early brief therapists (Davanloo, 1978, 1980; Malan, 1963, 1976, 1979; Mann, 1973; Sifneos, 1972, 1979/1987) developed stringent patient-selection criteria in order to identify those patients with the presumed potential to benefit from briefer treatments—those with the highest levels of ego strength, motivation, and object relatedness.

How have these selection criteria held up? First, it has been easier to acknowledge the relevance of such abstract concepts as ego strength than it has been to measure them (Binder et al., 1987). Second, performance-based approaches in early sessions (e.g., assessment of a patient's ability to engage in the psychotherapy process) have been only weakly predictive of therapeutic outcome in brief dynamic psychotherapy (Binder et al., 1987; Thackrey, Butler, & Strupp, 1985). While there is much agreement that patients with severe personality disorders are less likely to benefit from brief psychodynamic therapy than those without personality disorders (Pilkonis & Frank, 1988; Shea, Widiger, & Klein, 1992), it does appear that even these more disturbed patients can profit from brief therapy (see Bein, Levenson, & Overstreet, 1994; Thompson, Gallagher, & Czirr, 1988). Furthermore, such factors as acute onset, good premorbid adjustment, the ability to relate, a circumscribed problem, high desire for change, higher socioeconomic class, current crises, or other such patient variables have not been found to be uniquely predictive of outcome in brief therapy any more than they are in open-ended therapy (Lambert, 1983). It seems that a good patient is a good patient, regardless of the length of the therapy.

Therefore, the position of some teachers, researchers, and practitioners has been to use patient factors to inform the therapist as to how supportive or exploratory his or her interventions can be, rather than as a red light–green light indicator of suitability for brief therapy. This point of view is illustrated by the following conclusions from various brief therapists: "Virtually any psychotherapy with virtually any patient can benefit from a 'time-limited attitude' on the part of the therapist" (Levenson & Butler, 1994, p. 1018). "The best strategy, in my opinion, is to assume that every patient, irrespective of diagnosis, will respond to short-term treatment unless he proves himself refractory to it" (Wolberg, 1965, p. 140). "Although at this point we would like to list contraindications for brief therapy, it is not possible to do so. On the surface, many patients who seem to be poor brief therapy prospects may, with an appropriate patient–therapist match or with the correct brief modality, do extremely well in short-term treatment" (Budman & Gurman, 1988, pp. 24–25).

LEEDS METROPOLITAN UNIVERSITY LIBRARY

THERAPIST ACTIVITY

Many writers on brief therapy emphasize the need for the therapist to be active in the treatment. However, this does not imply that a certain quality and quantity of input from the therapist are required. The therapist should use only as much activity as is necessary to maintain the focus within the specified period of time. Many clinicians learning brief therapy mistakenly confuse therapist activity with confrontation, advice-giving, or directiveness, and this misunderstanding can result in unintended and adverse outcomes (Henry, Strupp, Butler, Schacht, & Binder, 1993b).

MODIFICATION OF PSYCHOANALYTIC CONCEPTS AND TECHNIQUES

Brief dynamic psychotherapy is founded on major psychoanalytic concepts such as the importance of childhood experiences and development; unconscious determinants of behavior; the role of conflicts; transference; the patient's resistance to the therapeutic work; and repetitive behavior. Many brief dynamic therapists, however, do not see the need to use highly inferential concepts (e.g., the Oedipus complex) or elaborate metapsychological models with unclear behavioral referents.

A striking modification of psychoanalytic technique for the brief therapist is the avoidance of patient regression and dependency. Instead, the therapist emphasizes the patient's strengths and keeps the therapeutic process more reality-based.

Another major modification of psychoanalytic technique involves the brief therapist's relative lack of interest in gathering genetic material for the sake of a "complete history." In brief dynamic psychotherapies, the therapist concentrates more on the here-and-now relationship between therapist and patient, and is more willing to make interventions based on incomplete information.

TRAINING IN BRIEF DYNAMIC PSYCHOTHERAPY

At my workshops on brief therapy, clinicians in the audience invariably come up to me to say that they had received little or no training in brief therapy theories and techniques and are now working in an HMO or other setting where short-term treatments are expected. These "confessions" have come from recent graduates as well as seasoned professionals, and from mental health practitioners of all disciplines (e.g., social work, psychology, psychiatry, nursing).

Despite its importance, training in brief therapy is far less researched and understood than brief-therapy techniques and outcome. Attempts to teach brief therapy as a form of psychotherapy have been limited (Schneider & Pinkerton, 1986). An early survey of psychiatric residency programs discovered that most programs combine brief-therapy training along with other training experiences (e.g., crisis intervention) rather than offering a specialized block rotation in brief psychotherapy (Clarkin, Frances, Taintor, & Warburg, 1980).

My colleagues and I have done two surveys documenting the extent and type of training in brief psychotherapy. In the first, we sent a questionnaire to 1,500 licensed psychologists in California and Massachusetts requesting information about their experience, training, and self-assessed skill in brief therapy (Levenson, Speed, & Budman, 1995). With a 58% return rate, findings indicated that 82% of the respondents were doing some amount of planned brief therapy (defined as therapy limited in focus or time—usually 10 to 20 sessions). In fact, 40% of their clinical time was spent doing brief work.

In the second survey, Donna Davidovitz (1995; Levenson & Davidovitz, 1995) broadened the scope. She conducted a national study of 3,600 psychologists, psychiatrists, and social workers. With a 57% response rate, she found that almost all clinicians in the three disciplines reported doing some planned brief therapy (89%, 77%, 84%, respectively), devoting 40% of their clinical time to it. Psychologists rated themselves as significantly more experienced and skilled in briefer interventions than psychiatrists or social workers, but they did not find it more professionally satisfying than the other two professional groups did. Interestingly, males were more involved in doing brief work (43% of their time) than females (38% of their time), and the location where the therapist practiced also had an effect. Therapists in metropolitan settings spent the least percentage of their time conducting brief therapy (37%) as compared to those in nonmetropolitan (44%) or rural (46%) locales.

It seems quite clear that a great deal of brief therapy is being done. But what training do those practicing brief therapy have? A disturbing but not unexpected finding was that one-third of those presently doing brief therapy reported that they had received little or no training in brief therapy theory or techniques (Levenson et al., 1995).

In order to assess whether brief-therapy training had increased over time in academic settings, the relationship between the therapists' years in practice and completion of brief-therapy courses was examined. Our two-state survey conducted in 1990 found that those psychologists who had recently graduated had not been exposed to more academic courses than their colleagues who had received their degrees 20 years earlier (Levenson et al., 1995).

Our national survey completed in 1994 showed that while there was a general increase over a 30-year period in the number of clinicians who had taken courses in brief therapy (from 51% to 68%), within the last decade there had not been such an increase for psychiatrists and psychologists (Levenson & Davidovitz, 1995). In fact, proportionally fewer psychologists who graduated from 1988 to 1994 have had brief-therapy courses as compared to those graduating between 1981 and 1987 (54% vs. 63%). This finding raises the question of whether training programs are really beginning to address the need of students to become more skilled and knowledgeable in time-sensitive theories and techniques. It is clear that graduate schools and residency/internship programs must encourage such training and accelerate their offerings if they are to meet the rapidly rising need for skilled brief therapists.

With many therapists working in managed care settings (estimates range from 40% to 70%), it seems logical that managed care organizations take some responsibility for providing brief-therapy training for their employees. However, such organizations generally view training as an expensive extravagance (Budman & Armstrong, 1992).

As we expected the survey of psychologists to show, the psychodynamically oriented therapists had received significantly less training in brief therapy than their colleagues with cognitive–behavioral or systems orientations. Nevertheless, since psychodynamically trained therapists comprised such a large proportion of practitioners (40% of the respondents), they were responsible for almost one-fourth of all the brief therapy being conducted.

These findings are alarming from a consumer perspective. It is now widely accepted that brief therapy is not dehydrated long-term therapy (Cummings, 1986) or just less of the same (Peake, Bordin, & Archer, 1988), but rather requires specialized training in its own methodology (Bauer & Kobos, 1987; Budman & Stone, 1983; Levenson & Butler, 1994). Therapists who are trained in brief therapy and follow specified methods have better outcomes than those who do not (Burlingame, Fuhriman, Paul, & Ogles, 1989; O'Malley et al., 1988; Rounsaville, O'Malley, Foley, & Weissman, 1988); and trained clinicians feel that they are better skilled in brief therapy than their untrained counterparts (Levenson et al., 1995). Yet it seems apparent that a major discrepancy exists between the provision of brief-therapy training and the need for professionals who are prepared to effectively use time-efficient methods.

THERAPY DURATION AND OUTCOME

Is outcome in therapy related to the amount of therapy? Looking at a sample of psychotherapy patients in long-term treatment, Kenneth Howard and his colleagues (1986) found that the more sessions the patients had, the greater was their chance of improvement. However, figure 2.2 shows that the plots of the actual percentage of patients who benefited as a function of length of therapy are negatively accelerated. Patients made the most gains early on, with diminishing returns (per unit of additional therapy) later in treatment.

These findings make intuitive sense to any clinician. Distressed patients coming for help seem to regroup quickly and feel much better (more hope, fewer symptoms) shortly after beginning treatment, but the gains achieved between the 56th and 58th sessions, for example, would be far less dramatic—even imperceptible.

Howard et al. (1986) also examined the outcomes of other research studies concerning improvement as a function of time in therapy. By combining data

Figure 2.2
Relation of number of sessions of psychotherapy and
percentage of patients improved

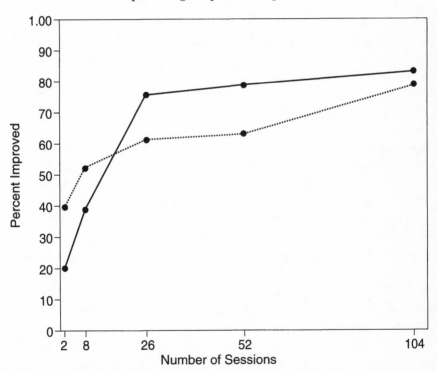

Note: Objective ratings at termination are shown by the solid line; subjective ratings during therapy are shown by the broken line.

(Howard, K. I., Kopta, S. M., Krause, M. S., & Orlinsky, D. E. [1986]. The dose-effect relationship in psychotherapy. *American Psychologist, 41,* p. 160. Copyright 1986 by the American Psychological Association. Reprinted by permission.)

from these studies, they were able to derive dose–effect relationship curves: how much treatment (dose) is necessary to get a certain outcome (effect). They estimated that by the 8th weekly session, 53% of patients would be expected to show measurable improvement, increasing to 74% by the 26th session. These figures are consistent with the 10-to-25-session limit of many brief dynamic therapies. From these findings, the investigators concluded that a typical patient could receive benefits from psychotherapy in 6 to 8 sessions.

A more recent study examined the dose–effect curves for different sets of presenting symptoms to ascertain the rates at which such symptoms remit to normal levels during psychotherapy (Kopta, Howard, Lowry, & Beutler, 1994). Symptom checklists were administered to 854 outpatients in open-ended psychotherapy. A vast array of symptoms were empirically grouped into three categories. As expected, acute distress symptoms (e.g., headaches, feeling restless, crying easily) responded well to psychotherapy, with the highest average percentage of recovery across sessions. Chronic distress symptoms (e.g., feeling worthless, feelings easily hurt, lonely with people) demonstrated the fastest average response rate; problems with hostility, paranoid ideation, and psychoticism (e.g., urges to harm someone, feeling watched, feeling something wrong with one's mind) responded the slowest to psychotherapy. Figure 2.3 presents the plots of the percentage of patients recovered as a function of number of therapy sessions for the three symptom classes.

It should be noted, however, that for both the Howard and Kopta studies, data were based on long-term or open-ended therapies, rather than on therapies that were specifically intended to be brief or time-limited (Hoyt & Austad, 1992). One might expect even more dramatic findings if the therapies had been designed to be brief (i.e., to make every session count).

A recent review of outcome research in brief psychotherapy indicates that empirical studies have failed to demonstrate that long-term (or open-ended) approaches achieve better outcomes than short-term (or time-limited) therapies (Koss & Shiang, 1994). And there are even some studies which indicate that briefer interventions are more effective. For example, William Piper and colleagues (1984) found that short-term individual dynamic psychotherapy (6 months) and long-term groups (24 months) produced better outcomes than long-term individual therapy or short-term groups. Furthermore, significant and enduring change has been shown to occur with brief interventions in a variety of clinical situations. (See Steenbarger, 1994, for another review.) Therefore, most investigators have concluded that "comparative studies of brief and time-unlimited therapists show essentially no differences in results. Consequently, brief therapy results in a great saving of avail-

Figure 2.3

Dose–effect relations, averaged across symptoms, for acute, chronic, and characterological symptom classes (N = 854).

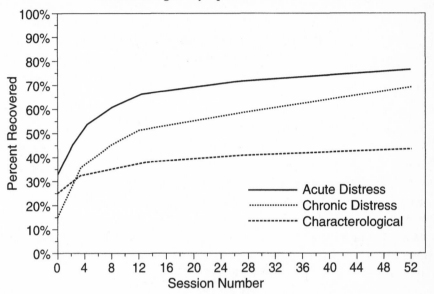

Kopta, S. M., Howard, K. I., Lowry, J. L., & Beutler, L. E. (1994). Patterns of symptomatic recovery in psychotherapy. *Journal of Consulting and Clinical Psychology, 62,* p. 1014. Copyright 1994 by the American Psychological Association. Reprinted by permission.

able clinical time and can reach more people in need of treatment" (Koss & Shiang, 1994, p. 692).

As someone who does both long-term and brief therapies, I am not arguing that the outcomes of the two are indistinguishable. Long-term treatment often seeks different ends (e.g., self-exploration) that are not easily measured, and research in this area is complex and time-consuming to do. What I am saying here, and elsewhere in more detail (Levenson & Butler, 1994), is that the present research literature provides strong support for the use of briefer forms of intervention.

Although positive-outcome data provide compelling motivation to try out new techniques, nothing is as convincing as one's own personal experience. Therefore, as a regular part of the Brief Psychotherapy Program, I include a clinical component, with each trainee assigned to work with one patient for 20 weeks. Trainees videotape each session and show portions from that week's session in a group supervision. This format allows trainees to receive peer and supervisory comments on their therapeutic technique as well as to observe the process of a brief therapy with other patient–therapist dyads.

THERAPIST VALUES

Despite advances in the theory and technique of brief dynamic psychother-apy, as well as a number of research studies demonstrating its overall effec-tiveness, many therapists are still reluctant to learn these methods. Therapists' values and assumptions regarding the nature and practice of brief psychotherapy contribute to this reluctance.

Simon Budman and Alan Gurman (1983) proposed that the values system of the long-term therapist is different from that of the short-term therapist. They suggested that one of the critical criteria for defining the nature of brief therapy is *"a state of mind of the therapist and of the patient"* (p. 278), rather than the number of sessions or length of treatment. These authors postulated eight dominant values pertaining to the ideal manner in which long-term therapy is practiced, and contrasted these with the corresponding ideal val-ues pertinent to the practice of short-term therapy. Table 2.1 lists the com-parative dominant values of the long-term and the short-term therapist. For example, Budman and Gurman postulated that one of the value differences between long-term and short-term therapists involves the idea of "cure." Whereas the long-term therapist seeks a change in basic character, the short-term therapist does not believe in the notion of "cure," preferring pragma-tism, and the least radical intervention, allowing the possibility of additional therapy in the future. (At least one large managed mental health care com-pany uses these eight values of the short-term therapist in evaluating poten-tial clinical providers. Mental health professionals seeking to be employed by that organization are sent a description of the values and informed that if they cannot subscribe to a majority of them, it is preferable that they not apply for that position.)

My colleagues and I (Bolter, Levenson, & Alvarez, 1990) sought to assess empirically whether, indeed, there were such value differences between practicing short-term and long-term therapists. We constructed an attitude scale designed to measure values pertaining to the nature and practice of psychotherapy. Items were written specifically to measure each of the eight value areas proposed by Budman and Gurman. In addition to the value items, we included a number of items relating to attitudes toward brief or short-term psychotherapy. Table 2.2 is a copy of the Beliefs and Attitudes Toward Therapy Questionnaire (BAT-Q). The reader may wish to respond to the BAT-Q as a way of stimulating an examination of how your attitudes and values may shape the type of the therapy you do.

We sent the BAT-Q to a random sample of 550 California psychologists, asking them to indicate their theoretical orientation and preferred therapeu-tic approach (e.g., brief, focused, or time-limited vs. long-term or open-ended). Fifty-four percent returned completed questionnaires. The results provide partial support for Budman and Gurman's proposal: In two of the eight areas, long-term and short-term therapists' responses differed significantly. Specifically, short-term therapists believed more strongly that psychological change could occur outside of therapy, and that setting time limits would intensify the therapeutic work. Furthermore, results indicate that

Table 2.1

Comparative dominant values of the long-term and the short-term therapist

Long-term therapist	Short-term therapist
1. Seeks change in basic character.	Prefers pragmatism, parsimony, and least radical intervention, and does not believe in notion of "cure."
2. Believes that significant psychological change is unlikely in everyday life.	Maintains an adult developmental perspective from which significant psychological change is viewed as inevitable.
3. Sees presenting problems as reflecting more basic pathology.	Emphasizes patient's strengths and resources; presenting problems are taken seriously (although not necessarily at face value).
4. Wants to "be there" as patient makes significant changes.	Accepts that many changes will occur "after therapy" and will not be observable to the therapist.
5. Sees therapy as having a "timeless" quality and is patient and willing to wait for change.	Does not accept the timelessness of some models of therapy.
6. Unconsciously recognizes the fiscal convenience of maintaining long-term patients.	Fiscal issues often muted, either by the nature of the therapist's practice or by the organizational structure for reimbursement.
7. Views psychotherapy as almost always benign and useful.	Views psychotherapy as being sometimes useful and sometimes harmful.
8. Sees patient's being in therapy as the most important part of patient's life.	Sees being in the world as more important than being in therapy.

(S. Budman & A. Gurman, 1988; reprinted with permission.)

clinicians with a psychodynamic orientation, in contrast to those having a cognitive–behavioral framework, were more likely to believe that therapy was necessary for change, that the focus of therapy should be on pathology, that therapy should be open-ended, and that ambitious goals were desirable. Thus, while the findings from our study suggest that one's preferred approach (short- vs. long-term) is related to therapeutic values, the therapist's theoretical orientation (psychodynamic vs. cognitive–behavioral) also plays a significant role.

Kay Bolter (1987) found that 91% of psychodynamic therapists indicated that they favored long-term therapy over brief therapy. Judith Speed (1992) similarly found that 87% of those therapists most comfortable with very long-term therapy were psychodynamically oriented. In the two surveys on prevalence of brief therapy (Davidovitz, 1995; Levenson et al., 1995), many respondents indicated that they were conflicted in their workplace. These are the therapists who felt that they did not have the necessary training, skill, or confidence in brief therapy, but felt forced to conduct brief work because of economic and/or administrative constraints.

Michael Hoyt (1985) proposed that dynamically trained therapists have resistances toward short-term psychotherapy. In trying to determine why many therapists are not learning and applying short-term dynamic methods as a treatment of choice, Hoyt rejected the idea that lack of awareness regarding recent clinical and research developments is chiefly to blame. Rather, he suggested that clinicians hold a number of myths or erroneous beliefs which make them resistant to learning briefer interventions. Hoyt organized these resistances into seven broad categories:

1. The belief that "more is better" (e.g., treatment must take a long time to be effective).
2. Myth of the "pure gold" of analysis (belief that other therapeutic techniques are second-rate).
3. Confusion of patient's interests (in the most efficient, effective help) with the therapist's interests (in uncovering all aspects of the patient's personality).
4. Demanding hard work (to be active and intensely alert).
5. Economic and other pressures (desire to hold on to that which is profitable and dependable).
6. Countertransference and related therapist reactions to termination (endings difficult for therapist as well as patient).
7. Therapists' negative reaction to being told what to do (i.e., reactance theory holds that people rebel when not given choices).

Table 2.2

Beliefs and Attitudes Toward Therapy Questionnaire

	Strongly Disagree	Somewhat Disagree	Slightly Disagree	Slightly Agree	Somewhat Agree	Strongly Agree
1) The primary goal of therapy is major character change.	−3	−2	−1	+1	+2	+3
2) For some patients, therapy can be harmful regardless of the expertise of the therapist.	−3	−2	−1	+1	+2	+3
3) Psychological pathology can usually be altered only through a significant and continuing therapeutic relationship.	−3	−2	−1	+1	+2	+3
4) It is important for therapists to be patient and willing to wait for their patients to change at their own pace.	−3	−2	−1	+1	+2	+3
5) In doing therapy, I tend to focus more on patients' existing strengths and capacities rather than on their deep-seated weaknesses and pathology.	−3	−2	−1	+1	+2	+3
6) Brief therapy is usually suitable only for minor disorders of recent onset.	−3	−2	−1	+1	+2	+3
7) I accept that most of a patient's significant changes will probably occur after the therapy is over.	−3	−2	−1	+1	+2	+3
8) An extended period of "working through" is necessary in order for a patient's gains to be consolidated.	−3	−2	−1	+1	+2	+3
9) In general, treating patients' immediate difficulty rather than their entire personality should be the major goal of therapy.	−3	−2	−1	+1	+2	+3
10) Quite serious, long-standing neurotic disorders can be resolved in brief therapy.	−3	−2	−1	+1	+2	+3
11) Setting a time limit in therapy increases and intensifies the work accomplished.	−3	−2	−1	+1	+2	+3
12) While a patient is in therapy, the therapy should be the most important event in the patient's life.	−3	−2	−1	+1	+2	+3
13) Therapists who practice brief therapy are under greater financial pressure than therapists who conduct open-ended treatment.	−3	−2	−1	+1	+2	+3
14) For someone who has had a lot of loss in his/her life, a time-limited therapy is contraindicated.	−3	−2	−1	+1	+2	+3
15) A patient's presenting problems are only a reflection of more basic pathology.	−3	−2	−1	+1	+2	+3
16) In the hands of a "good enough" practitioner, therapy is almost always helpful and not harmful.	−3	−2	−1	+1	+2	+3
17) Significant, enduring insight and personality change can be achieved in brief therapy.	−3	−2	−1	+1	+2	+3
18) Even without therapy, significant psychological change throughout life is inevitable for most people.	−3	−2	−1	+1	+2	+3
19) In most cases, the benefits of short-term therapy are relatively short-lasting.	−3	−2	−1	+1	+2	+3

The area of negative attitudes toward briefer modes of intervention is extremely important, since such beliefs could adversely affect therapists' willingness and ability to use brief-therapy methods effectively. Brief therapists and researchers have warned that a brief therapy could be undermined if the therapist does not feel optimistic and confident about the process (Flegenheimer, 1982; Ursano & Dressler, 1977). Similarly, Meir Winokur and Haim Dasberg (1983) suggested that

> when teaching professionals a new approach, it is not enough to rely on lectures, reading materials, or even live demonstrations and individual supervision. . . . In order to integrate a new approach into their professional identity, particularly if this identity is molded already, they need to work through the intellectual, quasi-intellectual, and emotional difficulties encountered in the learning process. (p. 51)

In another study, Bolter and I (1988) examined the values and attitudes of psychiatry residents and psychology interns before and after a 6-month seminar in brief dynamic psychotherapy. We found that after training there were significant differences in attitudes as measured by the BAT-Q. Specifically, post-training trainees were more willing to consider using brief therapy for other than minor disorders, more positive about achieving significant insight, more expectant that the benefits would be long-lasting, and less likely to think that an extended period of "working through" was necessary. Also they were more willing to be active, more likely to see that a time limit was helpful, and more prepared to believe that patients would change significantly after the therapy was over.

In a recent extension of this study, 167 experienced therapists responded to the BAT-Q before and after attending one of several daylong workshops on brief therapy (led by three different, experienced trainers using three different brief-therapy models) (Neff, Lambert, Lunnen, Budman, & Levenson, 1994). Results support the finding that an intensive training experience leads to more positive and optimistic attitudes toward brief therapy. In general, these studies support the notion that training in brief therapy is valuable not only didactically, but motivationally. It is my opinion that dealing with attitudes and values associated with short-term therapy is a necessary component for the success of any teaching or training program in brief psychotherapy. Fortunately, the importance of these "enabling attitudes" is beginning to be taken into consideration by trainers and supervisors (Bennett, 1994; Cummings, 1995).

CHAPTER 3

The Time-Limited Dynamic
Psychotherapy Model:
Premises and Goals

SINCE I BEGAN teaching brief psychotherapy in the late 1970s, I have searched for models of therapy that would be effective not only for conducting short-term dynamic therapies, but also for teaching and learning briefer interventions. Models of therapy get used (consciously or unconsciously) to filter our understanding of what transpires in psychotherapy. Having an explicit model helps the therapist to question premises, to evaluate what is happening in the therapy, and to know how to deviate from the model when necessary. All of these factors are especially critical when the therapy is brief.

My hunt for effective models eventually led me to time-limited dynamic psychotherapy (TLDP), developed by Hans Strupp, Jeffrey Binder, and colleagues (1984). A focused, contemporary psychodynamic approach, TLDP has at its core the examination of dyadic interactions between patient and therapist. TLDP makes use of the relationship that develops between therapist and patient to kindle fundamental changes in the way a person interacts with others and one's self. Its principles and techniques are broadly applicable regardless of time limits. However, its methods of formulating and intervening make it particularly well suited for the so-called difficult patient being seen in a brief or time-limited therapy.

WHY TLDP?

My reasons for choosing TLDP from all the available models include: (1) its applicability to the treatment of difficult patients (broad selection criteria); (2) its amenability to empirical scrutiny; and (3) its relevance and accessibility for psychodynamically trained clinicians who want to work more effectively and more efficiently.

BROAD SELECTION CRITERIA

TLDP is a flexible approach to brief therapy designed to treat people with chronic interpersonal problems or personality disorders—so-called difficult patients. These are the patients who do not seem to meet the therapist halfway—the ones who seem to thwart and inhibit the very help they manifestly need. They may seem incapable of insight, or if they are insightful, their wisdom has not freed them from their repetitive, maladaptive patterns of behavior. They certainly do not strike one as amenable to time-limited therapy.

Such individuals are often branded as difficult, dreaded, or worse because their treatment makes demands on therapists' skills and resources, and above all, challenges the clinicians' ability to manage their own (often negative) reactions to them. In a survey of psychiatrists regarding the "treatment-resistant" and "help-rejecting" patient, 100% of those interviewed said they reacted differently to the difficult patient than to other patients by setting too many limits, denying feelings of anger, being overly cautious and careful, overextending the treatment period or terminating prematurely, and outright rejecting or abandoning them (Bongar, Markey, & Peterson, 1991). Such patients often receive personality-disorder diagnoses, and frequently create management problems for those who are trying to treat them or oversee their care.

As a brief therapist, one can either eliminate these patients from one's practice (which is not very responsive to patient needs, nor very practical considering today's managed care environment), or one can use a therapeutic model with a rationale and interventions designed to deal with difficult patients in a time-sensitive manner.

One clinician who uses the highly restrictive selection criteria approach is Peter Sifneos, a pioneer in what is considered to be the second generation of brief therapists—when brief therapy began to emerge as a concerted therapeutic method (Crits-Christoph & Barber, 1991; Levenson & Butler, 1994). Sifneos (1979/1987) developed a short-term anxiety-provoking psychotherapy (STAPP) model that focuses on dealing with Oedipal issues. He screens prospective patients using the following criteria:

1. The ability of the patient to have a circumscribed chief complaint
2. Evidence of a give-and-take or "meaningful relationship" with another person during childhood
3. Capacity to relate flexibly to the evaluator during the interview
4. Ability to experience and express feelings directly during the interview
5. Psychological sophistication, defined by:
   (a) above-average intelligence
   (b) psychological-mindedness
6. Motivation for change (not symptom relief) indicated by:
   (a) willingness to participate actively in the psychiatric evaluation
   (b) honesty in reporting about oneself
   (c) ability to recognize symptoms as psychological in origin
   (d) introspection and curiosity
   (e) openness to new ideas
   (f) realistic expectations of the results of treatment
   (g) willingness to make a reasonable sacrifice of time and money (Sifneos, 1979/1987, pp. 30–45).

Whenever I present Sifneos's selection criteria to trainees, they react with incredulity, declaring that a STAPP-suitable patient sounds like he or she would not need therapy. Trainees comment that their caseloads are *not* composed of such patients. Sifneos himself told me that of the people who request treatment at his clinic, only 10% to 15% meet these STAPP selection criteria.

Rather than limiting the type of patient seen in a brief therapy, TLDP uses the approach of modifying the therapy and the training of therapists in an attempt to improve the treatment of difficult clients. A time-sensitive approach for patients with chronic dysfunctional interactional styles, it emphasizes brief psychodynamic strategies and methods in order to help the large majority of patients coming for treatment and not just those who are high-functioning. It has great applicability, therefore, for therapists who need to treat almost everyone who walks in the door and are not in a position to employ stringent selection criteria.

RESEARCH-BASED

TLDP is deeply rooted in empirical investigations focused on the therapist's contribution to the treatment process. The background for TLDP is a program of empirical research begun in the early 1950s (Strupp, 1955a–c, 1957, 1958, 1960). Strupp asked practicing therapists to pretend they were responding to patients' statements, which were presented in written form or on film. He was initially interested in the relationship between technique and therapist variables (e.g., theoretical orientation, level of experi-ence), but was intrigued with results which indicated that the therapists' immediate negative attitudes toward the patient were associated with a loss of empathy and unfavorable clinical judgments. "On the basis of these data, I hypothesized that the therapist's initial attitude toward the patient might give rise to a self-fulfilling prophecy and that the therapist's com-munications embodied both technical and personal elements" (Strupp, 1993, p. 431).

The following decade of Strupp's research focused on how outcomes were affected by the relative contributions of so-called specific (technical) and nonspecific (interpersonal) factors. As part of a program of empirical studies at the Vanderbilt University Center for Psychotherapy Research (Vander-bilt I), brief therapies conducted by trained psychotherapists were compared with those done by college professors who had no formal training in psy-chotherapy, but who had a reputation for being warm and understanding individuals (Strupp & Hadley, 1979). Results focusing on good and poor out-come cases treated by the same therapist revealed that patients who were hostile, negativistic, inflexible, mistrusting, or otherwise highly resistant uni-formly had poor outcomes, whether they were treated by trained therapists or by professors (Strupp, 1980a, 1980b, 1980c, 1980d). It should be noted that the professional therapists had good outcomes with those patients who were able to form good working relationships by the third session. However, even these therapists were relatively inept in adapting their approach to the needs of difficult patients.

Strupp reasoned from the results of these studies that the difficult patients had characterological styles that made it very hard for them to negotiate a good working relationship with their therapists. In such cases the therapists' skill in managing the interpersonal therapeutic climate was severely taxed. Since the therapies were brief, this inability to readily form a therapeutic alliance had deleterious effects on the entire therapy.

These findings from Vanderbilt I revealed that therapists made little progress dealing with the negative transferences of the more difficult patients. Furthermore, these therapists appeared to get entrapped into react-ing with negativity, hostility, and disrespect, and, in general, responded antitherapeutically to the patients' pervasive negativism and hostility. Such negative responses from their own therapists may only have served to heighten these patients' helpless and hopeless feelings and to solidify a neg-ative view of self and others.

The next body of research (Vanderbilt II) was designed to assess whether specialized training would help clinicians treat patients who have typically been rejected as suitable candidates for short-term dynamic psychotherapy. Vanderbilt II investigated the effects of training in TLDP for 16 experienced therapists (8 psychiatrists and 8 psychologists) and 80 patients. In the first year of the study, each therapist was asked to treat two patients (one relatively "easy," one relatively "difficult") in up to 25 weekly sessions as he or she ordinarily would. In the second year, the therapists were assigned to work with one patient each while they went through a TLDP training program (didactics and small-group supervision using audio- and videotapes of the training cases). In the third year, therapists again treated two patients, this time according to the tenets of TLDP. The main results indicate that the training program was successful in teaching therapists to use TLDP strategies (Henry et al., 1993b), even with the more difficult patients (Henry et al., 1993a).

The Vanderbilt II findings pertinent to the changes in therapists' behavior are quite complex, however. Although there were positive changes in therapists' skills following training, there were also indications of negative changes. For example, therapists had more opportunity to make mistakes, because of their greater activity level in the brief therapies. In addition, therapists after training appeared less approving and less supportive. The investigators speculated that there may be a post-training phase in which therapists' performance declines, as they grapple with integrating new techniques into their existing therapeutic mode.

The Vanderbilt II studies are commendable in that they are the only direct investigation into the effects of training on therapist performance. However, there are several problems with them, not the least of which is that the researchers recruited successful, local, private practitioners, who while they were motivated to participate in a prestigious study at Vanderbilt University, were less motivated to learn brief-therapy strategies. As chapter 2 points out, one's attitude toward brief therapy can affect how well one learns and competently implements this new knowledge. In addition, since these therapists were all experienced practitioners in long-term therapy, they probably had much to "unlearn." Supportive of this idea is the finding that that those therapists who had had *more* supervision in their own model before the training began were *less* likely to adhere to the new TLDP strategies (Henry et al., 1993a).

Among the more striking findings of Vanderbilt II were differences in training effects due to whether the therapist was in Trainer A's or Trainer B's group. Trainer A's therapists showed greater changes in adherence to TLDP. Inspection of differences between the two trainers indicates that Trainer A's approach was more directive, specific, and challenging. This finding led the investigators to suggest the following guidelines for maximizing gains from TLDP training (and presumably other manualized therapies).

1. Choose competent but relatively less experienced therapists.
2. Select therapists who are less vulnerable to negative training effects (e.g., less hostile and controlling).
3. Assume that even experienced therapists are novices in the approach to be learned.
4. Provide close, directive, and specific feedback to therapists and focus on therapists' own thought processes.

As part of the VA Short-Term Psychotherapy (VAST) Project, designed to examine various aspects of psychotherapy process and outcome as well as to study the process of training inexperienced therapists to conduct TLDP, 101 psychiatric outpatients received TLDP between 1986 and 1992 (Levenson & Bein, 1993). They completed measures prior to and just after treatment. Most of the patients were men seeking help for depression, anxiety, and/or long-standing interpersonal problems. They were likely to be unemployed or retired, single, middle-aged or older, not psychologically minded, diagnosed with various personality disorders in addition to Axis I problems. A history of substance abuse and psychiatric disabilities was quite common.

The therapists were psychiatry residents and psychology and social work interns who were receiving training in TLDP as part of a 6-month brief-therapy rotation. They completed measures on their patients pre- and post-therapy.

Each trainee was assigned to work with one patient for a maximum of 20 sessions. All therapy sessions were videotaped. Training consisted of a weekly didactic seminar and group supervision. The seminar covered for-mulation and intervention strategies illustrated by training tapes edited from real therapy sessions. In group supervision four to six trainees at a time presented their training cases and showed videotaped excerpts from that week's session. Supervision involved close, directive feedback around specific interventions. By stopping the videotape at critical or interesting junctures, the trainees explored alternative ways of proceeding and intervening consistent with TLDP.

David Overstreet (1993) found that approximately 60% of all patients in the VAST Project achieved positive symptomatic or interpersonal outcomes following TLDP (average of 14 sessions). At termination, 71% of the patients felt their problems had lessened. Furthermore, 21% of the patients achieved clinically significant interpersonal improvement (change of over two standard deviations on a measure of interpersonal problems), moving into the normal range of scores. This finding compares quite favorably with results of other investigators using different theoretical models with less difficult patient populations (e.g., Ankuta & Abeles, 1993).

A long-term follow-up study (Bein, 1995; Bein et al., 1994; Levenson &

Bein, 1993) that reassessed patients 6 months to 6 years (mean of 3 years) after their TLDP therapies were completed found that patient improvement in symptoms and interpersonal problems was maintained and slightly bolstered. At the time of follow-up, 80% of the patients thought their therapies had helped them deal more effectively with their problems ("somewhat," 48%; "a great deal," 32%). Only 20% reported that their treatment "really didn't help," and no one claimed it had made things worse.

Other analyses indicate that the patients were more likely to value their therapies the more they perceived that their sessions focused on TLDP-congruent strategies (i.e., trying to understand their typical patterns of relating to people, exploring childhood relationships, and trying to relate in a new and better way with their therapists). Interventions incongruent or at variance with TLDP (e.g., therapists' giving advice, focus on symptoms, homework assignments) were unrelated to patients' judged benefit.

In sum, then, these results suggest that TLDP holds promise for those patients who previously had been considered unsuitable for brief therapy, and that particular characteristics of the TLDP approach may make it more beneficial.

TEACHABLE/LEARNABLE

Many professionals attend workshops conducted by "therapist-gurus"— therapists who seemingly work miracles. Simply being in their presence seems curative (and may well be!). When trainees attempt the therapy being touted, however, they often mistakenly emulate the guru's personality, hoping that these stylistic changes in intonation, gestures, and appearance will foster the same results. But imitation just doesn't work.

TLDP, by contrast, does not depend on the charisma of the therapist to achieve results. Rather, it provides a flexible framework that therapists adapt to their own unique personalities. Furthermore, TLDP shuns lockstep techniques to which one must rigidly adhere and that make one feel more like a technician than a therapist.

As part of Vanderbilt II, a treatment manual was developed that was subsequently published in book form: *Psychotherapy in a New Key: A Guide to Time-Limited Dynamic Psychotherapy* by Hans Strupp and Jeffrey Binder (1984). It provided a clearer and more straightforward explication of formulation and technique than had previously existed. The TLDP principles and strategies presented in their manual are founded on clinical relevance and based on observable data. Because the book avoids complex metatheoretical constructs where possible, the therapist does not have to intuit what is meant by highly inferential concepts.

DEFINITION

TLDP is an interpersonal brief psychotherapy. Its goal is to help the patient move away from replicating dysfunctional interpersonal patterns by facilitating new experiences and understandings within the context of the therapeutic relationship. The intent is to modify the way the person relates to himself or herself and others. Thus the focus is not on the reduction of symptoms (although such improvements are expected to occur), but rather on changing ingrained patterns of interpersonal relatedness, or what has more traditionally been referred to as character structure.

In 1984 Strupp and Binder wrote about allotting 25 to 30 sessions for a time-limited therapy. In today's managed care environment, that number might be considered moderate or even long-term therapy! When I teach TLDP in a 6-month training rotation, I confine the therapies to a *maximum* of 20 weekly sessions, because this is the most the trainees can reliably have to see patients in those 6 months; the actual number of sessions is far fewer (average of 14 sessions) once vacations, illness, and holidays are taken into account. The experienced therapist will, no doubt, discover ways in which staying focused and attuned to the interactional process will alter the course of therapy, regardless of the actual number of sessions.

PREMISES

The TLDP model makes seven basic assumptions:

1. The patient needs an interpersonal therapy for problems stemming from disturbed interpersonal relationships.
2. Dysfunctional styles were learned in the past.
3. Dysfunctional styles are being maintained in the present.
4. The patient reenacts interpersonal difficulties with the therapist.
5. The therapist is a participant observer.
6. The therapist becomes hooked in to reenacting difficulties with the patient.
7. There is one identifiable, problematic relationship pattern.

INTERPERSONAL THERAPY

TLDP uses an interpersonal model of therapy. Historically, it is rooted in the object-relations tradition. It emphasizes the critical importance of an interpersonal perspective, as exemplified by the early work of Harry Stack Sullivan (1953), and consistent with the views of modern interpersonal theorists (e.g., Anchin & Kiesler, 1982; Benjamin, 1993; Greenberg & Mitchell, 1983). The search for and maintenance of human relatedness is considered to be a major motivating force in all human beings. This relational view is in sharp contrast to that of classical psychoanalysis, which emphasizes predetermined mental structures to deal with conflicts between gratification of instinctual impulses and societal constraints.

The TLDP interpersonal perspective reflects a larger paradigm shift occurring within psychoanalytic thinking and practice. This evolutionary trend (Cooper, 1987) or transitional period (Altman, 1993) is away from viewing the discharge of drives as determining the development of personality and toward focusing on the process of forming interpersonal relationships. In fact, most psychoanalytic schools are becoming less drive-oriented and more relational for various cultural, social, clinical, and scientific reasons (Aron, 1990; Messer & Warren, 1995). Such a shift affects the very basis of what is defined as pathology, how the therapist construes the clinical situation, and what interventions are considered appropriate.

The relational view focuses on transactional patterns where the therapist is embedded in the therapeutic relationship as a participant observer; transference is not a distortion, but rather the patient's plausible perceptions of the therapist's behavior and intent; and countertransference indicates not a failure on the part of the therapist, but rather his or her role responsiveness (Sandler, 1976) or interpersonal empathy (Strupp & Binder, 1984) to the pushes and pulls from the interaction with the patient.

It is beyond the scope of this chapter to describe all these evolutionary trends, but table 3.1 lists constructs that have been used by various theorists to delineate conceptual and procedural differences. The reader should note that there is a wide spectrum of psychoanalytic attitudes represented under each heading and these should not be taken as congruent with one another merely because they are in the same column. The approach of TLDP is clearly identified with the modernist view.

Not only psychoanalysis but other models of psychotherapy as well (e.g., cognitive therapy, Safran & Segal, 1990; behavior therapy, Kohlenberg & Tsai, 1991) are increasingly incorporating interpersonal perspectives. Human beings are interpersonal creatures by nature. Since we are dependent on others for our survival for an extended period of time after birth, it is not surprising that the manner in which we attach to others becomes the major force determining how we relate to the world and how we feel about ourselves. Congruent with this view is the finding that most of the problems we see in

Table 3.1

Evolutionary Trends in Psychoanalytic Thought and Practice

Historical	Modernist
Model	
Drive-Conflict Model	Relational-Conflict Model
Conflict between instinctual impulses and societal demands	Conflict between attachment needs and learned behaviors
Asymmetry in therapeutic relationship	Mutuality
One-person	Two-person
Intrapsychic	Interpersonal; interactional
Predetermined, internal structures	Interactional structures based on repeated interactions
Mind as structured from within	Mind structured from without; internal working model of interactions
Tensions between instinct, coping mechanisms, and society	Transactional patterns derived from interactive field
Role of Therapist	
Objective translator; decoder; decipherer	Participant observer; total participant
Objectivist, natural science	Perspectivist
Neutral screen; blank screen	Coparticipant; inevitable embeddedness of therapist in relationship matrix
Neutrality as equidistant from id, ego, and superego	Neutrality as balanced between old and new object
Transference	
Transference as distortion	Therapist's actual behavior strongly affects patient
Objective reflection of history	Activity of two individuals
Re-creation of the old	Patient's perceptions of therapist as plausible possibilities
Countertransference	
Countertransference as failure to remain neutral	Neutrality as an impossible position for the therapist
Product of therapist's unresolved conflicts and childhood residues	Interpersonal empathy
Therapist outside patient's relational matrix	Therapist plays roles assigned by patient; role responsiveness
Not joining the game is the principal task	Therapist cannot help playing the game
Countertransference disclosure as diversion away from focus	Countertransference disclosure as contribution to focus

Table 3.1 (continued)

Historical	Modernist
Type and Role of Intervention	
Accurate interpretation; emphasis on content and precision	Corrective emotional experience
Interpretation alters structures inside the patient	Interpretation as a complex relational event
Revealing historical truth	Narrative truth
Change through interpretation	Internalization of therapist; modifications of representations of self and others
Interpretation as truth revealing hidden content	Narrative; a way of understanding (one of several)
Insight; expansion of consciousness	Shared analytic reality; social constructivism
Cognitive enlightenment; allow unconscious contents to become conscious	Relativistic approach to truth; truth as invention
Communication made explicit	Need not be made explicit
Verbal transference interpretation	Implicit responsiveness of therapist to patient; therapist passes tests to disconfirm pathologic beliefs
View of Patient	
Reactive	Active construer of interpersonal world; interpretative

From Alexander & French (1946), Aron (1990), Beebe & Lachman (1988), Bowlby (1973), Burke (1992), Cooper (1987), Eagle (1984), Emde (1991), Fenichel (1941), Gabbard (1993), Gill (1982), Greenberg (1991), Hirsch (1992), Hoffman (1992), Mitchell (1988), Sandler (1976), Stern (1994), Strupp & Binder (1984), Sullivan (1953), Weiss et al. (1986), Wolf (1986), Wolstein (1983)

our offices and clinics are interpersonal in nature (Merikangas & Weissman, 1986).

In TLDP, psychological symptoms and problems are seen as arising from interpersonal difficulties. Often when people enter therapy, the presenting complaint involves some symptom (e.g., anxiety, depression) that forms the basis for an Axis I diagnosis (APA, DSM-IV, 1994). Only after the origin of such dysphoric feelings is tracked does its interpersonal source become apparent. For example, a patient enters therapy saying she's been nervous since the fall "for no good reason"; upon inquiry, however, the therapist learns that her only child left for college at that time. While some patients may actually enter therapy complaining of their lifelong interpersonal difficulties, this complaint is often embedded in a wish that the other people in their lives change (e.g., "If only my husband were more attentive, we would have a happy marriage").

Learned in the Past

How does someone develop a dysfunctional interpersonal style? The second assumption TLDP makes is that disturbances in adult relatedness usually stem from faulty relationships with early caregivers—usually in the parental home.* John Bowlby (1969) has eloquently described how a secure attachment to others (usually parents) satisfies the child's basic needs for nurturance, moderates the negative effects of anxiety, and fosters healthy development. Furthermore, Bowlby (1973) elaborated that these early experiences with parental figures result in mental representations of these relationships or working models of one's interpersonal world. The child learns that in order to maintain connections with others and feel secure, he or she must behave in certain ways. These "certain ways" compose the building blocks of what will become organized, encoded experiential and cognitive data (interpersonal schemata) informing one about the nature of human relatedness and what is generally necessary to sustain and maintain emotional connectedness to others.

Our fundamental working models (or schemata) of self, which determine our self-esteem and self-concept, are also derived interpersonally. "Just as we learn to see ourselves in a mirror, so the child becomes conscious of himself by seeing his reflection in the mirror of other people's consciousness of himself" (Popper & Eccles, 1977, p. 110). Guidano (1991) elaborates on this idea of the "looking-glass effect" by which human beings obtain self-knowledge chiefly through interacting with others.

Although I am emphasizing learned factors relevant to interpersonal styles, the influence of genetic and prenatal factors that promote certain individual temperaments cannot be ignored (Kagan, 1989). These temperaments are evidenced at birth and are modified (exacerbated or ameliorated) by interpersonal experiences. For example, the infant who is "hard-wired" to respond readily (e.g., with crying) to minimal changes in environmental stimuli (e.g., slight noises) may encourage an anxious and resentful caretak-

---

*Sometimes adult experiences of interpersonal or environmental trauma, especially over time, can result in dysfunctional relationships with others. For example, I have seen many Vietnam veterans who because of trauma associated with their combat experience have still felt alienated and suspicious of others some 25 to 30 years later. Their traumatic experiences of buddies being killed or disfigured resulted in their withdrawing into an isolated, hypervigilant existence, which was not characteristic of their attachment style before they went to war.

ing approach by the mother, which then in turn might lead the child to develop an insecure and frightened attitude toward others.

A corollary premise related to early learning of dysfunctional ways of relating is that such problematic behavior begins as adaptations the child learned to make in order to maintain any attachment to others. For example, Jim was raised by authoritarian, dogmatic, punitive parents. The boy learned that in order to maintain his connectedness to his parents (and this can run the gamut from gaining their approval to not getting beaten), he had to accommodate their wishes. He understandably became a placating and submissive child. Jim came to expect that his interpersonal world was safe only to the extent he stayed meek. However, this attachment style that might have served him adequately as a boy became anachronistic as an adult.

MAINTAINED IN THE PRESENT

This emphasis on early childhood experiences is consistent with the basis for much of psychoanalytic thinking as well as most other theories of human behavior. There is a major difference, however, between the relational TLDP model and a more classically psychoanalytic viewpoint, which holds that the individual's personality is crystallized by the end of the Oedipal phase of development.

In a TLDP framework, the individual's personality is not considered to be finished at a certain point, but dynamically changing as it interacts with others. One's dysfunctional interactional style is learned early in life, but for the interpersonal difficulties to continue this style must be fostered in the person's present adult life. What does this look like clinically? In the case of Jim, he developed a placating and submissive strategy as a child that he continued into adulthood because he expects (typically unconsciously, emanating from his interpersonal schema) that this is the only way to preserve his relationships with others. From a TLDP point of view, however, Jim's adult subservient style works only to the extent that he can fill his interpersonal world with others who behave toward him in dogmatic, authoritarian, and punitive ways.

Since Jim acts in such a subservient manner, he evokes, provokes, or invites people to behave toward him in a more overbearing manner. When confronted by such oppressive responses, Jim himself feels more comfortable, because others' domineering behaviors confirm his internal schema of himself—his self as it is reflected in the appraisals of others (Sullivan, 1953). It is a good match when his submissive style dovetails with others' dominance.

Jim is not behaving masochistically by "soliciting" such interactions;

rather, his submissive way of being in the world is confirmed by others' controlling behaviors. Such dissatisfying attachments feel better to Jim than his perceived alternative of being alone, but often symptoms and negative self-esteem result. Jim maintains continuity by "structuring social interactions so as to induce social patterns to engage in self-confirming interactional patterns" (Bartholomew & Horowitz, 1991, p. 241). What results is a dysfunctional interactive dance where all involved do their part to maintain a reciprocal system not of their conscious choosing.

The significance of the present is a major difference between TLDP and more classical psychoanalytic thinking. The TLDP position holds that while the dysfunctional style may have begun in the past, it gets maintained in the present. *This emphasis on the present has tremendous implications for treating such interpersonal difficulties in a brief time frame.* If such dysfunctional interactions are sustained in the present, then one can work in the present to alter the dysfunctional style. Working in the present allows for change to happen more quickly than assuming one needs to spend time working through childhood conflicts and discovering historical truths.

This focus is consistent with a systems-oriented approach, which holds that the context of a situation and the circular processes surrounding it are critical. The "pathology" does not reside within an individual, but rather is created by all the components within the (pathological) system. According to systems theory (Bertalanffy, 1969), if you change one part of the system, the other parts must also change, since the entire system seeks a new level of stabilization. If one does not respond to the pushes and pulls of the patient's style, then the patient's dysfunctional manner should also shift.

In our example, if the people who interact with Jim were able to resist the pull to respond domineeringly to his submissive and subservient behavior, then Jim would be influenced to become more independent and assertive.

In Vivo Reenactment in Therapy

A fourth premise is that the patient interacts with the therapist in the same dysfunctional way that characterizes his or her interactions with significant others. In psychodynamic terms we understand such behavior as transference. Obviously, patients do not leave their personalities outside the therapy office; rather, they end up responding to their therapists in the same stylistic manner that has been problematic for them their entire lives.

From an interpersonal-therapy perspective, this reenactment is an ideal situation, because it provides the therapist with the very scenario that gets the patient into difficulties in the outside world. The therapist is given the opportunity to observe the playing out of the maladaptive interactional pattern, and to experience what it is like to try to relate to that individual. Thus the therapist is able to enter the interpersonal world of the patient in an experiential manner and can attend to what develops. The patient's perceptions of the therapist's behaviors are not considered as static re-creations of the old (i.e., distortions), but as plausible possibilities (Gill, 1982) given the patient's frame of reference.

From this premise, one does not need to dwell on unearthing genetic material. It is not important to find out exactly what happened at every phase in childhood, because the crux of the therapy is the interaction in the room between the two of you. This does not mean, however, that historical information is ignored. If the therapist can combine observations of what is happening in the therapy with what the patient perceives of past and present relationships, then the therapist can feel more secure in formulating what has gone awry with this individual as he or she has interacted with others.

THE DYADIC QUALITY OF THE THERAPEUTIC RELATIONSHIP

A corollary premise to the TLDP concept of transference is that the therapist also enters into the relationship and becomes a part of the interaction. In Sullivan's terms (1953), the therapist becomes a *participant observer*. A participant observer is one who examines and attends to the interaction, but who also becomes a part of it and thus alters it. Others (e.g., Stern, 1994) speak of the therapist's being inescapably embedded in the relationship matrix.

In TLDP the therapist is viewed as contributing to the type and quality of the interaction. The therapist and patient are seen as constituting a dyadic unit (albeit one of whom is presumably in pain and the other presumably a helper) who are attempting to relate in order to accomplish some goal. They form an interactive system, much as a small (two-member) group would.

This premise represents another dramatic break with more classical psychoanalytic notions of the role of the therapist as an objective, neutral observer who does not (and should not) enter the system; in fact, in order to be of help, the analyst should remain detached from the dysfunctional presentation of the patient in order to allow the "inappropriate" transferences to occur to an object who is as much a blank screen as possible. In TLDP terms, the opposite applies: In order for a positive outcome to occur, the therapist cannot (and should not) remain detached and can be of help only to the degree that he or she becomes actively involved in the process of interlocking reciprocity.

INTERACTIVE COUNTERTRANSFERENCE

The classical view holds that countertransference is a manifestation of the therapist's own unresolved neurotic conflicts, which are stimulated by the patient but not germane to the working relationship. Thus countertransference is considered to be an impediment to the therapist's objectivity. From this point of view, the analyst needs to work through these conflicts in therapy and/or discuss them in case consultation.

The relational–interactionist position of TLDP holds that the therapist cannot help reacting countertransferentially to the patient—that is, the therapist inevitably will be pushed and pulled by the patient's dysfunctional style and will respond accordingly. Stephen Butler and colleagues (Butler, Flasher, Strupp; 1993) view this transactional type of countertransference as the "natural, role-responsive, necessary complement or counterpart to the transference of the patient, and to the patient's style of relatedness, suggesting that a transference response cannot be maintained without a corresponding, complementary countertransference response" (p. 347). As the contemporary interpersonal theorist Donald Kiesler (1982, 1988) would phrase it, the therapist inevitably becomes "hooked" in to acting out the complementary response to the patient's inflexible, maladaptive pattern.

Why does the therapist allow himself or herself to get pulled into a dysfunctional interaction with the patient? Cannot the therapist, with appropriate supervision, therapy, and/or training, rise above the pushes and pulls of the patient's dysfunctional presentation? The premise here is that if a therapist enters into a collaborative relationship with the patient, the therapist begins relating to that patient as an individual. Initially, the therapist is really quite naive as to the patient's dynamics and the patient may be quite adept at his or her role, having been reenacting this interpersonal scenario for decades. In the therapist's attempts to understand and relate to the patient, the therapist begins responding to the patient's interpersonal cues in analogous ways.

The assumption made here is that the patient is more dysfunctional than the therapist; therefore, it is expected that the patient's more inflexible, extreme, and chronic interpersonal style will outweigh the therapist's more flexible, moderate, and tempered style and will thus exert a greater influence on the relationship. If the reverse is true, deleterious therapeutic outcomes will most assuredly occur.

As an example of getting hooked in the initial sessions or the engaged stage (Kiesler, 1982), consider the treatment of Jim, the placating patient. A therapist might find in the give-and-take of the early sessions that he or she is behaving somewhat more actively than usual, is feeling a little more confident and self-assured than is customary, and sounding more like an authority than is typical for him or her—maybe even dogmatically so. The therapist's manner dovetails nicely with Jim's presentation, and encourages him to respond in an even more acquiescent and tentative fashion, which in turn facilitates the therapist's even more assertive and expert demeanor, and so on.

The TLDP perspective assumes that this transactional countertransference has several positive aspects. First, in becoming so unavoidably co-opted, the therapist is able to appreciate experientially what it is like to interact with this person. This gut-level knowledge can then direct the therapist to contemplate what might need to shift in the here and now to improve the interaction. Second, in the heat of the sessions, these countertransferential feelings serve as a sensitive compass signaling the therapist when interactions are headed in a beneficial direction.

Third, the therapist's initial collusion with the patient's maladaptive style quite likely promotes the development of one aspect of the therapeutic alliance, the patient's affective bond to the therapist. How is this so? Patients have learned that they need to present themselves in a certain way in order not to threaten their attachments with others and have come to expect that others will respond in a corresponding manner. When their therapists react in ways similar to those of significant others, their behavior is familiar and, therefore, less threatening (i.e., it is consistent with the patient's underlying interpersonal schema).

This does not mean that the therapist's initial complementary response is ultimately what the patient desires or wishes, but rather that this behavior (e.g., acting authoritatively in response to the patient's submissiveness) is what is expected, and therefore understood and tolerated by the patient. Can you imagine how Jim might have felt upon entering therapy to discover his therapist was even more submissive than he? He might well have quit therapy because of the anxiety generated by the mismatch of roles. However, a patient who had a more dominant style might be quite comfortable with the complementarily submissive clinician.

Fortunately, the therapist does not have to expend great effort determining what would be a good "dysfunctional" fit. It happens naturally and does not (and should not) have to be manipulated by the therapist. It is the therapist's "reasonable and socially expected" response to the patient's interpersonal presentation (Butler & Strupp, 1991, p. 93).

Getting oneself unhooked from responding countertransferentially, however, is more problematic and very much at the heart of training in TLDP, since what the patient does not need is yet one more maladaptive relationship. It is essential that the therapist eventually realize how he or she is fostering a replication of the dysfunctional pattern and then use this information to change the nature of the interaction in a positive way and collaboratively invite the patient to look at what is happening between them.

Findings from one study indicate that in therapies with successful outcomes, therapists were able to shift from initial complementary roles to non-complementary positions by the middle of therapy (Dietzel & Abeles, 1975). However, this same study also found that the more maladjusted the patients were (i.e., the more difficult), the more effective they were in eliciting complementary reactions from their therapists throughout therapy.

The TLDP transactional view of countertransference needs to be differentiated from what Strupp and Binder (1984) call the conservative interactive view (p. 147). This view, espoused by several brief-dynamic theorists (e.g., Davanloo, 1978; Mann, 1973; Sifneos, 1979/1987), holds that while the therapist can learn much by being aware of the feelings the patient arouses, the therapist should keep these feelings "under control" and not "join the game." The conservative interactive position is similar to the classical analytic view, in that the therapist's role is defined as that of an objective observer who stays outside the patient's interpersonal space.

One Chief Problematic Relationship Pattern

While patients may have a repertoire of different interpersonal patterns depending on their states of mind, who they are interacting with, etc. (see Horowitz, 1987), the emphasis in TLDP is on comprehending what is a patient's most pervasive and problematic style of relating (which may need to incorporate several divergent views of self and other). This is not to say that other relationship patterns may not be important, but rather that focusing on the most frequently troublesome type of interaction should have ramifications for other less central interpersonal schemas and is pragmatically essential when time is of the essence.

GOALS

TLDP has two major goals: (1) providing a *new experience* for the patient and (2) providing a *new understanding* for the patient. I give more attention to the first goal, which is somewhat of a departure from the emphasis presented in *Psychotherapy in a New Key* (Strupp & Binder, 1984). I will elucidate this difference in the next section.

New Experience

The first and primary goal in conducting TLDP is for the patient to have a new experience. *New* is meant in the sense of being different from and more functional (i.e., healthier) than the maladaptive pattern the patient has become accustomed to. And *experience* emphasizes the affective–action component of change—behaving differently and emotionally appreciating behaving differently. From a TLDP perspective, behaviors that signify a new manner of interacting (e.g., more assertively) rather than specific, content-based experiences (e.g., being able to go to a movie alone) are encouraged. Of course, one cannot manifest a new way of interacting without its being expressed through content of some kind, but the TLDP therapist wants to promote fundamental changes in interacting that will block or defeat maladaptive patterns, rather than instituting specific, concrete behaviors per se.

This new experience emphasizes change through doing. It has two reciprocal parts. First, in the give-and-take of the encounter between therapist and patient, the patient should have a different sense of himself or herself. The patient should have a set of experiences in the therapy sessions in which he or she takes some risks in behaving differently with the therapist. For example, the goal for the subservient Jim could be to gain an increasing sense of himself as acting more assertively and independently as the therapy progressed.

The second part of the new experience involves the patient's having a different experience of the therapist than he or she has had of other significant people in the past. For example, in Jim's therapy, we would hope that he would have a series of experiences in which he observes and feels the therapist to be less punitive, less judgmental, and less rigid than others in his life.

Thus the new experience is actually composed of a set of experiences throughout the therapy in which the patient has a different appreciation of himself or herself, of the therapist, and of the interaction between them. Since the patient's original, dysfunctional interactional style was learned interpersonally through a series of antecedents and consequences, it is assumed that a more functional interpersonal style can be learned through another series of antecedents and consequences.

The function of positive interpersonal experiences (e.g., more assertive patient interacting with less judgmental therapist) is to provide the patient with firsthand learning so that old patterns may be relinquished and new patterns may evolve. This in vivo learning is a critical component in the practice of TLDP. The patient has the opportunity actively to try out new behaviors in the therapy, to see how they feel, and to notice how the therapist responds. This information then shapes the patient's interpersonal schemata of what can be expected from self and others.

These experiential forays into what for the patient has been frightening territory make for heightened affective learning. A tension is created when the familiar (though detrimental) responses to the patient's presentation are not provided. Out of this tension new learning takes place. Such an emotionally intense process is what heats up the therapy and allows progress to be made more quickly than in approaches that depend solely on more abstract learning (usually through interpretation and clarification). As Frieda Fromm-Reichmann is credited with saying, what the patient needs is an experience, not an explanation.

There are parallels between the TLDP goal of a new experience and procedures used in some behavioral techniques, such as exposure therapy, where clients are subjected to feared stimuli without negative consequences. Modern cognitive theorists voice analogous perspectives (e.g., Safran & Segal, 1990) when they talk about *experiential disconfirmation* (disconfirming dysfunctional beliefs about the self and others through new experiences). Similarities can also be found in the *plan formulation method* of Joseph Weiss and Harold Sampson (Sampson & Weiss, 1986; Weiss, 1993), in which change occurs when therapists pass their patients' tests.

The concept of a *corrective emotional experience* described 50 years ago is also applicable. In their classic book, *Psychoanalytic Therapy: Principles and Application* (1946), Franz Alexander and Theodore French challenged the then prevalent assumption concerning the therapeutic importance of exposing repressed memories and genetic reconstruction. In commenting on a case similar to that of Jim's, they wrote:

> The patient had to experience a new father–son relationship before he could release the old. This cannot be done as an intellectual exercise; it has to be lived through, i.e., felt, by the patient and thus become an integral part of his emotional life. Only then can he change his attitudes. (p. 63)

Alexander and French's concept of the corrective emotional experience has been criticized for promoting manipulation of the transference by suggesting that therapists provide a response diametrically opposite to the one the patient expects. For example, if the patient had been raised by an intrusive mother, then the therapist should maintain an aloof stance.

The TLDP concept of the new experience does not involve a direct manipulation of the transference as suggested by Alexander and French; nor is it solely accomplished by the offering of a good therapeutic relationship. Specifically, a therapist can promote a new experience by selectively choosing from all of the helpful, mature, and respectful ways of being in a session those particular aspects that would most undermine a specific patient's dysfunctional style.

By this I do not mean that the therapist changes his or her way of being or personality to provide what the patient's parents did not. Rather, the therapist needs first to have a thorough understanding of the patient's maladaptive pattern (see chapter 4) and from that formulation identify what the therapist could say or do (within the therapeutic role) that would be most likely to subvert the patient's maladaptive interactional style. Consistent with this way of conceptualizing a new experience, Merton Gill (1993) suggests that what is needed are *specific* mutative transference–countertransference interactions. The therapist–patient "interaction has to be about the right content—a content that we would call insight if it became explicit" (p. 115).

For example, Marjorie's maladaptive interpersonal pattern suggested she had deeply ingrained beliefs that she could not be appreciated unless she were the entertaining, effervescent ingenue. When she attempted to joke throughout most of the fifth session, her therapist directed her attention to the contrast between her joking and her anxiously twisting her handkerchief. (New experience: The therapist invites the possibility that he can be interested in her even if she were anxious and not cheerful.)

Jill's lifelong dysfunctional pattern, on the other hand, revealed a meek stance fostered by repeated ridicule from her alcoholic father. She also attempted to joke in the fifth session, nervously twisting her handkerchief. Jill's therapist listened with engaged interest to the joke and did not interrupt. (New experience: The therapist can appreciate her taking center stage and not humiliate her when she is so vulnerable.) In both cases the therapist's interventions (making an observation about nonverbal behavior; listening) were well within the psychodynamic therapist's acceptable repertoire. There was no need to do anything feigned (e.g., laugh uproariously at Jill's joke), nor was there the demand to respond with a similar therapeutic stance to both presentations.

In these cases the therapists' behavior gave the patients the opportunity to disconfirm the patients' interpersonal schemata. With similar experiences of sufficient quality and/or quantity, patients can develop different internalized working models of relationships. In this way TLDP promotes change by altering the basic infrastructure of the patient's transactional world, which then reverberates to influence the concept of self. There is growing empirical evidence that patients internalize their therapeutic relationships. Stephen Quintana and Naomi Meara (1990) found that patients' intrapsychic activity became similar to the way they perceived their therapists treated them in short-term therapy. Steven Harrist and colleagues (1994) went one step further, and found that patients internalized both their own and their therapists' contribution to the therapeutic interaction and that these internalizations were associated with positive outcomes.

My emphasis on the goal of creating a new experience as first and foremost in TLDP has tremendous implications for the selection criteria governing the type of person considered amenable to this brief psychotherapy. If having such a reparative experience facilitates change, then we do not need to select for brief dynamic therapy only the most introspective, intelligent, and verbal of those seeking help. Even those who are concrete thinkers and not psychologically minded usually know when they have had a new experience.* They know when something is happening that is outside their usual frame of reference. They might not be able to conceptualize this new experience fully, abstract it, or even talk about it, but they usually have some "felt sense" (Gendlin, 1991) that they are encountering something unexpected and potentially worthwhile. This emphasis on having a new experience as a major goal allows us to accept a wider range of patients into treatment than many other types of psychodynamic brief therapies, which emphasize understanding through interpretation.

Another reason for my stressing the new experience as a major goal speaks to the relevance of experiential learning. One does not have to be a clinician very long to encounter patients who can talk very knowledgeably, even insightfully, about their dynamics. This is especially true with patients who have been through several insight-oriented therapies. Some can wax eloquent about their fears of surpassing their fathers, inhibitions about commitment, Oedipal conflicts. A few can even provide their DSM-IV diagnoses. And yet they are not leading happier, more fulfilled, more rewarding, or more functional lives. The truth has not set them free.

NEW UNDERSTANDING

The goal of providing a new understanding focuses much more on cognitive changes than the new-experience goal, which emphasizes more the affective–behavioral arena. The patient's new understanding usually involves an identification and comprehension of his or her dysfunctional pattern. To accomplish this the therapist uses common psychodynamic techniques such as interpretation, clarification, and confrontation.

To facilitate a new understanding, the TLDP therapist can point out repetitive patterns that have emerged with the therapist, with past significant oth-

---

*Sometimes therapists need to facilitate patients' perceptions that they have had new therapeutic experiences. Some deprived patients have had so few positive interpersonal experiences in their lives that they have trouble encoding such an experience when it occurs. As one patient of mine stated it, "I have no file folder in which to store these experiences, so they get lost." The therapist's underscoring, emphasizing, and otherwise making new interpersonal behaviors prominent enables the patient to create such a "file folder," and therefore be able to appreciate this taste of something new.

ers, and with present significant others. Patients begin to recognize how they have similar relationships with different people in their lives. This new perspective enables them to examine their active role in perpetuating dysfunctional interactions with others. In Jim's case, he began to appreciate why his wife behaved in a harsh, domineering manner. Previously, he had just thought of her as a "demanding bitch" who was too selfish to comprehend how hard he was trying to win her love.

In TLDP the most potent intervention capable of providing a new understanding is the examination of the here-and-now interactions between therapist and patient. It is chiefly through the therapist's observations about the reenactment of the cyclical maladaptive pattern in the sessions that patients begin to acquire an in vivo understanding of their behaviors. By ascertaining how the pattern has emerged in the therapeutic relationship, the patient has, perhaps for the first time, the opportunity to examine in a safe environment the nature of those behaviors that make up the pattern.

The therapist can help depathologize the patient's behavior and symptoms by helping him or her to understand their historical development. From the TLDP point of view, symptoms and dysfunctional behaviors are the individual's attempt to adapt to threatening situations. For example, in therapy Jim began to understand that as a child he had to be subservient and hypervigilant in order to avoid beatings. This learning enabled him to view his present interpersonal style from a different perspective and allowed him to have some empathy for his childhood plight.

Of course, the degree to which a patient can comprehend, generalize, and expand on any new understanding is limited by such factors as his or her intellectual ability, capacity for introspection, and psychological-mindedness. For some concrete-thinking patients, the most they can understand is a linear connection between their behavior and another's response. Others with more psychological sophistication can appreciate the nuances of their interactional patterns, can delineate how their patterns of relating began, and can discern the subtle manner in which they might be manifested in the present.

A RAPPROCHEMENT

Although I have presented the two TLDP goals as separate entities, in actuality the new experience and the new understanding are parts of the same picture. Both perspectives are always available, but at any one time one becomes figure and the other ground. New experiences, if they are to be more than fleeting sensations, have elements of representations (understandings) of self and others. Similarly, new understandings, if they are to be more than mere intellectualizations, have experiential and affective components.

In teaching TLDP I make a conceptual division between the idea of a new experience and a new understanding for heuristic reasons; it helps the trainees attend to aspects of the change process that are helpful in formulating and intervening quickly. In addition, I have found that psychodynamically trained therapists are so ready to intervene with an interpretation that placing the new experience in the foreground helps them grasp and focus on the big picture: how not to reenact a dysfunctional scenario with the patient.

Procedurally, a therapist encourages a different type of processing depending on whether he or she seeks to promote a new understanding or a new experience at any particular point in the therapy. The emphasis on getting to underlying emotional material by challenging the patient's conceptual framework directly represents *top-down processing;* the approach of accessing the emotional experience directly through facilitating behavioral change or experiential awareness is a *bottom-up* approach (Safran & Greenberg, 1991). The goals outlined in this book involve encouraging both bottom-up and top-down processing.

STRATEGIES

It is not the purpose of this one chapter to outline all the ways a therapist can intervene to accomplish the TLDP goals. Much of the rest of the book will focus on such strategies. At this point, however, I refer the reader to the appendixes, containing the Vanderbilt Therapeutic Strategies Scale (VTSS) and its extensive manual. I have included the VTSS for readers who wish to have a shorthand list of TLDP interventions. The VTSS was designed by Stephen Butler and members of the Center for Psychotherapy Research Team at Vanderbilt University (1986) to measure therapists' adherence to TLDP principles. It was devised because the researchers needed a means for assessing how faithfully the therapists in the Vanderbilt II studies were conducting TLDP. The VTSS was used by raters, not the therapists themselves, to evaluate the degree to which the therapists were using particular TLDP strategies and their skill in implementing them. Research indicates that the VTSS is able to reflect changes in therapists' behaviors following training in TLDP (Butler, Lane, & Strupp, 1988; Butler & Strupp, 1989; Butler, Strupp, & Lane, 1987; Henry et al., 1993b).

Because TLDP is not considered to rely on a set of techniques, the focus of the Scale is on therapeutic *strategies*, which are useful only to the extent that they are embedded in a larger interpersonal relationship. The VTSS is divided into two sections. The first is concerned with a general approach to psychodynamic interviewing and the second with therapist actions specific to TLDP.

Readers may wish to use the VTSS to assess the degree to which they use TLDP strategies in their practices (before and/or after learning about TLDP), or to keep them on track as they try to implement TLDP with a patient (as a sort of before-session checklist). In order to accomplish these aims, you will need to have audio- or videotapes of your sessions with a patient. You can then serve as your own rater by referring to the VTSS manual while listening to or watching your tape. The manual provides rating guidelines for each item, with specific examples and rules to assist in making the ratings. In fact, using the VTSS and its manual can be a learning process in itself because it helps the therapist gain a clinically relevant, action-anchored understanding of TLDP.

CHAPTER 4

Case Formulation: Finding a Focus

T HE MAJOR CONCEPT that distinguishes brief dynamic psychotherapy approaches from long-term psychotherapy is the limited focus of the treatment. Brief therapists need a central theme, topic, or problem to serve as a guide in keeping them on target. Brief therapists cannot pay attention to all clinical data; even fascinating clinical material must sometimes be ignored. Practitioners working with short-term models must learn to use *selective attention* (Malan, 1963) and *benign neglect* (Pumpian-Mindlin, 1953), or run the risk of being overwhelmed by the patient's rich intrapsychic and interpersonal life.

But how does one discern a focus for the therapeutic work? Is it the patient's presenting complaint? For example, "I don't want to be unhappy any more." Or is it a specific behavior? "I have trouble speaking up in a room full of people." Or is it a circumscribed problem? "I am too intimidated by authority figures."

In TLDP the focus for the therapeutic work is the recurrent interpersonal patterns that create and maintain dysfunctional relationships in the patient's life; these in turn are thought to lead to symptoms and problems in living. In other words, the TLDP focus is the maladaptive interactional style of the patient. Given such a large and inclusive focus, how does one go about identifying this style?

In the past, psychodynamic brief therapists used their intuition, insight, and clinical savvy to devise formulations of cases. While these methods may work wonderfully for the gifted or experienced clinician, they are impossible to teach explicitly (and untenable to test empirically). One remedy for this situation was the development of a procedure for deriving a dynamic, interpersonal focus, or *cyclical maladaptive pattern* (CMP) (Schacht, Binder, & Strupp, 1984).

The CMP outlines the idiosyncratic "vicious cycle" a particular patient gets into in relating to others. These cycles or patterns involve inflexible, self-perpetuating behaviors, self-defeating expectations, and negative self-appraisals, which lead to dysfunctional and maladaptive interactions with others (Butler & Binder, 1987; Butler, Strupp, & Binder, 1993). The CMP is composed of four categories that are used to organize the interpersonal information about the patient:

(1) *Acts of the self.* These include the patient's thoughts, feelings, wishes, and behaviors of an interpersonal nature. For example, "When I meet strangers, I can't help thinking they wouldn't want to have anything to do with me" (thought). "I am afraid to take the promotion" (feeling). "I wish I were the life of the party" (wish). "I yell and scream at my kids when they get in my way" (behavior). Sometimes these acts are conscious, like those just mentioned, and sometimes they are outside awareness, as in the case of the woman who does not realize how jealous she is of her sister's accomplishments.

(2) *Expectations of others' reactions.* This category pertains to all the statements having to do with how the patient imagines others will react to him or her in response to some interpersonal behavior (act of the self). "My boss will fire me if I make a mistake." "If I go to the dance, no one will ask me to dance."

(3) *Acts of others toward the self.* This third grouping consists of the actual behaviors of other people, as observed (or assumed) and interpreted by the patient. "When I made a mistake at work, my boss shunned me for the rest of the day." "When I went to the dance, guys asked me to dance, but only because they felt sorry for me."

(4) *Acts of the self toward the self (introject).* In this section belong all of the patient's behaviors or attitudes toward herself or himself—when the self is the object of the interpersonal dynamic. How does the patient treat himself or herself? "When I made the mistake, I berated myself so much I had difficulty sleeping that night." "When no one asked me to dance, I told myself it's because I'm fat, ugly, and unlovable."

Figure 4.1 is a schematic form for categorizing patients' CMPs. Actually writing down the CMP following the initial session(s) can be a very helpful way for trainees to keep focused and to track changes in their formulations. Some institutions have even required this form to be a part of their psychi-

Figure 4.1
Form for the cyclical maladaptive pattern (CMP)

ID:	
1. Acts of the Self	
2. Patients' Expectations of Others' Reactions	
3. Acts of Others Toward the Self	
4. Acts of Self Toward the Self	
5. Countertransference Reactions	

GOALS:
New Experience
New Understanding
Patient Name: Date:

atric inpatient charts, so that whoever is working with the patient on a particular shift can be apprised of a specific patient's current CMP.

By putting the data from these four categories together, the therapist can
usually grasp a particular patient's idiosyncratic interpersonal story or scenario. While people might have several role-relationship patterns (depending on their mood, setting, other people, and so on), the CMP centers around
the person's major, pervasive, preemptive interpersonal pattern. This pattern

describes the predominant dysfunctional style that gets the patient into difficulties and/or leaves him or her feeling anxious, depressed, or unfulfilled.

The therapist frames the CMP information in a narrative fashion: Patients are described as feeling, thinking, wishing, and acting in such-and-such ways; imagining other people will react to them in such-and-such ways; observing that other people do react to them in such-and-such ways; all of which relates to how they treat themselves. For example, "I distrust other people (acts of the self) and stay away from them (acts of the self), because I have come to expect that other people are cold and thoughtless (expectations of others); others ignore me (acts of others), which leaves me having to protect and isolate myself (acts of self toward the self) since I can rely on no one (expectations of others)."

The therapist can start with any of the four categories and build a similar scenario, since they all interlock to form one dynamic framework. For example, one could begin describing the patients' introject, or how they treat themselves, and relate this to how they act toward others and how others react back, which is reflected in what they feel they can expect from their interpersonal world. "I have to protect myself; since I cannot get my needs met by others, I isolate myself; other people respond by ignoring me; and, therefore, I have come to expect the world to be a cold and thoughtless place."

These categories serve two purposes: (1) to provide an organizational framework—to make comprehensible a large mass of data; and (2) to provide a heuristic system that can lead to fruitful hypotheses and other useful models. A CMP should not be seen as an encapsulated version of Truth, but rather as a plausible narrative that incorporates major components of a person's interactional world. As such, it is possible for there to be a number of equally feasible dynamic formulations (Messer & Warren, 1995).

To the four categories of the CMP, I add a fifth one: the therapist's countertransference. How are you feeling being in the room with this patient? What are you pulled to do or not do? The therapist's countertransferential reactions are a very important source of information for understanding the patient's lifelong dysfunctional pattern. One's reaction to the patient should make sense given the patient's dynamic focus. How others react to the patient and the patient's expectation of others' behaviors should have parallels with how the therapist is feeling and acting toward the patient, because the therapist is now a part of that individual's interpersonal world.

As discussed in chapter 3, TLDP uses countertransference in a very specific way. The assumption is that the therapist cannot help becoming entangled in the patient's dysfunctional interactions—not as a helpless fly caught in a spider's web, but rather as an active, responsive, and responding force that contributes to the dysfunctional dynamic. The image is more like the tennis server who puts spin on the ball causing it to bounce in a manner unanticipated by the opponent who swings full force and "whiffs," hitting only air.

If the countertransferential responses to the patient seem inconsistent with the interpersonal narrative, one possibility is that the therapist is experiencing the patient in terms of the therapist's own unique history (more in line with the classical definition of countertransference). If the patient looks like the therapist's brother with whom she's been competitive since she was 5 years old, for example, such an idiosyncratic reaction would have less to do with the patient's CMP than with the therapist's personal issues.

Another reason for countertransferential reactions that do not fit with the CMP is that there may be more information to be learned; that is, the CMP needs revision. The patient might be too vague for the therapist to get a good handle on the situation or may be purposefully obfuscating (e.g., "malingering"). When the therapist's reaction to the patient is not understandable given the patient's acts, expectations, actual behavior of others, and introject, something is amiss.

In the assessment phase of the treatment (which begins with the first contact with the patient—even by phone), the therapist listens to *how* the patient tells his or her story (e.g., deferentially, cautiously, dramatically) as well as the content. The therapist then explores the interpersonal context of the patient's symptoms or problems. By using the four categories of the CMP and his or her own affective, cognitive, and behavioral reactions, the therapist begins to develop a picture of the patient's idiosyncratic, interpersonal scenario. The therapist attends to themes in the emerging material, identifies transactional patterns, and from these develops a narrative of the patient's major, cyclical maladaptive interpersonal pattern. Table 4.1 contains the various general steps involved in formulating and intervening in TLDP.

A CLINICAL APPLICATION

In order to make the concept and usefulness of the CMP come alive, I present to brief-psychotherapy trainees the case of a patient, Lydia Ludlow. I then work with the trainees to generate a dynamic focus for Ms. Ludlow.

Ms. Ludlow came to therapy with multiple problems, which she discussed in a tangential, unfocused manner. I like discussing her case early in the training because if the trainees can learn how to derive a focus for her, they should have less difficulty with patients who present more cogently and concisely.

Table 4.1

Steps in TLDP Formulation and Intervention

1. Let the patient tell his or her own story in his or her own words.

2. Explore the interpersonal context related to symptoms or problems.

3. Use the categories of the CMP to gather, categorize, and probe for information.

4. Listen for themes in the patient's content (about past and present relationships) and manner of interacting in session.

5. Be aware of reciprocal reactions (countertransferential pushes and pulls).

6. Be vigilant for reenactments of dysfunctional interactions in the therapeutic relationship.

7. Explore patient's reaction to the evolving relationship with the therapist.

8. Develop a CMP narrative (story) describing the patient's predominant dysfunctional interactive pattern.

9. From this CMP outline the goals for treatment.

10. Facilitate a new experience of more adaptive relating within the therapeutic relationship consistent with the patient's CMP (Goal 1).

11. Help the patient to identify and understand his or her dysfunctional pattern as it occurs with the therapist and others in his or her life (Goal 2).

12. Assist the patient in appreciating the once adaptive function of his or her manner of interacting.

13. Revise and refine the CMP throughout the therapy.

Ms. Ludlow was an overweight woman who looked and acted younger than her 45 years. She was recently separated from her husband. Besides marital difficulties, her numerous problems included compulsive eating, financial woes, an alcoholic mother, and "I don't know what love is." Her previous therapist had recently increased her fee to an amount Ms. Ludlow felt she could not afford, so she came to the Outpatient Clinic.

I purposely do not give more information about Ms. Ludlow's background, because I am interested in preparing the trainees to attend to what they are seeing, hearing, and feeling in the session as a way of obtaining sufficient information to derive a dynamic focus. It is obvious from the way the CMP is obtained that the emphasis is not on DSM-IV diagnoses nor on the specific content of the problem, but rather on the patient's *interpersonal processes*.

[IN THE CLASSROOM WITH THE TRAINEES]

[Setting: A seminar room in the psychiatric outpatient clinic of a large teaching medical center. There is a circle of eight chairs around the periphery of the room with a videotape playback machine and a blackboard at one end. I sit near the VCR; the other chairs are occupied by the various trainees: three psychology predoctoral interns, two psychiatric residents, one social work intern, and one clinic staff member.]

LEVENSON: Now that I have told you a little bit about the patient, Ms. Ludlow, let me tell you some things about the therapist, Margaret Ellison. Dr. Ellison, at the time of this therapy, was a third-year psychiatry resident. She had just rotated off the inpatient unit. Not only was Ms. Ludlow her first brief-psychotherapy patient, she was also her very first outpatient case. Dr. Ellison came into training, much as you have, with a brief introduction to TLDP.

I advise the trainees to let the patients tell their own stories in the beginning session(s) rather than rely on the traditional psychiatric interview or clinic intake form, which structures the patients' responses into categories of information (e.g., developmental history, schooling, medical history). With the patients' interactions less confined, therapists can learn not only from the content of the patients' stories, but also from the manner in which they convey this information (for example, emphasizing minute details; externalizing all responsibility for events; seeking guidance and reassurance from the therapist). In this way the trainees will learn firsthand the content *and* process of any dysfunctional patterns.

I ask the trainees to videotape their first session and to inform patients that this is an evaluation session to see whether TLDP is appropriate for them. Patients are further told that the therapists in the brief program work as a team, showing portions of the videotape and consulting with colleagues and a supervisor during a group supervision session. Therapists let patients know at the second session (which is scheduled for the following week) the decision of the team regarding the suitability of TLDP for them. If the team decides that the brief, interpersonally focused treatment is not appropriate (e.g., the problem does not have interpersonal roots, the patient is psychotic, the patient is not willing to maintain regular appointments), alternatives are discussed with the patient. (A fuller discussion on selection criteria is contained in chapter 5.)

[CLASSROOM]

LEVENSON: I will play for you the first 5 minutes of Dr. Ellison's first evaluation session with Ms. Ludlow. I have written the four categories of the
dynamic focus on the blackboard. As we listen to Ms. Ludlow on tape,
I will write down some of what she has to say under one of the four
groupings. I will place enough of what she has to say under each of the
four categories so that you can get an idea of how I listen and organize
material in order to derive an early formulation of a case.

When we have seen these initial five minutes of the first session on
videotape, I will then ask you for your own countertransferential reactions to this patient. We will then practice using information about Ms.
Ludlow's thoughts, feelings, and behaviors, her expectations of others'
behavior, the behavior of others toward her, and her attitude and behavior toward herself, along with your reactions to Ms. Ludlow to derive an
interpersonal narrative of her interactional style. This will enable us to
formulate Ms. Ludlow's lifelong, cyclical maladaptive pattern.

[VIDEOTAPE]

Therapist: Well, maybe you can tell me a little bit about what's going on
for you in getting into this program.

Ms. Ludlow: Um. (pause) I've never been in with any kind of psychology until I was married. I used religion to try to get better. I didn't
hate psychologists, but I just didn't turn to them. I've gone to Stay
Well, my HMO, and most recently to the Care Center. The lady's leaving the Care Center and their fees were going up. She said she'd keep
me on, but she's caught in the middle.

Therapist: Where is this Care Center?

Ms. Ludlow: Downtown Funston.

Therapist: How long have you been working with her?

Ms. Ludlow: Not that long. There was a long waiting list. I did an intake
at Mount Rushmore Clinic and the Care Center and they both said
that's fine, but there was a long waiting list. And when I needed it the
most, I've had to wait and wait. And I lost my HMO coverage, so I've
been making do. But I've done a lot of reading. Alice Miller's book on
child abuse and Scott Peck's *People of the Lie*. That's my parents. I can't
get all the answers. Positive affirmations aren't enough. I need more.

Therapist: Can you say what's troubling you now and what brought you
into therapy?

Ms. Ludlow: When I see what my parents did and what they taught
me—I don't know what love is with my husband. I'd like to get back
with him. It isn't manipulation. I'm a compulsive eater. If I'm on a

strict diet, honest to God, my metabolism changes. It really does. I'm eating measured protein. I'm on the edge of answers. I watch Bradshaw on TV and they talk about compulsive behavior and manipulation. And I think I've almost got it.

Therapist: You said you don't know what love is with your husband. Can you say more about that?

Ms. Ludlow: Well, a real duck soup example is if I say "I love you," in the old days, he was supposed to say "I love you" right back. It called for it. And sometimes he would say "I know that." And it would drive me up the wall. And, of course, I can laugh about that now. But I really don't know what being together and being OK is. Because my parents are like this [interlocks her fingers and pushes and pulls hands together in front of her]. My mother's drinking; Dad's pouring. I don't feel loved; I don't feel OK.

[A few minutes later in the same session]

Ms. Ludlow: I realized my parents weren't there for me. They're self-centered and holier-than-thou. They've concentrated on my problems all my life. My dad is a doctor; he specializes in weight control. My mother is a health fanatic and a size four. They concentrated on my physical defects. I was beautiful. But then it was one damn thing after another. My lip curled so they made me massage it, and then they got me braces. And I was grateful for that. But it's one thing after another. They've been trying to fix me all my life.

Therapist: What was that like for you, when you were younger?

Ms. Ludlow: They were perfect. I didn't see them as human beings until a few years ago.

[CLASSROOM]

LEVENSON: Let me get your countertransferential reactions first. Imagine you are the therapist—you are Dr. Ellison. How are you feeling and thinking about Ms. Ludlow? How are you being pushed and pulled to react to her?

TRAINEE: Well, I hear Ms. Ludlow saying that she is here, but she doesn't expect much from the therapy.

LEVENSON: And how are you feeling hearing that this patient does not expect much from you or the therapy?

As this trainee's response exemplifies, it is often difficult for the therapist, especially a less experienced one, to focus on his or her own reactions to the patient. We have been trained to concentrate primarily on what is going on with the patient. Not attending to one's countertransference can rob the therapist of a critical source of information about the patient's chief problem.

TRAINEE: I'm kind of irritated.

TRAINEE: I am really frustrated and annoyed. I want to shake her and say "Why are you here?"

TRAINEE: Yes. And I'm feeling overwhelmed by her hostility. I feel insecure, especially when she made that remark, "I don't hate psychologists"!

This trainee was able to pinpoint exactly what statement by the patient engendered the feeling of insecurity. The therapist's being able to specify what causes certain thoughts, feelings, and/or behaviors can be especially helpful in understanding how the patient elicits unrewarding interactions with others.

TRAINEE: (continuing) I feel set up. Everyone has tried to fix her and I am going to fall into the same situation. I felt a pressure to fix her and to keep her on track. But how can I compete with Bradshaw and Alice Miller? If these experts didn't help her, I can't do any better. I am going to let her down too. So I feel helpless and hopeless.

TRAINEE: She seems so childlike. I had trouble remembering she is 45. I guess I feel frustrated.

TRAINEE: I can see what you mean. Initially I felt compassionate toward Ms. Ludlow. She is just so needy that I want to take care of her. But then I starting feeling like she was asking for so much. My caretaking turned to irritation.

TRAINEE: I, too, thought her needs seemed so great. She feels like an empty pit which I am never going to fill up. And then, of course, that makes me feel ineffectual, but also like I want to avoid her.

TRAINEE: I agree. She is so hostile and demanding that I felt like distancing myself. She seems accustomed to keeping people at bay.

LEVENSON: So now we have an idea of some of the reactions she might pull from the therapist. In a group supervision we can get the sense of agreement among the participants—consensual validation. This patient is causing a reaction that seems more consistent than divergent. We all have our own complex personalities with unique backgrounds, and yet, for the most part, imagining being with this patient resulted in feelings of irritation, frustration, helplessness, and distance.

TRAINEE: Her voice put me on edge. It's like she's in a fog. She uses this little helpless voice, and you're supposed to reach your hand to her and know where to lead her. Yet she won't give you the information or permission to do that. The way she presents herself is this vague way where she starts to answer the question, and she even said something like, "I'm on the edge of answers," and it seems like this is her theme.

LEVENSON: Can you expand on that more?

TRAINEE: This is where I feel set up. She calls out, "Here, come and help me," but I get a sense she won't let me—that she is going to sabotage every move. Even if you manage to help her a little bit, she might take it as a comment that she is defective. I feel like my hands are tied behind my back.

LEVENSON: It seems like your comments are expanding from your countertransferential reactions into the area of Ms. Ludlow's cyclical maladaptive pattern. Let's take a look at the four CMP categories and see how I organized the data from these initial interactions.

> *Acts of the self:* used religion, went to an HMO, had to wait and wait, making do, done a lot of reading, watch TV, on the edge of answers.

> *Expectations of others:* husband was supposed to say "I love you."

> *Acts of others toward the self:* my therapist is leaving the mental health center, there was a long waiting list at the clinic, my mother's drinking and Dad's pouring, my parents have concentrated on my problems all my life, they've been trying to fix me.

> *Acts of the self toward the self (introject):* I don't feel OK, I don't know what being OK is, I was beautiful, I massaged my lip, I am a compulsive eater.

Under *acts of the self* I placed such behaviors as Ms. Ludlow's reading books about psychological issues and watching educational "pop psychology" TV programs. Usually such activities as reading and watching TV are not thought to be interactional, but for Ms. Ludlow they have interpersonal meaning. It seems she wants to learn about how others relate and their motivations so she can better understand what is going on in her interpersonal world. Ms. Ludlow seems to convey by the tone and phrasing of her material that it is the others in her life who need the help. She is more the innocent bystander.

We know far less about Ms. Ludlow's *expectations of others* than about her own thoughts and behaviors. The CMP structure can be helpful in alerting the therapist to areas of scant information. The therapist can then follow up with questions designed specifically to elicit the relevant material. For example, "When you go home for a visit now, what do you expect from your parents?"

Ms. Ludlow does allude to her unfulfilled desire to have her husband tell her that he loves her when she says "I love you." One also gets a pervasive feeling that she believes others will not come through for her or meet her needs. However, I give less emphasis to clinical inference in this initial attempt at developing a working formulation, preferring to stay close to the descriptive data. This does not mean that one cannot form hypotheses (and even make some far-fetched guesses), but at the outset, when one's information about a patient is so limited, it is wise not to fill in too many blanks.

Ms. Ludlow gives us much information about how she interprets the *acts of others.* For example, she sees that her parents bought her braces (and she is grateful for that), but she views their attempts to fix her as designed to deflect attention from their own problems by highlighting her deformities. Ms. Ludlow views her parents as self-centered and holier-than-thou. They were not there for her. Similarly, we hear of how her previous therapist increased her fee and also how other mental health professionals were not there for her "when I needed it the most."

The fourth category, *acts of the self toward the self,* or introject, I have found to be the most difficult category to fill in. Patients often do not disclose how or why they treat themselves in certain ways until the treatment is well under way and a positive therapeutic alliance has been established. Butler and Binder (1987) make the point that the action component of the introject is critical for understanding the patient's active role in developing his or her CMP. For example, if a male patient stated, "When she approached me, my self-esteem fell to zero," the therapist should try to clarify what *behaviors* (public or private) the patient engaged in which resulted in this deflation. (For example, the therapist could ask, "What did you say to yourself that made you feel so unworthy?") In this way, the therapist not only begins to understand the patient's automatic thoughts (Beck, Rush, Shaw, & Emery, 1979) that contribute to the dysfunctional dynamic, but also conveys to the patient that the patient is *actively* doing something to promote or encourage the very feeling he or she finds intolerable.

In addition to using the content of what Ms. Ludlow says to understand her customary way of interacting with people, we can also use the *way* she presents her story to formulate her case. For example, we know much more about what Ms. Ludlow is *passively* doing (waiting, making do) and what others are *actively* doing to her (fixing her, concentrating on her problems) than we know about her expectations of others' behavior or how she treats herself. From these process data, we can hypothesize that Ms. Ludlow may be externalizing responsibility for her problems and personalizing others' reactions to her. And Ms. Ludlow's manner of talking (voice quality, phrasing, tone) and nonverbal behavior contribute to the therapist's estimation of her interactional style (as resembling that of a little girl).

When initially formulating the CMP, some therapists become concerned about whether they have placed what the patient is saying in the right category. There are simple guidelines, such as, the patient's own behaviors toward others usually go under *acts of the self,* whereas behaviors directed toward the self usually go under *acts of the self toward the self.* But sometimes the meaning of a particular behavior (whether it is directed at others or toward the self) is not so obvious. For example, does Ms. Ludlow eat compulsively to annoy her diet-doctor father (acts of the self) or to soothe herself (acts of the self toward the self), or both? Fortunately, one need not become obsessed with the correct placement, because these categories are primarily to help the therapist organize large amounts of data and eventually they will all be combined into one narrative. What is important is to understand the patient's behaviors, thoughts, attitudes, and motivations and how these interrelate to form the resulting interpersonal dynamic.

[CLASSROOM]

TRAINEE: I can see how you got the acts of the self based on what the patient said, but I thought she wanted someone to love her and take care of her.

LEVENSON: Yes, I can certainly see how you drew that inference. But initially what I like to do in formulating the case is to stay very close to what the patient says and the descriptive data. Ms. Ludlow never really says directly that she wants someone to love her. Later when you step back and examine all the information you have gathered, you can *abstract* a CMP. Then I feel more comfortable making inferences which connect the basic data to form a narrative. What I would like to push you to do now is to take the basic data for Ms. Ludlow's CMP and combine them with the manner and process with which she presents them and our own countertransferential reactions to derive a narrative about this woman's dysfunctional maladaptive interaction patterns. Why are Ms. Ludlow's relationships so unsatisfactory?

TRAINEE: She is trying and trying to improve herself. People try to help, but they fail, confirming her expectation that people cannot help her.

TRAINEE: I see that she is searching for self-worth. She is constantly being disappointed by others. Others can't do enough. They tell her what to do or try to fix her or ignore her, but these very behaviors leave her feeling flawed, unloved, broken, and unaccepted.

TRAINEE: This is a woman who does not have much worth. She feels criticized by others and this leads her to retaliate as a way to deal with rejection. She is then left feeling needy and like a victim, but this only puts others off even more and confirms Ms. Ludlow's worst fear that she is worthless.

TRAINEE: This is a woman who makes weak attempts to understand herself. She approaches others for help but does not really believe they can be there for her—because no one ever has. She therefore stays helpless, causing herself and others to believe she really does need fixing. When others try to help, Ms. Ludlow resents them because the underlying message is that they find her unacceptable the way she is. This attitude of needy resentment causes others eventually to abandon her. This leaves Ms. Ludlow feeling faulty, angry, confused, lonely, and disappointed.

TRAINEE: She has the expectation that someone will be perfect and take care of everything. When that expectation is not confirmed, she is disappointed. She sees that other people let her down.

TRAINEE: It seems the only attention she gets is from overeating and complaining and failing.

TRAINEE: Because she was rejected by her parents, she has this overwhelming dependency and neediness, which she fills up with food and books and other people's advice. But nothing makes the needy feel better. People eventually disappoint her.

LEVENSON: Leaving her feeling how?

TRAINEE: Leaving her feeling unsatisfied and unsatiated. That's this being on the edge. If she felt better about herself, the failures of others would not be so important to her.

One can see from the trainees' attempts to understand the pattern of Ms. Ludlow's interpersonal scenario that while each narrative is somewhat different in focus, scope, and completeness, they all seem to be on the same wavelength. Some of the main themes of these variations:

Acts of the self: Ms. Ludlow sees herself as trying to "improve herself" and deal with her "problems," but she feels very needy and victimized by others. Her resentment about the way she has been treated by others keeps her waiting for someone who could give her what she needs.

Expectations of others' reactions: While Ms. Ludlow hopes that someone perfect will provide for her, she has come to expect that others will find fault with her and reject her at worst, and try to "fix" her at best. However, both of these approaches convey to her that she is defective and unacceptable as she is.

Acts of others toward the self: Others find Ms. Ludlow's passive–aggressive behavior, resentful neediness, and diffuse presentation irritating and overwhelming. If they try to help, Ms. Ludlow interprets their behavior as nonempathic attempts to humiliate her; if they leave her alone, she understands this as evidence that they see her as unlovable.

Acts of the self toward the self: Ms. Ludlow sees herself as a victim in a world of nonempathic people. Putting other people down in righteous indignation helps her to feel vindicated and special, but her self-defeating behaviors (e.g., overeating) only serve to confirm her own fears that she is truly defective and unlovable and, therefore, in need of someone to fix her.

THE 5-MINUTE FORMULATION

I call these initial attempts to formulate the case the *5-minute formulation.* I am not promoting the formulation of a case after only 5 minutes with a patient; rather, I use the rudimentary or 5-minute formulation as a didactic device to demonstrate how much a therapist might know at the end of only 5 minutes of interacting with a patient. As each of the successive 5-minute segments unfolds, additional information could either strengthen, modify, or negate one's previous understanding of a patient's dysfunctional interpersonal scenario. In this way, for most cases, one can derive a working formulation of the case by the end of the first session.

Since the CMP should form a blueprint for the therapy, I continue the didactic exercise by having the trainees use the initial formulation of Ms. Ludlow's case to derive the goals of her therapy. If Ms. Ludlow displays the maladaptive style we described, then what *new experience* and what *new understanding* would be helpful for her to have in the process of the brief therapy? First, what new experience would be conducive to derail her hypothesized repetitive interaction sequence?

[CLASSROOM]

TRAINEE: She should be able to find a way to ask for what she needs directly.

TRAINEE: She could set up her own boundaries more successfully so that she does not need to depend on others to do that for her.

TRAINEE: What about, "It's OK to be flawed"?

LEVENSON: To accept who she is? Perhaps she does not have to massage her upper lip to be acceptable to others. She does not have to be perfect.

TRAINEE: To feel less like a victim. To be able to get what she wants more directly instead of depending on the kindness of strangers.

TRAINEE: To experience herself as less helpless in a relationship with Dr. Ellison, the therapist. To have some sense that she is enough or could get more of what she wants on her own.

TRAINEE: To experience herself as effective, not defective.

TRAINEE: Yes. And that's related to Dr. Ellison's not being pulled into fixing her or seeing her as defective.

What this trainee is discovering is that the new experience is really composed of at least two components: The first is how the patient will experience herself in the interaction, and the second is how she will experience the other person in the give-and-take of the relationship.

[CLASSROOM]

TRAINEE: The patient should have the experience of herself as an autonomous adult able to find her own answers and meet her own needs. And also to experience the therapist as not critical—as interested in her without trying to fix her. The therapist should not abandon her.

TRAINEE: Yes, then she would have the experience of someone telling her she is OK and worthwhile.

LEVENSON: Alright. So Dr. Ellison should not try to fix Ms. Ludlow, but should somehow convey her interest in the patient. And then hopefully Ms. Ludlow would have a sense of herself as someone who did not need to define herself by others' criteria, feel prey to their needs, and then feel resentful.

As you can see, the goal is not content-based, such as encouraging Ms. Ludlow to join Weight Watchers; rather, it is a process-focused goal. The therapist is not constrained to imagine or define specifically how this new experience might be accomplished. The precise form such new experiences might take in the actual therapeutic situation can rarely be predicted. The process-focused TLDP goal facilitates the therapist's awareness and sensitivity to recognize and promote *anything* that transpires between patient and therapist which fosters movement in the desired direction.

The trainees appear to have some agreement about the type of experiences (of self and other) that might facilitate change: Ms. Ludlow's experience of Dr. Ellison as trying to understand and collaborate with her without trying to fix her and her experience of herself as effective and not defective.

[CLASSROOM]

TRAINEE: I would also like her to realize what she does affects other people—or would that be something that would be more of a long-term goal?

LEVENSON: What you are now addressing is what I see as the second goal of TLDP: the new understanding. What do we want Ms. Ludlow to understand? What would we like her to have some awareness of, some insight into, by the time the therapy is completed? What faulty thinking would you want her to be on her way to correcting as the therapy concludes?

TRAINEE: How she pushes people away.

TRAINEE: That she can't rely on others to make life OK for her.

TRAINEE: I'd like her to see that she tries to get others to help her because she feels so inadequate.

TRAINEE: I guess I hope she can realize how she sabotages herself by presenting in a childish way and then gets a parental response.

TRAINEE: Also she might be operating under the idea that being needy and flawed might be the only way to have a relationship. This was the way she related to her parents. I would like her to see that there are other bases for relationships besides presenting oneself as a needy child.

LEVENSON: Whenever possible, I like to include as part of that new understanding the patient's awareness of the general origin of the dysfunctional pattern. Why did this maladaptive way of relating to others begin? I make the presumption that what now seem like dysfunctional ways of relating began as functional ways of maintaining relationships, usually with parents. Perhaps being a defective, overweight child was the only way to get any attention in her diet-doctor-father and size-four-mother home. The understanding of the adaptive function of one's past behavior can promote empathy for oneself and help alleviate the self-blame that can often come with increased responsibility for one's behavior.

In general, the trainees' comments indicate they would like Ms. Ludlow to have some understanding of how she pulls others to respond as chastising parents when she presents as a needy, frustrating child. They would like for her to be able to see she could have relationships that were not founded on her being defective.

Now that we have our dynamic focus and two goals for the therapy, I push the trainees to use the 5-minute formulation—this time to predict what might be the nature of the transference–countertransference interaction. If they were Dr. Ellison's consultants and could warn her of impending problems in her work with Ms. Ludlow, how would they advise her? If one can use the CMP to anticipate the nature of the unfolding therapeutic relationship, then truly the dynamic focus can become a blueprint of the entire therapy.

[CLASSROOM]

LEVENSON: Now, based on our formulation of this case, let's consider what will be the nature of the interaction between Ms. Ludlow and Dr. Ellison.

TRAINEE: Ms. Ludlow will let Dr. Ellison know that she is not doing a good enough job. She will be expecting that Dr. Ellison will try to fix her. Then Ms. Ludlow will feel betrayed.

TRAINEE: I would warn Dr. Ellison not to go with the pull to rescue, organize, and ultimately fix Ms. Ludlow, because it will boomerang. The pull is for Dr. Ellison to put emotional braces on Ms. Ludlow and send her off all rehabilitated, but then Ms. Ludlow will feel victimized by someone who cannot accept her for who she is.

TRAINEE: Also there is the danger that Dr. Ellison will be pulled to abandon the field—if not in reality, then emotionally, as she becomes frustrated with Ms. Ludlow's passive resistance.

TRAINEE: Also, the therapist could feel so attacked by Ms. Ludlow that she could retaliate by saying some subtly hostile things back to the patient.

TRAINEE: I would advise Dr. Ellison to avoid plans, advice, and getting caught in "yes-buts." Dr. Ellison has to maintain her own sense of being worthwhile. Otherwise she might end up feeling helpless and incompetent.

By this time, the trainees have anticipated the entire therapy. They have generated the CMP, the two goals, and ideas about transference–countertransference reenactments, all from 5 minutes of videotaped material. This way of categorizing data enables the therapist to outline the interaction dynamic from the outset. As one learns more in the next 5 minutes and all the subsequent minutes, the dynamic formulation gets altered to better fit the incoming data.

A recent study using the VAST Project data has relevance for the meaningfulness of TLDP case formulation in a real clinical situation (Hartmann, 1994, Hartmann & Levenson, 1995). CMP case formulations written by the treating therapists were read by five experienced clinicians who did not know anything about the patients or their therapies. These raters were able to agree on the patients' interpersonal problems just based on their reading of the CMP narratives. There is also a statistically significant relationship between what interpersonal problems the raters felt *should* have been discussed in the therapy (based only on the patients' CMPs) and those topics the therapists said actually *were* discussed. Perhaps most meaningful is the finding that better outcomes were achieved the more these therapies stayed focused on topics relevant to the patients' CMPs. Thus, these preliminary findings indicate that the TLDP case formulations can convey reliable interpersonal information to clinicians otherwise unfamiliar with the case, guide the issues that are discussed in the therapy, and lead to better outcomes the more therapists can adhere to them.

However, difficult patients provide challenges for their therapists with regard to deriving and maintaining a focus. For example, in a study examining the treatment records of patients, every difficult patient (but no control patient) lacked a comprehensive formulation of problems and a treatment plan (Neill, 1979). As the following chapters will show, the clarity of the formulation permits the therapist to intervene in ways that have the greatest likelihood of being therapeutic. Thus the therapy can be briefer *and* more effective at the same time.

CHAPTER 5

Selection Criteria and CMP Reenactments

THIS CHAPTER will look at the case of Ms. Ludlow and Dr. Ellison as a way of exploring how selection factors and the working CMP are employed clinically. After the first session with Ms. Ludlow, Dr. Ellison considered the suitability of TLDP as a format for Ms. Ludlow's treatment. After seeing her videotape and discussing her case in supervision, I asked Dr. Ellison whether she felt Ms. Ludlow was an appropriate patient for TLDP. We will return to Dr. Ellison's reply after a brief introduction to TLDP selection criteria.

SELECTION

The first session is presented to patients as an evaluation session to assess the appropriateness of TLDP treatment for them. However, as has already been stated, the evaluation actually begins with the very first contact with the patient, whether directly (e.g., by phone) or indirectly (e.g., through a referral). How a patient handles the first contact with the therapist can be very telling about the patient's hopes, expectations, fears, attitudes, and overall style. For example, the patient who responds in a deferential and obsequious manner to that first phone call from the therapist ("Oh, Doctor, I so much appreciate your willingness to see me; I have heard what a marvelous therapist you are and I am so looking forward to meeting you and am so glad you will be able to see me although you are so busy with more important things") is already affecting the therapist differently than the patient who replies in a challenging, argumentative way ("I can only come in for appointments on Thursday afternoons, and I cannot work with anyone who is going to be late. Are you late for sessions?").

And in the face-to-face meeting, much can be learned about dysfunctional patterns of relating to others by observing the nonverbal and paralingual behavior of patients right from the outset. For example, structural family therapists (e.g., Minuchin, 1974) have been trained to observe how family members arrange themselves in the waiting room, and who walks down the hall with whom and in what order. Such "structures" can be revealing about how the family functions. In individual therapy, too, the therapist gains valuable information about the patient's possible characteristic ways of relating by his or her demeanor.

For example, does the patient's wife appear with him in the waiting room? Does she answer for him when you introduce yourself to him? And does he ask her permission when you suggest that you and he initially meet alone for the first part of the hour? Such a situation confronted one particular trainee and will be discussed in chapter 13.

Of course, there are several caveats, lest first impressions become snap judgments frozen in perpetuity. First of all, there is the reality that the therapy situation involves someone in a needy position coming for help from someone who has expertise in helping. Approaching a professional for assistance when one is in pain and feeling vulnerable concerning intimate, embarrassing, or shameful issues can cause a good deal of anxiety. In our society, going for therapy is still stigmatized as a sign of weakness and personal failure for most people. The initial interaction between therapist and patient should be understood in this context, where anxiety, deference, and caution may be the rule or baseline behavior.

Second, the manner in which a person interacts is not solely determined by his or her idiosyncratic pattern of living. It is also a product of culture, society, economic status, race, gender, and age, just to mention a few. The therapist must be cautious not to pathologize or seek to change what might be a culturally acceptable, and even prescribed, way of relating, for example. Chapter 7 discusses how one might be able to differentiate a maladaptive pattern indicative of dysfunction from a manner of interacting that is normative for one's particular referent or membership group.

Five major selection criteria are used in determining a patient's appropriateness for TLDP. These are listed in table 5.1.

First, patients must be in *emotional discomfort* so they are motivated to change and make the sacrifices of time, effort, and money that therapy requires; they need to be willing to endure the sometimes difficult and

Table 5.1

Selection Criteria for TLDP

1. *Emotional discomfort.* The patient is in sufficient emotional pain because of his or her feelings and/or behavior to seek therapeutic help.

2. *Basic trust.* The patient has sufficient trust and hope for relief from distress that he or she is willing to come for regular appointments to talk about his or her life.

3. *Willingness to consider conflicts in interpersonal terms.* The patient can entertain the possibility that his or her problems reflect difficulties in relating to others.

4. *Willingness to examine feelings.* The patient is open to *considering* the possibly important role that his or her emotional life plays in interpersonal difficulties. Furthermore, the patient is able to distance emotionally from possibly intense feelings so that they can be examined.

5. *Capacity to relate to the therapist in a "meaningful way."* The patient is able to experience and relate to others as separate, whole persons, so that new interpersonal experiences can be perceived and that reenactments of dysfunctional relationships within the therapeutic situation can be examined. In cases where the patient persists in relentless, intractable dysfunctional interactions with the therapist, the therapist may be prevented from functioning in a psychotherapeutic role.

Modified from Strupp & Binder (1984)

painful therapeutic process. Most therapists have confronted the enormous (and often insurmountable) problem of trying to treat people who are court-referred or dragged in to the consultation room by an exasperated family member. Systems-oriented family therapists (e.g., Haley, 1976; Weakland, Fisch, & Watzlawick, 1974) are adept at transferring the highly vocalized pain from some family members to others within the same system. For example, the overwrought parents who are in turmoil concerning their misbehaving but blasé son learn how to cause him some "pain" (to motivate him for change) by imposing a curfew.

Second, patients must be *willing to come for appointments and engage with the therapist*—or at least talk. Initially such an attitude may be fostered by hope or faith in a positive outcome. Later it might stem from actual experiences of the therapist as a helpful partner.

Third, patients must be willing to consider how their *relationships* have contributed to their distressing symptoms, negative attitudes, and/or behavioral difficulties. The operative word here is *willing.* Suitable patients do not actually have to walk in the door indicating that they have difficulties in relating to others. Rather, in the give-and-take of the therapeutic encounter, they must show signs of being *willing to consider the possibility* that they have problems relating to others.

Fourth, patients must be willing to *examine feelings* that may hinder more successful relationships and may foster more dysfunctional ones. Also, Strupp and Binder (1984) elaborate that the patient needs to possess "sufficient capacity to emotionally distance from these feelings so that the patient and therapist can jointly examine them" (p. 57).

And fifth, patients should be capable of having a *meaningful relationship* with the therapist. Again, it is not expected that the patient initially relates in a collaborative manner. But the potential for establishing such a relationship needs to exist. Patients cannot be out of touch with reality or so impaired that they have difficulty appreciating that their therapists are separate people. It would be impossible to conduct an interpersonal therapy if the patient did not know where he or she ended and the therapist began.

Compared to the selection criteria from other psychodynamic models (e.g., M. Horowitz, 1976; Mann, 1973; Sifneos, 1979/1987), the five outlined by Strupp and Binder are quite broad. They do not focus on static patient variables (e.g., psychological-mindedness, above-average intelligence). No mention is made of specific diagnoses or symptom clusters. Rather, these selection criteria emphasize qualities that can be judged only as they emerge in the therapeutic relationship. For example, with the therapist's help, is a patient able to begin to realize that his depression is not solely due to the pain in his lower back, but is predominantly related to his fears of becoming incapacitated and dependent on his children? Through interactions with the therapist, can a patient begin to let herself feel how angry and disappointed she is with her less than perfect helper, and see that her therapist does not punish her for having these feelings?

The empirical literature supports such a notion of selection built on knowledge that emanates from the interactive therapeutic process. Investigations have consistently found the state of the therapeutic alliance to be correlated with therapeutic success (e.g., Eaton, Abeles, & Gutfreund, 1988; Gaston, 1990; Marmar et al., 1989; Orlinsky & Howard, 1986). And the helping alliance has been found to be the best predictor of therapeutic outcome, outweighing the contribution of other factors, such as theoretical approach or specific techniques (Luborsky et al., 1985).

However, in TLDP it has been my experience that patients who have long-standing, dysfunctional ways of relating to others have problems forming positive therapeutic alliances. Rather than rejecting such "difficult" patients for TLDP because they have impediments to forming working relationships with therapists, the TLDP work focuses on the very reasons these patients find being collaborative a challenge.

Therefore, difficulties in forming a therapeutic bond are not obstacles to benefiting from TLDP, but instead provide therapeutic opportunities. Problems in relating to the therapist that emerge in the therapist's office become the in vivo setting for change. From this behavioral–systems perspective, patients can profit from an interactional therapy without being as introspective, psychologically minded, or even verbal as required by models of brief dynamic therapy that place more of an emphasis on insight and understanding.

The exclusionary criteria for TLDP (see table 5.2) are very similar to those for red-flagging patients in other brief dynamic approaches. These criteria are quite minimal and would apply to most psychodynamic approaches, long-term or short-term. (For a cogent discussion of selection and exclusionary criteria for a wide variety of dynamic models, see Crits-Christoph & Barber, 1991, pp. 328–330).

Now let us return to Dr. Ellison, who at the outset of this chapter was considering the appropriateness of TLDP for her patient. I asked the training group what they thought Dr. Ellison would say about the advisability of accepting Ms. Ludlow into treatment.

[CLASSROOM]

TRAINEE: Well, the patient seems to be suitable. She meets the selection criteria—she is definitely stuck right now and seems to be distressed.

TRAINEE: Yes. She already sees that her issues are interpersonal ones.

TRAINEE: And she is not suicidal or drinking—so I don't think she meets any of the exclusionary criteria.

Table 5.2

Exclusionary Criteria for Time-Limited Dynamic Psychotherapy

1. The patient is not able to attend to the process of a verbal give-and-take with the therapist (e.g., the patient has delirium, dementia, psychosis, or diminished intellectual status).

2. The patient's problems can be treated more effectively by other means (e.g., the patient has a specific phobia or manic-depressive illness).

3. The patient cannot tolerate the active, interpretative, interactive therapy process, which often heightens anxiety (e.g., the patient has impulse-control problems, abuses alcohol and/or drugs, or has a history of repeated suicide attempts).

Adapted from MacKenzie (1988)

TRAINEE: She's certainly ready to talk about her feelings, but I don't know how motivated she is to work on her problems. She is such an externalizer.

LEVENSON: Externalizer?

TRAINEE: Yeah, she sees her problems as due to mistreatment by everyone else. And she is the innocent victim.

LEVENSON: That appears to be the case. But then this was part of her dysfunctional style as we outlined it in the previous session. I would not disqualify her from treatment because of her externalizing attitude; in fact, it would probably provide excellent opportunities for much of the therapeutic work.

TRAINEE: I can see that. I think, however, that the treatment will be difficult.

LEVENSON: So you can see that this patient might be appropriate for TLDP, but that the process will not be easy. What do you think Dr. Ellison will say about Ms. Ludlow's suitability?

TRAINEE: She should see her as an OK candidate, I think.

TRAINEE: Hmm. Maybe the therapist will see her as not suitable because this patient was so hard to focus. There was so much going on with her.

TRAINEE: Yeah. This patient is a handful. I remember my reaction to seeing her on tape was to back away because she was so irritating and frustrating.

LEVENSON: When I asked Dr. Ellison what she thought about the patient's appropriateness for TLDP, she replied that she wanted another patient! Dr. Ellison saw Ms. Ludlow as "very tangential, very circumstantial, very overwhelming, very unfocused, and perhaps prepsychotic."

TRAINEE: Prepsychotic?

LEVENSON: Yes, Dr. Ellison felt that if she challenged this patient's defenses, whatever was holding her together would disintegrate, and Ms. Ludlow would be left even more disorganized and impaired than before the therapy.

TRAINEE: So was Ms. Ludlow accepted for treatment or not?

The training team of which Dr. Ellison had been a part was undecided as to whether to accept Ms. Ludlow for treatment. It appeared that Ms. Ludlow technically met the selection criteria, but Dr. Ellison, who was the only one to interact with the patient, felt doubtful about the usefulness of TLDP with her. Dr. Ellison and the training team compromised and decided that perhaps more information would enable them to make an accurate evaluation. It was decided that Dr. Ellison would meet with the patient again for a second evaluation session. Dr. Ellison would then bring this additional material back to her team and a final determination about the patient's suitability for TLDP could be made.

At the beginning of this second session, Ms. Ludlow had been expecting to hear whether she had been accepted into the program. Instead, Dr. Ellison informed her at the outset that the team felt more information was needed in order to make a judgment about the appropriateness of brief therapy for her. Dr. Ellison went on to explain that this second session should be considered a part of the evaluation, and that she thought she would have an answer for Ms. Ludlow regarding her acceptance into the brief program at the next session.

CMP REENACTMENTS

At this point, I show a videotaped portion from the second session. At the end of this segment, I ask the trainees what they think is transpiring in this therapist–patient exchange.

[VIDEOTAPE]

Therapist: What do you want to work on for yourself?

Ms. Ludlow: I thought we talked about that.

Therapist: Well, we're working on it. We're making progress.

Ms. Ludlow: Are we? It's frustrating.

Therapist: (coughing repeatedly through the session due to a cold) Do you feel like it's frustrating to, um, for yourself to try to reflect on what it is that you want to work on or change or find as a problem area?

Ms. Ludlow: No, I want to do all these things. Sometimes your questions, I can't believe you're that dumb. I know you are a smart lady. Would you ask me again?

Therapist: Um. What is there about my questions that seem dumb to you?

Ms. Ludlow: I just thought my problems were obvious.

Therapist: Do you . . . What makes you think that they are obvious to other people?

Ms. Ludlow: Well, I have already told you a lot. And I thought you would have figured some things out. I don't know.

Therapist: Do you think that happens with other people? Do you sometimes get, um, frustrated with them because you think they should know more about what's going on with you or have you figured out?

Ms. Ludlow: Oh, I suppose that's happened with my husband. And also with my folks. They're off in left field. But no. I'm finding out that most people are coming from their own inadequacy. Like in the office. If I use good manners and good cheer, and just try to communicate the work stuff, um (pause), I just want to be sure that people know that I am not going to do them in or hang them or betray them. I just want to make my own way. I don't want to step on anybody while I'm doing it.

Therapist: Uh huh.

Ms. Ludlow: And I see people afraid. I have a co-worker I am having trouble with. She's messed up and she's clearing her throat and discrediting me.

Therapist: Do you think she's afraid of you?

Ms. Ludlow: Yeah. She's cringing inside. But she's hurting me pretty bad. I am angry at her.

Therapist: Why would she be afraid of you?

Ms. Ludlow: Well, I'm good, but she's good, too. And if she doesn't know it, that's her problem. And I don't want to make her look bad, but I just want to do good myself. And uh, she ridiculed me in front of a dozen people in one room. And she interrupts, and she just, I just don't like it and I don't need it.

Therapist: Do you think she does this intentionally to you?

Ms. Ludlow: Yeah. This goes back to the same experience—I came through grade school with a girl who did this. She was conniving, grasping. She wanted the boys to like her. Her own daddy wasn't there for her. And our mothers were friends. I had to suffer this little bitch all the way through school. And I would just go cold inside. I would be talking to a boy. She would come up and butt in and get the guy's attention. And he would look at her. And I would just freeze up. And that's how it is. I lost. I just get cold. But on the work situation with this woman, I just don't want to be her friend.

Therapist: Do you think that it feels like people want to make you feel stupid or wrong in a way very similar to what your parents used to do?

Ms. Ludlow: (nodding) Sure.

Therapist: Do you get that sense with my questions that I have been asking you, that you somehow feel that I might be making you look stupid?

Ms. Ludlow: Yeah. (giggling) I feel like I'm something that just came from the moon and you never saw anything quite like this before. (laughing) And I think really that a lot of my challenges can be put in neat little slots.

Therapist: Your challenges?

Ms. Ludlow: My little problems. Yeah.

Therapist: 'Cause I'm just wondering why you would think—why you would expect me to sort of know all these things, the questions I have been asking trying to get information from you. Why would you expect me to know all these things and not have to ask?

Ms. Ludlow: Just, well, you kind of ask them another way. (pause) It's been done before to me, I mean.

Therapist: What is that—that's been done?

Ms. Ludlow: I went through a laborious intake procedure at Mount Rushmore Clinic, and then I didn't go through with it. And the guy asked questions the way you are. So . . .

Therapist: Was there something about the way he asked questions that made you uncomfortable?

Ms. Ludlow: I had so much happen to me, he just looked amazed. He looked a little like, my goodness, I'm a walking soap opera!

[CLASSROOM]

LEVENSON: So what do you see going on here?

TRAINEE: It's already started.

LEVENSON: What is "it?"

TRAINEE: Devaluing the therapist.

TRAINEE: This portion you showed us was right after Dr. Ellison told her she was not yet accepted into the brief program, right?

LEVENSON: Yes. Why do you ask?

TRAINEE: Because in a way Dr. Ellison is rejecting her—at least by saying they have to have another evaluation session, that she cannot be accepted right away for treatment.

TRAINEE: Yes. Ms. Ludlow probably saw this as a slap in the face, like she wasn't good enough in some way to be acceptable.

TRAINEE: Rejection is so critical for this patient. In terms of her dynamic focus, she fears she will not be acceptable to people—that somehow they will find her wanting and defective—damaged goods.

TRAINEE: That's what I meant by "It's already started"! The dynamic between therapist and patient is unfolding in a rather predictable way. The patient feels rejected and is reacting by getting angry with the therapist and devaluing her attempts to help.

TRAINEE: All the incidents the patient talked about had a similar theme— of people rejecting her and her getting hurt.

I point out to the trainees that the patient's experience of others did not happen in a vacuum. For example, Ms. Ludlow's unfocused, alienating style caused a countertransferential reaction in her therapist. The therapist wanted to reject this patient. Not only had Ms. Ludlow's presentation made it difficult to assess whether she met the selection criteria, but it had also engendered a negative reaction in her therapist. Dr. Ellison wanted another, easier patient; one who might know how to ask for and utilize help. Dr. Ellison felt wary of trying to help Ms. Ludlow, because so many others had failed to be of assistance to this overwhelmingly needy person, who sounded more like a whiny child than a 45-year-old woman.

I and the rest of Dr. Ellison's team also colluded with Dr. Ellison in acting out her countertransferential reaction. We suggested the therapist hold a second evaluation session rather than accepting the patient into treatment. In essence, Dr. Ellison and the brief-therapy team reenacted a significant portion of this patient's cyclical maladaptive pattern with others—we rebuffed her because of her diffuse, critical, and needy presentation.

As part of the TLDP model introduced in chapter 3, it was stated that the therapist cannot help acting out the role into which a patient with entrenched, persistent, maladaptive modes of relating casts the therapist. The therapist gets drawn into a destructive "game" (Berne, 1964) with the patient, becoming a participant and not merely an observer. "The patient unwittingly behaves in ways that tend to provoke others (including the therapist) to respond reciprocally. This has the effect of confirming the patient's expectations of how the kind of person he or she is evokes certain responses in others. In other words, the patient's behavior becomes a self-fulfilling prophecy. This unconscious and self-defeating conduct is the *action* component of the transference . . . " (Strupp & Binder, 1984, p. 142). Similarly, Dr. Ellison's almost rejecting the patient for treatment is the action component of her countertransference.

In addition, it should be remembered that Ms. Ludlow was Dr. Ellison's first outpatient case and that she might have felt overwhelmed by almost any patient. But clearly, Dr. Ellison's inexperience has nothing to do with Ms. Ludlow's presenting style; if Dr. Ellison's reaction to Ms. Ludlow, however, was based solely on her lack of training and experience, then it would not be of help to us in delineating the patient's CMP.

Since Dr. Ellison's reaction to Ms. Ludlow seems rather understandable based on the dynamic formulation derived for the patient, we can proceed on the assumption (until proven otherwise) that Dr. Ellison has become ensnared in a dysfunctional scenario with the patient that is driven by engaging in the patient's style. In this case, the therapist almost acted out her countertransference in a major, destructive manner: rejecting the patient for treatment. The Brief Psychotherapy Program team suggested having another evaluation session. We were also drawn into the patient's CMP in not immediately accepting her for treatment, but this "acting out" was less extreme and permitted the relationship to continue, at least for another session.

It should be emphasized that from the TLDP point of view, the therapist's strong countertransferential reaction to this patient was not a "mistake." Rather, it would have been a mistake not to use such internal data as a source of information about what it is like to interact with this patient. It would have been a mistake to deny that one was having such negative reactions, in order to maintain a view of oneself as an all-accepting, empathic helper. It also would have been a mistake to see such reactions as idiosyncratic manifestations of neurotic conflicts that the therapist needed to work through in her own therapy or in consultation (in the absence of a compelling reason to come to this conclusion).

Thus it appears that Dr. Ellison's telling the patient a second evaluation session was needed is an example of how the therapist can be drawn into the patient's self-defeating style of getting others to reject her. Further, we saw how this "rejection" caused a series of angry responses in the patient. What emerged here in the second session illustrates how transference–countertransference patterns become apparent very early in a therapy and can be worked with almost immediately. I ask the trainees what else they observed on the videotape.

[CLASSROOM]
TRAINEE: I saw the patient repeatedly telling the therapist how much she had been rejected by others.
LEVENSON: Specifically, what references were made to other rejections?
TRAINEE: There is the co-worker who is discrediting and hurting the patient.
TRAINEE: She ridiculed the patient in front of a dozen people in one room.
TRAINEE: And also the girl in grade school.
TRAINEE: The "little bitch."
TRAINEE: Who took the boys' attention away from her.
LEVENSON: What was the patient's reaction to these rejections and humiliations?
TRAINEE: She got angry, felt hurt.
TRAINEE: Got cold inside.

As the trainees' responses indicate, an interpersonal pattern is emerging in which the patient observes others as rejecting and hurting her for no good reason; this perception results in the patient's anger and disappointment. We see the exact same pattern unfolding at the beginning of the second session. The patient feels rejected by the therapist and responds by getting angry

("Sometimes your questions, I can't believe you're that dumb") and feeling disappointed ("Well, I have already told you a lot. And I thought you would have figured some things out").

In fact, we can view the beginning of this second session as the patient's experience of being hurt and frustrated by the therapist unconsciously evoking memories of similarly upsetting interpersonal interactions. Thus the patient's stories about the co-worker and grade school companion serve as allusions to what is happening in the transference (Gill, 1979).

From an object-relations perspective, it is assumed that the patient's experience of the therapist is mirrored in what the patient says about transactions with others. Sometimes these parallels are obvious (as with the co-worker and childhood companion examples); sometimes the similarities are more subtle. An example of a possible subtle allusion to the transference occurs when Ms. Ludlow, in discussing her experience with her co-worker, says that this person is "clearing her throat and discrediting me." If one realizes that Dr. Ellison, the therapist, has been coughing and clearing her throat (because she has a cold) throughout the session, this subtle, unconscious reference may been seen as having relevance for Dr. Ellison.

Another possible example of a subtle allusion to the transference within this segment occurs when Ms. Ludlow refers to the co-worker's "ridiculing her in front of a dozen people in one room." The patient had been informed by her therapist in the first session that videotaped segments of her therapy would be shown to the Brief Psychotherapy Program team, composed of other trainees and a supervisor. She does not know exactly how many people will be observing her via tape, but perhaps it is reasonable to think there might be a dozen such people in one room.

While such transferential allusions cannot be proven in the clinical situation, they provide useful hypotheses for the therapist to consider, offering invaluable glimpses into the unconscious or censored areas of the patient's mind. Is the patient concerned that Dr. Ellison might be ridiculing her behind her back? Is she afraid that her therapist is trying to discredit her? Does she get cold inside when she does not get the attention she wants from Dr. Ellison? Does she see her therapist as afraid of her and, therefore, intentionally trying to hurt her?

Such connections between interactions with others and with the therapist can be made explicit to further the patient's awareness and understanding of her patterns. Dr. Ellison makes this kind of connection when she asks Ms. Ludlow whether she sees people such as her co-worker as making her feel stupid in a way very similar to what her parents did (a connection between present significant others and past significant others). Dr. Ellison then goes further and asks whether Ms. Ludlow had the sense that she (Dr. Ellison) might also be trying to make her look stupid (a reference to what is happening within the transference between therapist and patient).

These interpretations connecting emotionally charged interactions with present significant others, past significant others, and one's therapist (transference) form what has been called the *triangle of insight* (Malan, 1979; Menninger, 1958). Figure 5.1 is a diagrammatic representation of this connection between past, present, and the therapeutic situation for the general case. One can readily see why linking the various corners of the triangle might be a powerful intervention, since it ties together a pattern that has occurred with different significant people over a great expanse of time (from childhood to adulthood).

Figure 5.1

Malan/Menninger model of psychoanalytic process

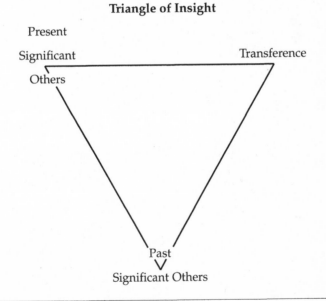

Triangle of Insight

Present

Significant   Transference

Others

Past

Significant Others

(Butler & Binder, 1987; reprinted by permission.)

The procedure for discerning a patient's CMP is totally consistent with the triangle of insight. In both cases, identifiable, predictable patterns of interactional behavior are seen to occur with important people throughout the patient's life. Butler and Binder (1987) perceived parallels between the two constructs and put forth a conceptual integration of cyclical psychodynamics and the triangle of insight, explicating how at each corner of the triangle

Figure 5.2

Integrated model: CMP and triangle of insight

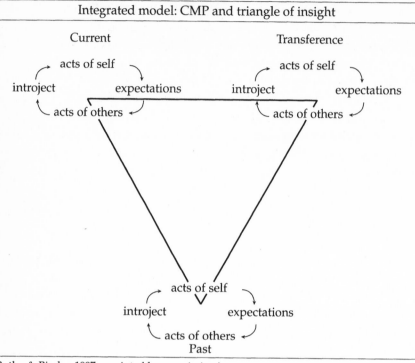

(Butler & Binder, 1987; reprinted by permission.)

(past significant others, present significant others, and therapist) one could delineate a dysfunctional interaction (CMP). This integration is presented in diagram form in figure 5.2.

To return to Ms. Ludlow's second session, Dr. Ellison perceived that a dysfunctional interaction was transpiring with a present significant other (co-worker) which seemed similar to relationship patterns with parents. Seeing these similarities allowed Dr. Ellison to recognize (and possibly to anticipate) the form the transference was likely to take. This ability to comprehend readily and even to anticipate what will happen as the therapy unfolds is critical for a brief psychotherapy.

INTERVENTIONS

Usually at this point in the training, one of the trainees asks how soon one can start making interpretations in a brief therapy. In session two we see Dr. Ellison making a triangle-of-insight interpretation. Is this a "premature" interpretation? Shouldn't the therapist wait until more information has been gathered?

Of course, the answer is not a simple one. The shorthand reply is that the decision must be left to one's clinical judgment. But this is an unsatisfactory explanation for beginning clinicians or practitioners who have little experience with short-term interventions. I use five principles to guide the therapist concerning the timing of interpretations.

First, in a brief therapy one must accept that interventions (including interpretations) must occur even if the therapist has incomplete information. Of course, this is also true in a long-term or open-ended therapy, where one never knows all the relevant "facts." But it is especially true in time-efficient therapies, where if the therapist is to intervene at all, it must be done based on "educated guesses." The saving grace comes in the therapist's deliberate use of a focus. Because the therapist focuses on a *circumscribed area*, he or she is able to know more in a shorter period of time than in an open-ended therapy in which the therapist follows all leads.

The second principle is that interpretations are not discoveries of truth as known and uncovered by the therapist, but rather as plausible possibilities based on what the patient is saying and doing. From a TLDP point of view, interpretations help make sense of events. They do not need to be "correct" in an absolute sense. The way a therapist frames interpretations can convey this "multiple truth" perspective. Comments such as "Based on what you are saying, I wonder if . . . " or "You immediately went from talking about your mother's hostility to talking about your wife—could it be that you are concerned about your wife's disapproval of you?" provide ways of introducing parallels to be considered by the patient, without making pronouncements that serve to short-circuit investigation rather than promote it. Dr. Ellison delivers her triangle-of-insight interpretation in this fashion: "Do you get that sense with my questions that I have been asking you, that you somehow feel that I might be making you look stupid?" This interpretation gives the patient leeway to reflect on what the therapist has said.

The third principle stems from the second one. A well-timed interpretation (i.e., one that furthers the therapeutic process) should not be judged solely by whether or not the patient agrees with it. In fact, for patients with a particularly deferential style, agreement may be only an indication of their acquiescent CMP. Even if patients disagree with the interpretation, the therapist has accomplished at least two things: Patients learn that they can disagree with their therapists and not be punished, and therapists acknowledge the seed of an idea that may germinate at a later time. (The next chapter will discuss how the therapist can judge whether an interpretation works.)

The fourth principle is especially critical for judging the timing of a transference interpretation in TLDP. The therapist needs to allow ample time for the therapeutic relationship to evolve. The therapist and patient need to have experiences between them that occur naturally in the course of the therapy. These interactions are usually germane to the patient's CMP. Sometimes these interpersonal episodes are abundant and emotionally charged even in the first session (or even over the telephone in setting up the first session).

Although there is no litmus test for determining when there has been a sufficient amount and degree of interaction, a rule of thumb is to allow enough repetitions of a particular dynamic interaction so that a pattern of patient behavior and/or expectation and therapist response is subjectively recognized by the patient. Whereas the therapist might be able to perceive (or even to anticipate) such a pattern quite readily, one needs cues from the patient indicating that he or she has come to expect certain responses from the therapist. Sometimes these cues are directly stated (e.g., "You sure keep asking a lot of dumb questions!"); sometimes they are more covert (e.g., the patient repeatedly avoids eye contact with the therapist, expecting to be blamed for some transgression).

A quite common error in technique is for the therapist, who is alert to discerning interactional themes, to point out such transferential patterns to the patient long before the patient has had the opportunity to experience a series of interactions with the therapist. I have found that therapists need more practice learning how to comment on here-and-now transactions between themselves and patients within the context of the actual experienced relationship. Similar occurrences were found in the Vanderbilt II studies (Henry et al., 1993b), where therapists grasped a more mechanical, or cookbook, application of delivering a transferential interpretation without understanding how to embed it within a relationship framework.

For example, one past trainee of mine saw so clearly that his patient wanted to compete with and defeat the efforts of others that he asked during a second session, "And how will you manage to destroy my attempts for this to be a good therapy for you?" The therapist had (correctly) anticipated that this patient's competitive style would emerge in the therapeutic relationship, but at this point in the treatment the patient had not repeatedly attempted to sabotage the therapy. The patient responded in shocked dismay that he had no such plans and thought the therapist had completely misunderstood his motivation in coming for help. Because this dysfunctional interaction had not had the opportunity to be played out again and again between therapist and patient, it was no wonder the patient felt totally misunderstood and maligned. These types of premature interpretations are usually met with surprise, hostility, and/or confusion on the part of the patient and can lead to gross ruptures in the working alliance.

What this patient *had* repeatedly done in the first two sessions, however, was to indicate that he was superior to the therapist in terms of knowledge, athletics, and moral values. Perhaps if the therapist had interpreted the parallels between the patient's customary practice of competing with others and his tendency to compare himself favorably to the therapist, the patient would have been more willing to examine the possibilities, because the patient himself had already had the experience of claiming he was better than the therapist on several occasions.

The fifth principle is especially related to the previous point. In deciding when to use transference interpretations, the therapist needs to wait until he or she can make them as detailed and concrete as possible (Strachey, 1934). Such specificity helps the patient experientially recognize himself or herself in the situation. For example, saying "It seems you are acting toward me the same way you acted toward your father" is not as affectively or intellectually compelling as saying "You have smiled and complimented me several times during our session today even while I am saying some hard things to you. This seems similar to what you said you did with your father to get him to stop berating you."

Before leaving the topic of transference interpretations, lest the reader get the idea they are used abundantly in TLDP, I must note Strupp's admonition that the supply of transference interpretations far exceeds the demand. A few go a long way. I have placed the emphasis in TLDP on the new experience, in part because of the deleterious effect repeated transference interpretations can have on psychotherapeutic process and outcome. Patients often hear such interventions as reproach and criticism (Henry et al., 1993b; Piper, Azim, Joyce, & McCallum, 1991). A recent review of the research literature on psychodynamic interventions by William Henry and colleagues (1994) questions the effectiveness of transference interpretations in general. Of course, the accuracy or correspondence of the interpretation to the patient's focus, in addition to the frequency of such interpretations, is a critical variable (Crits-Christoph et al., 1988; Silberschatz et al., 1986). To the extent that difficult patients may be more vulnerable to the negative effects of transference interpretations (Piper, Joyce, McCallum, & Azim, 1993), extra caution is warranted in using them.

Returning to the case of Ms. Ludlow and Dr. Ellison, I ask the trainees what else struck them about this vignette.

[CLASSROOM]

TRAINEE: I was curious about the way Ms. Ludlow initially expressed her anger toward Dr. Ellison. She was criticizing her by calling her dumb. And yet she is the one who is very sensitive to others trying to make her, the patient, look dumb.

TRAINEE: Yeah. It looks like she is doing to the therapist what her parents did to her.

TRAINEE: Is this like Control Mastery's idea of passive into active?

LEVENSON: It is difficult to capture the relevancy of one concept taken out of context of its own theory, but let's attempt to examine your idea.

One way of understanding the form of Ms. Ludlow's attack on the therapist can be derived from the *plan formulation method* (formerly *control mastery theory*) developed by Joseph Weiss, Harold Sampson, and the Mount Zion Psychotherapy Research Group (Weiss, 1993; Weiss et al., 1986). According to their model, patients unconsciously seek to disconfirm unconscious pathological beliefs (schemata) by testing such beliefs as they interact with their therapists. One way patients may do this is by *turning passive into active*, behaving toward their therapists as they had been treated or perceived themselves to have been treated by their parents, with the hope (again, unconscious) that their therapists will not be traumatized by such actions.

From a TLDP perspective, recognizing such role reversal reenactments is helpful. Patients do not always or only present from the point of view of their position within their parental home; they may present as they were treated or perceived to be treated. However, the TLDP model does not hold that patients come to therapy with an unconscious plan of how to get better and as part of this plan provide their therapists with opportunities to disconfirm their pathogenic beliefs. Rather, it is assumed in TLDP that patients' attitudes and behaviors are a reflection of their best efforts at trying to make sense out of relating to their therapists, given their views of the world and themselves. Ms. Ludlow had grown up in a home where anger and frustration were expressed in terms of put-downs and name calling; it would not be surprising that she might model her behavior after that observed and over-learned in her parental home.

At this point I suggest that the trainees think about how Dr. Ellison responded to the patient's contentious statement challenging her intelligence.

[CLASSROOM]

TRAINEE: I don't quite remember what she said, but I remember I really liked what she did.

TRAINEE: I think she said something like, "What about my questions seems dumb to you?"

TRAINEE: Now I remember that I thought Dr. Ellison was doing a remarkable job of stepping back, looking at the here-and-now interaction, and just asking for information, rather than getting defensive. I would have felt intimidated and put on the spot if a patient of mine had said that to me.

TRAINEE: Yes. Dr. Ellison's response was to be open and curious. If I were the patient I would have felt like my therapist was really interested in my point of view.

LEVENSON: What if Dr. Ellison instead had simply explained to Ms. Ludlow that she needed to ask such questions to get to know her better in order to understand her and be of help?

TRAINEE: That sounds like something I have said to patients in the past. But when I hear it from a patient's point of view, it seems like a subtle put-down. Like I'm not entitled to an opinion; that the therapist is merely doing what she needs to do, and I'm the dumb one if I don't understand that!

LEVENSON: Yes, there can be a defensive quality about telling the patient the simple truth that you need more information. Dr. Ellison's response validates the patient's right to have such opinions. Furthermore, Dr. Ellison's asking why her questions seem dumb conveys to the patient that there is something to be learned from examining her (the patient's) reactions.

TRAINEE: Also, Dr. Ellison demonstrated that she would not retaliate or withdraw from the patient because of her hostility.

TRAINEE: And her voice is very calm. The patient's is very childish and bratty. But Dr. Ellison's tone is inquisitive and collaborative.

TRAINEE: Dr. Ellison's question elicits more material from the patient—to try to understand her processing of information. If the therapist smoothes over the situation with an explanation, then she never obtains this data, which might be important.

TRAINEE: Dr. Ellison is not falling into the trap of responding in an authoritarian or angry way. She is not being put off by the patient's hostility. If she had had an angry comeback, then it would have been a repetition of other people's reactions to the patient.

LEVENSON: So in this way, Dr. Ellison is providing a mini–new experience for the patient. Later in the same vignette, Ms. Ludlow gives us many examples of what happens with other people: the bitch from school, her co-worker, her parents. All of these people reject her in some form. From the patient's point of view, the theme seems to be, "I do something perfectly fine, and for some unknown reason having to do with their own stuff, other people take it out on me." By asking about her thoughts and opinions, Dr. Ellison is changing the nature of this interaction. She seems eager to hear what Ms. Ludlow has to say, willing to be flexible in how she asks questions, and respectful—a very different response from what usually gets elicited.

The four categories that make up the CMP can be used as prompts to suggest possible interventions. In this example, after the patient has criticized her, Dr. Ellison could ask: "What is there about my questions that seem dumb?" (*acts of the self*); "What do you think might happen now that you have said that?" (*expectations of others' reactions*); "When you made that comment, I felt like retreating" (*acts of others*); or "Right now, are you aware of saying anything to yourself?" (*acts of the self toward the self*). Each of these questions invites information about a different facet of the interactional pattern. In delivering such interventions, the therapist must be careful through tone and content not to come across as blaming, but rather as curious as to the interactional process through the patient's eyes.

Dr. Ellison's willingness to explore her own "dumbness" also exemplifies another aspect of working within brief-therapy limits. It is quite important for the therapist who is under time constraints to address immediately any indications of negative transference when they emerge in the therapy. A brief treatment affords no time to deal with the aftermath of a major disruption in the therapeutic alliance and the regression in functioning that usually accompanies it.

In the initial formulation of this case discussed in chapter 4, Ms. Ludlow revealed quite a bit of information about her acts of the self and acts of others. Little was directly stated about her expectations of others' reactions or her introject. In the second session we learn more about both of these.

[CLASSROOM]

TRAINEE: In addition to the rejection theme, there is another theme that somehow the therapist should know what is wrong with her and already have her categorized.

LEVENSON: Yes. The patient states that she thought that by the second session the therapist already "would have figured some things out." The therapist then explores the patient's expectations of others' reactions by asking questions about the types of interactions the patient anticipates (e.g., "What makes you think that they are obvious to other people?" "Why would you expect me to know all these things and not have to ask?").

TRAINEE: Dr. Ellison finds out that Ms. Ludlow expects others to be able to put her "little problems" into "neat little slots."

TRAINEE: From her experience with her parents, who had no shortage of opinions about her problems, she has probably learned that the only way she can get attention is by presenting as a problem to be fixed.

TRAINEE: She's an interesting contradiction. On the one hand, she states that she has simple problems with simple solutions. But on the other hand, she seems to be saying that her problems are so large and so complex, people look amazed.

TRAINEE: She's a "walking soap opera!"

LEVENSON: In fact, these expectations are dynamically intertwined with her introject. What do we know about her introject?

TRAINEE: Well, from the first session, it appeared she saw herself as a victim. From this session it is clearer that she sees herself as a *special* victim—a complex person who can astonish professionals and parents alike.

LEVENSON: Yes. When she talks about being from the moon and the therapist's never seeing anything quite like her before, she is laughing. And when she explains how she overwhelmed the last intake worker she saw because she is a "walking soap opera," she says it with bravado and pride. In her problemhood she is special; she is someone to be reckoned with; she has power.

This presentation of the introject suggests that the patient has a positive attachment to the way she treats herself. Her introject is not all negative. Although she is depressed and feels unloved, she has a powerful way of defending herself from feeling too vulnerable. If she is to be a problem, then she can be the biggest problem. She can defeat her diet-doctor father (and be her own person) by being fat. If others can see her only as a project to be fixed, she will defy the fixing. Anything that might challenge this self-view will be seen as threatening, in that she might not know how to feel secure about herself without presenting herself as a "problem."

By the end of the second session, Dr. Ellison can clearly comprehend how the patient's CMP has been reenacted in the therapeutic setting. Her countertransference has not shifted significantly—she still would have preferred another patient—but she understands how her feelings of being overwhelmed and frustrated by this patient are part of the pull of Ms. Ludlow's CMP. Accordingly Dr. Ellison accepts her for TLDP.

CHAPTER 6

Use of Process and Countertransference Disclosure

I N CONTRAST TO A MORE classically psychoanalytic view, the therapist's behavior in TLDP is thought initially to contribute significantly to maintaining the dysfunctional interaction between patient and therapist. Not only is the therapist unconsciously invited by the patient to enter into a dysfunctional dynamic interaction, the therapist's unwitting involvement in the maladaptive scenario further promotes the patient's self-defeating behaviors.

What is the way out of this interactive rut? Recognizing one's contribution, changing one's behavior, and commenting on the process provide three antidotes. This chapter explores how the therapist, once he or she is aware of participating in the patient's CMP, can metacommunicate about that interaction, promoting a new experience and a new understanding. Chapter 9 will examine how the therapist can become aware of his or her contribution to the transactional cycle within the therapeutic context.

Practitioners often become adroit at identifying and pointing out the patient's contribution to the clinical process and getting therapeutic mileage from it. Their ability and inclination to use their own affective, cognitive, and behavioral reactions to further the therapeutic work are often less well developed. Since the interactive operation of therapist's and patient's behavior is of paramount importance in TLDP, TLDP therapists must become comfortable with when, where, and how to comprehend their own internal processes and when, where, and how to share these perceptions with patients. Dr. Ellison's dilemmas with Ms. Ludlow provide a rich clinical example of the therapist's quandaries in discerning the appropriate use of self-disclosure in TLDP.

In classical psychoanalytic work with neurotic patients, the therapist's "self-revelations" are limited to what the patient can discern from the therapist's choice of decor, visible books, clothes, and so on. However, Sallye Wilkinson and Glen Gabbard (1993) make the point that when working with more disturbed patients, a different standard of self-disclosure is needed:

> Honesty about feelings in the here and now may be essential in allowing the therapist to develop and maintain a therapeutic alliance with the patient. We are advocating limited self-disclosure that is designed to inform the patient of the interpersonal and intrapsychic use that the patient is making of the therapist. The need for this form of countertransference disclosure can be narrowly defined as *clinical honesty* that focuses on the therapist's experience of the patient's impact in the here-and-now moment of the session. (p. 282)

A distinction between *purposeful self-disclosure* and *inadvertent self-disclosure* is helpful. The former pertains to the therapist's conscious choice to make some self-revealing statement, usually about his or her feelings about the patient; the latter applies to cues the therapist gives off indirectly to the patient through verbal and nonverbal behaviors, such as specific words used, gestures, facial expressions, voice quality. All in all, self-disclosure "is not an option; it is an inevitability" (Aron, 1991, p. 40).

Returning to Ms. Ludlow's case, after the second session it was obvious to Dr. Ellison that her patient's long-standing dysfunctional interpersonal style might be well suited to TLDP. During the first half of the 18-session therapy, Dr. Ellison obtained much more information about Ms. Ludlow's interactional style—the dynamic focus became clearer and more understandable as it unfolded.

However, Dr. Ellison continued to work very hard in the sessions to keep Ms. Ludlow organized and focused. Dr. Ellison tried unsuccessfully not to feel overwhelmed by the patient's negativism and vagueness. Every week in group supervision Dr. Ellison shared her experience of the patient and how frustrating it was to deal with Ms. Ludlow's challenging manner. Her colleagues, watching segments of each week's session on videotape, identified with Dr. Ellison's plight. On several occasions I suggested that perhaps Dr. Ellison could convey to her patient the frustration she experienced in repeatedly rescuing Ms. Ludlow from the depths of muddled and diffuse thinking.

Dr. Ellison was not enthusiastic about this idea of disclosing her interpersonal difficulties to Ms. Ludlow and therefore did not make use of opportunities to do so for several sessions. Why might Dr. Ellison have been so reluctant to reveal her feelings to Ms. Ludlow?

[CLASSROOM]

TRAINEE: Well, the first thing that comes to mind is that there is the idea in doing therapy that the therapist should be polite—be nice—not say negative things. As I say that, I realize that this was not something I was taught specifically in my graduate training, but rather probably something that comes from my upbringing.

LEVENSON: Perhaps from your unique home, but also in our society in general, there is the idea that "if you can't say something nice, don't say anything at all." So there may be some societal pulls for not revealing negative thoughts or feelings aroused in us by our patients.

TRAINEE: Along those lines, I *was* trained that at the very least the therapist should be supportive.

LEVENSON: And what does that mean, "supportive"?

TRAINEE: I don't think I've ever clearly thought about it before. I guess I was assuming that it meant being pleasant and respectful to patients without challenging their usual defenses needlessly. If I'm honest with myself, I think I've operated like it implied being kind and helpful.

TRAINEE: Therapists could really wound patients by saying they had negative reactions to them.

TRAINEE: I'm more concerned about getting an angry response. Sharing how I was really feeling, assuming it was negative, might make a patient mad. I don't want things to get out of hand and have the patient explode with anger directed at me. I would find it quite difficult to say something of a revealing nature if I thought the patient would verbally attack me in return.

TRAINEE: Yes, that connects with what I was going to say. I would be hesitant to reveal something of a personal nature to the patient who is hypercritical. I'd be hesitant because I'd be afraid the patient might quit therapy.

TRAINEE: I believe in using my countertransference for my own information—to understand better what might be going on with the patient—but I, too, would be reluctant to put it out there.

LEVENSON: Because?

TRAINEE: Because when therapists self-disclose what is really going on with them, they give up their therapeutic neutrality.

TRAINEE: Yes. Such openness contaminates the transference.

TRAINEE: I have a different reason for not saying much about my feelings or reactions in doing therapy. I think it's risky business. Perhaps what you are feeling about the patient has nothing to do with him or her. Maybe it has more to do with your unresolved issues with people in your own life.

TRAINEE: How do you know when it *is* your stuff that has no business being talked about in the therapy?

TRAINEE: I've always thought that I should be focusing more on the patient than on me—trying to understand the patient. When I bring up my own reactions, it could be taking away time and attention from the patient. It seems rather narcissistic for therapists to be so concerned with their own process. If I were the patient, I would feel slighted.

TRAINEE: My own lack of comfort about distinguishing what is my issue and what is the patient's would prevent me from revealing much about my own feelings. Also, how does one know when to stop revealing? I might end up disclosing more than I really planned to.

LEVENSON: So far you have mentioned concerns about hurting patients, or receiving hostile reactions from patients, diluting or otherwise altering the therapist's neutral stance, and difficulties recognizing when your feelings have to do with your own un-worked-through conflicts. Any other reasons for being reluctant to disclose one's reactions to patients?

TRAINEE: Using countertransference disclosure as a part of the process of doing therapy really involves shifting gears to a different way of interacting with patients.

LEVENSON: Can you say more?

TRAINEE: Stating your own feelings in the session means that you as the therapist join the patient in the trenches. The role of therapist as observer provides a safe, protected position. Disclosing how you feel means putting yourself in the patient's frame of reference.

TRAINEE: I see what you mean. There is a vulnerability involved.

TRAINEE: Also, it means that if I put my own thoughts and feelings on the line, my ability to interact will be on the line. Am I capable of healthy interactions? Can I be accessible—to the patient and to my own process?

TRAINEE: It is scary to acknowledge how one is contributing to a dysfunctional process. I can see that by self-disclosing, you take a risk. When I share with a patient, I don't know what will happen. Is this what is meant by collaboration?

As a reason for censoring one's own feelings and not disclosing them, the trainees first mention their motivations not to hurt the patient. The research of Henry et al. (1993b) suggests that even a few unintentionally belittling, disparaging statements from a therapist can nullify any positive therapeutic work. The clinician who gives personal feedback in a manner that conveys blaming the patient (e.g., "See how you are making me feel?") will probably cause an irreparable rift in the therapeutic alliance.

The trainees next consider the reverse of fears of hurting the patient—namely, fears of having the patient hurt the therapist. Here the trainees are concerned that patients will perceive therapists' self-disclosures to be an attack and will retaliate with verbal hostilities of their own. Almost all therapists have had a patient (in many cases diagnosed as having a borderline personality disorder) who has responded to an intervention with biting sarcasm or even rage.

Many patients are adept at sensing when the therapist is feeling vulnerable or not being truthful with them (e.g., trying to disguise countertransferential reactions). It is not that these patients have uncanny perceptive abilities, but rather that they often arouse marked reactions in their therapists—reactions that are impossible to conceal. Patients who feel that their therapists are angry with them, bored, or otherwise negatively predisposed react strongly to these covert messages, especially when they perceive that these therapists are not acknowledging their own affective states. Sometimes the therapist's very attempts to avoid the patient's anger only engenders it more.

Clearly there are some patients for whom a therapist's forthright openness or "clinical honesty" would not be helpful. Fragile, narcissistic patients are exquisitely vulnerable to being wounded by a therapist's negative reaction to them. Patients who are easily humiliated or who feel very responsible for others might feel ashamed to have caused the therapist any pain or discomfort. And therapists who candidly reveal their own processes to sadistic or antisocial patients may actually be furnishing ammunition to be used against themselves.

In general, however, clinicians usually overestimate patients' negative reactions to countertransference disclosures. If the therapist can enlist the patient's dispassionate examination of the interactive process between the two of them, the patient is usually grateful for someone's willingness to talk frankly about the effect he or she has on others. For people with dysfunctional styles, the others in their lives tend either to react in a reciprocal fashion (e.g., hostility begetting hostility) or to leave the field. Rarely do they provide the person with feedback about their reactions in a tactful, helpful, and compassionate manner. And without such feedback, people operate in a vacuum built upon their fears and untested expectations.

Another reason the trainees propose for not using self-disclosure about countertransferential feelings has to do with the implications for loss of neutrality or "contamination of the transference" (Curtis, 1981; Palombo, 1987). Sigmund Freud (1915/1957) maintained that analysts who developed "real" relationships with patients would lose their objectivity. Furthermore, psychoanalytic technique required that the therapist provide a "blank screen" on which the patient would project feelings, thoughts, and behaviors more appropriate to parental figures. To the extent this blank screen was not so blank, it was thought that the usefulness of the transference and hence the transference interpretations would be hindered. However, when dealing with characterologically disturbed patients, such a blank screen can induce projections that are inflexible, nonreflective, and all-encompassing; this can inhibit therapeutic progress rather than facilitate it. Self-disclosures can be particularly helpful in preventing a patient's regression, reminding the patient that his or her therapist is a separate person, and allowing the patient to consider that his or her own view of the world is not necessarily veridical.

Perhaps the reason therapists give most frequently for not saying more about their feelings in sessions is the fear that their input is inappropriate—that it has more to do with their own dynamics than those of the patients. Of course, the sine qua non for a therapeutic relationship is that the therapist defer his or her own needs to concentrate on the needs of the patient.

We can think of therapist disclosure as encompassing a range from less to more personal—from focus on the interaction to focus on the self. Figure 6.1 diagrams this disclosure continuum. At the far left are those therapist utterances that focus on the therapeutic process in general (e.g., "I notice that frequently as I am about to speak, you cringe as though I were going to strike you"). Usually such interventions are thought of as process comments rather than self-disclosures, but, of course, since the therapist chooses to put forth these statements, they do reveal some aspect of what is going on with the therapist.

Figure 6.1

Therapist purposive self-disclosure

Process Statements	Self-Involving Responses	Present Personal Information	Past Behavior/ Personal Feelings
Focus on Interaction	← —————————————→		Focus on Self

One step to the right on this self-disclosure continuum are those statements we have been calling countertransference disclosures. Patricia McCarthy and Nancy Betz (1978) refer to these as *self-involving disclosures*, which they define as direct expressions (usually in the present tense) of the therapist's feelings about or reactions to the statements or behaviors of the client. In this grouping are comments by the therapist that convey the affective state of the therapist, usually in the context of some interaction with the patient. ("When you talk about the disappointing way people have treated you, I feel an urge to reassure you everything will be OK.")

The next step on the continuum might include information about the therapist's present state that has nothing to do with what is being evoked in the give-and-take between therapist and patient, but is told to the patient because it might be helpful in maintaining the therapeutic alliance or preventing regressive patient fantasies. ("You may notice I am talking funny in today's session—it's because I just came from the dentist.")

The final category pertains to statements made by the therapist (usually in the past tense) referring to his or her own relevant history or personal experiences, what McCarthy and Betz (1978) call *self-disclosing disclosures* (e.g.,"Alcohol almost wrecked my life, too"). Proponents of this type of self-disclosure believe that it improves rapport (Bradmiller, 1978), facilitates trust (Johnson & Noonan, 1972), and increases patient disclosure (Truax & Carkhuff, 1965). Psychodynamic therapists, in contrast to those with other theoretical orientations, use this type of self-revelation the least because they believe it interferes with transference (Anderson & Mandell, 1989).

Omitted from the diagram are those therapist self-disclosures that emanate from the therapist's own personal problems and are motivated by his or her own needs. ("I am lonely because my wife doesn't understand me.") These are viewed by all schools of psychotherapy as inappropriate violations of the therapeutic frame and contract and as harmful to patients.

Of particular relevance for TLDP are self-involving statements or countertransference disclosures. How does the TLDP therapist know when such an intervention might be relevant and is not coming from his or her own needs or idiosyncratic reactions? The dynamic focus provides a touchstone for preventing the wild and wanton use of self-disclosure. Specifically, a therapist can assess whether his or her reactions to a patient are consistent with how others act toward that patient as described in the patient's CMP. If there is a parallel, then it is more likely that the therapist's responses are interactionally countertransferential and not personal. For example, does the therapist want to protect the patient, similar to the behaviors of significant others in the patient's life? Or is the therapist submissive toward the patient because he looks like her chastising professor?

The last reason for not using disclosure mentioned by the trainees has the greatest relevance for the practice of TLDP: the vulnerability the therapist feels when he or she is accessible to the patient as another human being trying to engage in a relationship. As one trainee put it, "It involves shifting gears to a different way of interacting . . . the therapist joins the patient in the trenches." The trainees invoked the concept of safety; it is safer and easier for the therapist to remain emotionally uninvolved, intrapsychically and inter-personally. Of course, from a TLDP perspective, such a detached position inhibits the therapist's contribution to the therapeutic task and thereby impedes therapeutic progress. Specifically, it prevents therapist and patient from having a new (and corrective) interactive experience of one another.

The work of Clara Hill and colleagues (1988, 1989) empirically corrobo-rates the fear of accessibility as the reason for the reluctance of therapists to use disclosing comments. Studying therapist self-disclosure in eight cases of brief therapy, these investigators found that disclosures, although used infrequently, were rated by patients as the most helpful response mode; such disclosures were also associated with greater patient involvement in the therapy. However, the therapists rated their own disclosures as the least helpful response mode. "Based on our examination of specific disclosures, we would now speculate that disclosures were threatening to therapists because they felt vulnerable [in] sharing part of themselves with clients" (Hill, Mahalik, & Thompson, 1989, p. 294).

Returning to the case of Ms. Ludlow, Dr. Ellison finally decided to disclose the frustration she had been feeling in the sessions. She was driven to reveal these feelings because she was beginning to realize that if she did not com-ment on her own process, both she and the patient would remain stuck in a continuous reenactment. The videotape of the beginning of the ninth session shows the patient describing a number of symptoms she is having, with Dr. Ellison initially asking questions about these symptoms. Seeing that this line of inquiry was taking them far afield from any productive work on the focus, Dr. Ellison built up her courage as she took a deep breath with an audi-ble sigh, then put forth her feelings about what it was like to interact with Ms. Ludlow.

> [VIDEOTAPE]
> *Ms. Ludlow:* Yeah, I puff. I get heartburn. My stomach puffs. In fact, I feel—sometimes my gut just grinds. It's another thing I'm starting to really notice with the anxiety, and it feels just a little bit like menstrual cramps—just for a minute. And I think I wonder if in the past I inter-preted that as hunger and it wasn't. I don't know.
> *Therapist:* Are these uncommon symptoms for you? Is this something new that's started recently?
> *Ms. Ludlow:* I've ignored and discredited my body for years. I was rough on myself; I mistreated myself. (pause) Um, I don't know how to answer that. (pause) I'm just trying to listen better.

Therapist: (deep sigh) You know, I think what's apparent that's happening here and that happens a lot is that, um, sometimes you go from one thing to another and it's often hard for me to follow you, and, therefore, I become frustrated with you—like you're waiting for me to come in and organize you. And yet, ah, when I do that, it's very much like your parents and what it does . . .

Ms. Ludlow: (shrieking/laughing) Oooooh!

Therapist: . . . is leave you feeling, um, or rather not feeling like an adult, but rather like that child who needs to be rescued.

Ms. Ludlow: And I'm hoping that you can make some sense out of all of this. I'm giving you what I have, which is only pieces of a puzzle (Mmm hmm), and I mentioned the box—I reach in that box and I think, well, there's three more pieces of sky that I've gotta find and there are no more sky pieces in the box and so what's going on? You've got them over there in your pocket. I don't know.

Therapist: When I said that, you laughed. You had a pretty strong response.

Ms. Ludlow: Yeah, I could see . . .

Therapist: What was that? What were you thinking when I made that comment?

Ms. Ludlow: Well, you did give me something. You didn't organize my life, but you did give me something. You showed me . . . (pause)

Therapist: Mmm?

Ms. Ludlow: Yeah.

Therapist: Was there anything else there that you feel like when you heard what I was saying that you were responding to when you laughed like that?

Ms. Ludlow: It's just a nifty idea. I think you're right. (laughs)

Therapist: What . . . (stopping herself midsentence and beginning anew) How do you understand what I just said?

Ms. Ludlow: Well, I can see my folks sitting me down in the evening on our visit, telling me, "We care about you, tell us about this, tell us about that." And my father would even say, "Well, keep talking," and I'd say, "Damn it all, you talk. I have nothing else to say." I could hardly go on a visit and just sit and listen. They wanted me to spill my guts and then they would tell me what was wrong. And I didn't pick up on the fact that I was doing that with you. I, I just think of you as a friend and helper, who's going to help me see—you just did, you did what I really needed, I think. (pause) I'm trying to think of everything that can contribute, looking for new truths and, um, I didn't realize I was expecting you to jump in the way my folks do. OK, that's what I understand.

Therapist: Do you see how that happens in here? [Mmm hmm] How that is sort of re-created with me and similar to what you do with your parents? Why do you think that might happen in here for you?

Ms. Ludlow: It's the only way that I know to be. (pause) In fact, there was a time if somebody said, Lydia, how are you—I would give them 6, 8, 10 unrelated facts, instead of drawing it all up, tying it with a string and saying, "fine" or "pretty good."

Therapist: So, again presenting yourself, hoping perhaps the other person is sort of going to pull you together and make sense out of these 8 or 10 unrelated facts . . .

Ms. Ludlow: Yeah. (laughing excitedly and nodding in agreement)

Therapist: And what then happens? Why do you do that in order to secure a relationship?

Ms. Ludlow: (nodding) Yeah.

Therapist: What would it be like for you in here if you—if that wasn't happening—if you weren't pulling me to rescue you? What do you think would happen?

Ms. Ludlow: I don't know. I'm realizing that there are other ways to talk about things. In fact, I'm getting all new pleasure in life watching how other people converse . . . watching (pause) all sorts of things.

Therapist: You know, again, I brought this up a couple of weeks ago, but, again, I wonder if what you're feeling is that if you can't—if you don't present yourself as sort of disorganized and needing someone to step in and organize and rescue you, then that there might be some concern on your part that you wouldn't be able to have a relationship, if that were the case.

Ms. Ludlow: Yeah. I can hardly imagine how you and I would talk if we didn't talk in that way. Because talking around a problem and exploring, thinking in connections and new insights—this is the only way I know to talk with you about it.

[CLASSROOM]

LEVENSON: Reactions?

TRAINEE: She hit the jackpot there!

LEVENSON: What do you mean?

TRAINEE: The patient really got what Dr. Ellison was trying to say. It's incredible. I mean, when you told us that's what she was going to try to do—self-disclose—I anticipated all kinds of negative reactions on Ms. Ludlow's part.

TRAINEE: It was very powerful. They were not talking about the past. They were talking about what has happened between the two of them in the short time they have known each other, and it was very alive and real.

TRAINEE: The right interpretation and the patient came through.

The trainees emphasize the interpretative nature of what Dr. Ellison said—that the patient is responding to the content of Dr. Ellison's intervention. In a study of general interpretations vs. therapist-related (transferential) interpretations and defensive and affective responding in focused, time-limited therapy, Leigh McCullough et al. (1991) found that patient–therapist interpretations followed by affect are positively related to outcome, while patient–therapist interpretations followed by defense are negatively related to outcome. Therefore, when transferential interpretations (e.g., Dr. Ellison's comment on the process between therapist and patient being reminiscent of parental interactions) are followed by emotional responses (e.g., Ms. Ludlow's dramatic "Oooooh!"), therapists may justifiably feel that they are on the right track.

In this case, certainly the content of Dr. Ellison's interpretation (framed as a self-involving disclosure) had a very strong effect on Ms. Ludlow—she responded emotionally and was able to see parallels between how her parents had treated her and what she pulled for from the therapist. But it also seemed that in addition to the content, an important part of this intervention was the process of providing another new experience for the patient.

Dr. Ellison's sharing her countertransferential feelings—displaying clinical honesty with the patient—resulted in her becoming more real to Ms. Ludlow as a true participant in the interaction. Dr. Ellison's self-involving disclosure about how she felt and about her role in the give-and-take of the sessions made her appear more as an interactive partner than a disapproving parent to Ms. Ludlow.

In addition, Dr. Ellison's disclosure of her predicament implicitly suggests that she thought Ms. Ludlow could deal with communicating with her on a more straightforward basis. The manner of Dr. Ellison's intervention invited Ms. Ludlow to join her in a different mode of relatedness: more adult–adult than child–parent. In essence, Dr. Ellison was saying to Ms. Ludlow, "Here is my dilemma and what I am dealing with as a result of trying to relate to you. Can we work together to discover another, more fruitful way I can be helpful to you?" The trainees begin to see this other experiential layer (the new experience) supporting the more cognitive one (the new understanding).

[CLASSROOM]

TRAINEE: I think the patient is responding very positively to being treated like an adult. Ms. Ludlow can't quite formulate it clearly in words, but I get the message she has the idea.

LEVENSON: What does she say?

TRAINEE: She talks about the therapist's giving her something—not organizing her life or giving her the answers . . .

TRAINEE: Or the three pieces of sky!

TRAINEE: . . . but giving her what she really needed.

TRAINEE: Perhaps being treated with respect and understanding.

TRAINEE: Also with the therapist's expectation that the two of them could figure something out together.

TRAINEE: And that was precisely what we had indicated for the goal of this brief therapy—that Dr. Ellison would not jump in to fix her but not abandon her either.

TRAINEE: Well, I don't know if I agree that she has had a new experience or a new insight. I don't think she knows how to have a new experience yet. That's something which takes more time. If you have been a certain way all your life, and then someone points that out, you can have a moment of understanding and say "Ah ha," but that doesn't mean you are going to act differently. I wonder if Ms. Ludlow is just being compliant with the therapist.

LEVENSON: I certainly agree that if people have been habitually interacting in a certain way, motivated by trying to avoid pain, preserving their identity and worldview, and maintaining a sense of connectedness, we should be suspicious of seemingly dramatic and sudden changes. With regard to your skepticism, however, we have not conceptualized Ms. Ludlow's primary dysfunctional stance as that of a compliant, dependent person. Let's examine what are the data as to whether Ms. Ludlow's behavior is reflective of a new experience and understanding or is instead a manifestation of superficial compliance.

This trainee's incredulity reminds us that the therapist must constantly watch for signs that he or she is colluding in a dysfunctional interaction. Patients can be adept at seeming to make therapeutic progress while actually manifesting incredibly subtle forms of resistance. Is Ms. Ludlow's agreement with her therapist's interpretation a way to short-circuit the therapist's intent?

In a brief therapy it is especially critical for the therapist to see therapeutic progress as a set of mini-outcomes interspersed throughout the whole therapeutic process. Since time is so short, if corrections need to be made in approach, focus, or the type of treatment in general, the therapist needs to make them midstream. Judging outcome session by session ("Did I make the most of this session?") and intervention by intervention ("Was this a helpful thing to have said or done?") allows the therapist to use data within sessions to inform himself or herself about what worked and what did not.

[CLASSROOM]

TRAINEE: I thought her interpretation and the context in which it was embedded did create a new experience. That was quite an outburst from Ms. Ludlow.

TRAINEE: It seemed like a shriek of recognition; it was obvious that Dr. Ellison's comments affected her greatly.

TRAINEE: The sound of the shriek made me think Ms. Ludlow was both fascinated and relieved.

TRAINEE: I thought so, too. And after her outburst, Ms. Ludlow had a different demeanor. She seemed more her age and had more spontaneous affect which was congruent with what she was saying.

TRAINEE: Even her voice quality changed. It isn't that whiny, childish voice. It's more modulated.

TRAINEE: Also there is a feeling of a connection between Ms. Ludlow and Dr. Ellison. They are having a back-and-forth conversation.

TRAINEE: Ms. Ludlow did seem more adultlike. She was definitely more collaborative—less of a child to be fixed.

TRAINEE: What Dr. Ellison said really seemed to resonate with Ms. Ludlow. Following it, the patient was more relaxed and involved.

TRAINEE: Also she is owning more of the process. She didn't realize she was pulling for Dr. Ellison to act as her parents did.

TRAINEE: And she takes responsibility for giving confusing answers to people when she was asked how she was feeling—giving them 8 or 10 unrelated facts. Before, she was projecting it outward—it was others' fault or some quirk of fate.

TRAINEE: My countertransference to Ms. Ludlow before Dr. Ellison's intervention was of being bored and frustrated. I had a hard time following the patient. Afterwards, it was easier to understand her. She seemed more organized.

TRAINEE: And my countertransference feelings also changed. I felt warmer toward her. I even had some sympathy for her.

TRAINEE: Her associations were rich. She produced more material. She gave Dr. Ellison examples spontaneously of how she replicates her dynamic of being vague and disorganized in her everyday life. She doesn't just agree that Dr. Ellison is right and that's all she can say. She has put the concept into her own words with her own examples. This makes me feel she is not just being compliant with the therapist as a person in authority.

As evidence of behavioral changes in the patient, the trainees have pointed to the shift in Ms. Ludlow's emotional tone and voice modulation, nonverbal behavior, cognitive flow and organization, collaboration, and associations, and their own countertransferential reactions. The trainees conclude that something significant happened in this session which was precipitated by Dr. Ellison's self-involving disclosure.

Invariably one of the trainees will ask whether Dr. Ellison could have or should have made this interpretation in a previous session and whether it would have had the same effect. I think the answer must again rest with the therapist's judgment regarding the nature of the relationship between patient and therapist. Have the two of them repeatedly and/or intensely experienced this dysfunctional dance? Has the therapist repeatedly felt the pull to behave in a complementary manner? Does the therapist feel stuck and unable to keep from being lured into a detrimental series of interactions? Does the patient seem pressed to perceive the therapist *only* as a representation of past significant others? If so, then a self-involving disclosure seems appropriate.

To paraphrase Jay Greenberg (1986), if the therapist cannot be experienced as an old object, the analysis never begins; if the therapist cannot be experienced as a new one, it never ends. Countertransference disclosures can create a bridge enabling patients to see their therapists as new objects and to permit an exploration in the here and now of the cyclical maladaptive pattern.

As the trainees further discuss this clinical vignette, two other observations can be made. First is the recognition that the patient seems increasingly sad as she continues to talk about her need to present herself as disorganized as a way to maintain a relationship. Such sorrow and even anguish can be a natural outgrowth of recognizing how one's own actions have contributed to one's misery. Patients can go through a mini–grief reaction, mourning lost opportunities. To keep patients from becoming depressed and morbidly remorseful, it is important that they comprehend the past adaptive nature of such behaviors (see chapter 3).

The second observation has to do with how many rapid-fire questions Dr. Ellison seems to be asking, taking rather large conceptual leaps. She also seems to be emphasizing the reasons for the patient's pattern of behaving, rather than feelings. It should be pointed out that Ms. Ludlow is able to keep up with Dr. Ellison, but what about Dr. Ellison's technique here? Is this brisk, more cognitively focused pace a necessary part of doing a brief therapy?

Dr. Ellison's reaction to this session, which became known during her own supervision, helps us understand. She was quite astounded by Ms. Ludlow's positive response to her self-involving disclosure. As you will recall, Dr. Ellison was quite hesitant to present so much of herself in the session; she felt it was a risky thing to do. When her intervention worked, and had an obvious emotional and cognitive impact on her patient, Dr. Ellison became very encouraged. She felt, for the first time, that she was talking to an adult, an adult who was collaborative and able to take a look at her own processes.

Therefore, Dr. Ellison felt she was on a roll. Her rapid-fire behavior suggests a strike-while-the-iron-is-hot phenomenon. Dr. Ellison was now stimulated to ask all of those questions she had been curious about, but had been afraid to ask or were previously met with resistance. "Why do you do this?" "What would happen if . . . ?" "Do you see how this happens in here?" Any one of these questions could have been developed further—examining feelings surrounding it, examples, associations, and so on. Just as the therapist had been pulled to treat her patient as a child earlier, here she is inspired to go deeper and faster by Ms. Ludlow's responsiveness and availability.

In closing the training module on this ninth session, I inform the trainees that Dr. Ellison's interventions have not resulted in a magical transformation of Ms. Ludlow. It is not smooth sailing from here on. Shortly after the segment I played, Ms. Ludlow again became somewhat diffuse and tangential. Dr. Ellison again (briefly) became frustrated and felt defeated. However, since the therapist and patient both knew they had experienced each other in a more mature and related way, they reminded themselves of that fact, and used this experience in the broader context of their relationship to get back on track.

Dr. Ellison and Ms. Ludlow worked together for another nine sessions. They repeatedly dealt with Ms. Ludlow's ambivalence about defining herself as a problem in order to get the attention from and connection with others she desired. Increasingly, but not without its setbacks and difficult moments, Ms. Ludlow began to experience her therapist as an adult collaborator—as someone who was willing to meet her halfway, but not rescue her or desert her. She experienced herself as more capable, while at the same time comprehending how she had contributed to an unrewarding pattern of disappointed relationships.

EPILOGUE

As part of a quality-assurance component of the Brief Psychotherapy Program, patients respond to various self-report instruments pre- and post-therapy. Ms. Ludlow's scores indicated that following TLDP she was much less distressed by symptoms (as measured by the Symptom Check List-90R: Derogatis, 1983) and interpersonal problems (as measured by the Inventory of Interpersonal Problems: Horowitz, Rosenberg, Baer, Ureno, & Vallasenor,

1988). For example, at intake she had indicated that feeling blue was extremely distressing for her; at termination she reported that this problem was only slightly distressing. At intake she responded that getting along with people was extremely distressing for her; by termination it was markedly less so. At termination she rated her overall problems as maximally improved.

In addition to gathering the pre- and post-therapy data, I try to interview patients 6 months to 1 year after they have completed their time-limited therapies. I do this for three reasons. First, I want to assess whether these chronically troubled patients have been helped by TLDP. Second, I like to provide the trainees with some feedback as to how their former patients are doing. Such data are valuable for therapists who often do not get to see dramatic changes by the time a brief therapy ends. I encourage therapists who undertake a TLDP (or other model of brief therapy) to inform themselves by doing follow-up interviews whenever possible. And third, the act of having patients return for a follow-up interview can sometimes consolidate and strengthen therapeutic gains. The collaborative nature of the interview reinforces the TLDP therapist's stance.

When I contacted Ms. Ludlow, she declined to come in for a 1-year follow up. No reasons were asked for or given. However, 6 years later when we were conducting a long-term follow-up study (Bein et al., 1994), Ms. Ludlow readily agreed to return. Such long-term follow-up studies are critical when working with difficult patients, because research has indicated that quite often positive changes do not become apparent until years after the therapy is concluded (Lambert & Bergin, 1994).

As part of the long-term follow-up procedure, patients participated in a semi-structured, videotaped interview and completed several psychometric instruments, and a questionnaire designed to measure how they saw their therapy and therapist. On the questionnaire item designed to assess overall evaluation of the therapy, Ms. Ludlow indicated that she thought her brief therapy had "helped a great deal" (highest rating) to deal more effectively with her problems. When asked what she remembered focusing on in her therapy, she checked the following "a great deal": trying to understand my typical patterns of relating to people; the influences that past experiences had on my current life; and my relationships with people when I was a child. She thought the following were discussed "a fair amount": my attitudes and feelings about my therapist; my relationship with people in my life at the time of the therapy; giving me a chance to relate in a new and better way with my therapist. Ms. Ludlow thought there was little or no focus in her TLDP on her symptoms, advice-giving by her therapist, or specific tasks she should do outside therapy. Clearly Ms. Ludlow's perception, some 6 years later, of what transpired in her therapy had a strong correspondence with the strategies and techniques of TLDP.

Responses to the self-report inventories revealed that not only did Ms. Ludlow maintain the gains she had achieved, but she had made even further symptomatic and interpersonal improvement.

On a section of the follow-up questionnaire reserved for additional thoughts or feelings about the therapy, Ms. Ludlow wrote in:

> It was *too* brief and I disliked the way it was administered. However, Dr. Ellison showed—made me figure out—how I was the family scapegoat, how I kept my parents together by being and presenting a problem. At the dinner table they worked on me rather than look at their own stuff. I was also trying to be perfect, so—great tension for me. I've learned how to be a friend without presenting a problem or giving status reports. My parents are both in nursing homes and no longer in the game. My sister is mistreating me as she administers the family trust. Five years ago my husband was killed in a terrible swimming accident. But the basic knowledge stated above was a priceless revelation to be given at age 45 after a lifetime of trying to do better, be more, and show love by being a problem.*

Although she had been through some horrendous stressors, including the death of her husband, with whom she had reunited following the therapy, Ms. Ludlow had managed not to become clinically depressed. She attributed her positive attitude to having developed a better support system, which helped her feel loved and appreciated. She viewed her TLDP experience as fundamental to these changes.

---

*It is interesting to note that the patient did not relinquish her pre-therapy understanding of her family dynamics ("I was the family scapegoat"), but rather blended it with her therapy-acquired understanding (trying to get love and/or attention by being a problem).

CHAPTER 7

The Therapist's Stance

WHAT QUALITIES IDEALLY describe the attitude and behavior of the therapist in TLDP? Because so much of the "technique" of TLDP has to do with the therapeutic relationship, the therapist's stance is critical. To illustrate therapist attitudes and behaviors that facilitate treatment, the case of Mrs. Follette will be presented.

At the time of her therapy, Mrs. Follette was a 59-year-old employed, widowed, African-American woman, who had three grown children. She had been in individual and group therapy several times in the past. Her therapist was Dr. David, a Caucasian male, who was a fourth-year psychiatry resident. During his first session with Mrs. Follette, Dr. David was unsure how he could be of help to her. She presented with no clear agenda—only saying that she had some memory difficulties. She had been referred by the Neurology Service when they could find no evidence of an organic problem. Dr. David did some formal mental-status testing, but also did not find any discernible memory impairment. And by the third session, Mrs. Follette said her memory difficulties had disappeared and were "no longer bothering me."

Mrs. Follette was prompt for her appointments, but it was unclear what she hoped to accomplish in the therapy. By the third session she had not stated what her goals were or even what she wished to talk about in a particular session. As a result, Dr. David was feeling lost, helpless, and superfluous.

However, based on her manner of interacting with him, what she said about her relationships with others, and his reaction to her, Dr. David was able to discern a style of relating that was quite problematical for Mrs. Follette. Dr. David's working formulation of her CMP was as follows:

Acts of the self: Patient feels self-conscious in the presence of others, particularly peers in a nonworking environment. Patient maintains a "shell" around herself that allows her to keep others at "arm's length." Although she longs for closeness and acceptance, she fears intimacy. ("I don't want to be depending on anyone.") As a result, she remains somewhat isolated and alone. ("I need to get out and do things.") Patient believes she does not need other people. ("I don't care what other people think.") She repeatedly sets professional goals for herself that she eventually meets, but is then left feeling unfulfilled. ("Once I reach my goals, I feel unsatisfied.")

Expectations of others' reactions: Patient believes others are not dependable. ("If you depend on people, it hurts you when it's not there.") She believes others are not willing to provide closeness and nurturance when needed. ("When you need someone, they will not be there.") She expects others will be hurtful to her if she depends on them, and thinks others will treat her better the more she is independent. Patient believes others are often not honest with her. ("All the support I've gotten in the past has been misleading.") She also expects that others will perceive her as inferior. ("They said I wasn't college material.")

Acts of others toward self: Patient's fears of allowing others to get close to her or to know her by revealing things about herself leads others to feel alienated and distanced. (I felt put off by her seeming self-sufficiency and lack of interest in my help.) Others view the patient as being strong and independent and not interested in or in need of their help or friendship. Some others treat the patient as if she were inferior.

Acts of the self toward the self (introject): Patient sees herself as having an inferior mind, and therefore feels she is inadequate. ("Maybe I am the way I am because my umbilical cord was wrapped around my neck when I was born.") She considers herself to be unlovable. Patient feels guilty. She sees herself as vulnerable, with a need to preserve control and appear strong. She has a heightened sense of responsibility for her own well-being.

Since Dr. David was able to derive a dynamic focus, and Mrs. Follette met the five basic selection criteria for TLDP and none of the exclusionary criteria, she was accepted into treatment in the Brief Psychotherapy Program. She could not come to therapy on a weekly basis, however. Every other week she had to take computer classes during the time she would ordinarily meet with Dr. David. So a revised schedule was agreed on; Mrs. Follette would come to therapy every other week.* In total, she was to receive 10 sessions over 20 weeks.

To illustrate how Dr. David's stance as a therapist was helpful to this patient, I show the trainees three videotaped vignettes from the same session. These excerpts come from the first 5 minutes, the middle 10 minutes, and the last 5 minutes of the fifth session. Following these, I present portions of a 6-month follow-up interview I conducted with Mrs. Follette.

FIRST 5 MINUTES

[CLASSROOM]

LEVENSON: I will now show you the first 5 minutes of this fifth session. Remember, at this point the therapy is half over. I think you will see how Dr. David's dynamic focus for this patient, derived some weeks previously, captures her interactional style. Just to summarize that CMP: This is a woman who puts out signals that she does not need anything from anyone, because she fears no one will be there for her if she is vulnerable. She keeps her guard up, so as not to get harmed, but her distancing style (her pseudoindependence) puts others off, ensuring the very reaction she most fears.

[VIDEOTAPE]

Therapist: Any thoughts?

Mrs. Follette: Not really. No. Not any real thoughts. Things are just moving along. Do you got any thoughts? What about your thoughts? (laugh) Oh, goodness!

Therapist: What kind of thoughts were you speaking of?

Mrs. Follette: You mean what kind of thoughts, that I was speaking of when I asked you what your thoughts were?

Therapist: Uh huh.

Mrs. Follette: Oh, your thoughts about me [Uh huh], and what we've been doing. (pause) If it is helping you.

---

*I generally use the traditional weekly, 50-minute-hour format in training since it keeps all the trainees in the group at approximately the same developmental pace. However, many brief therapists are experimenting with the frequency and duration of sessions as they take into account the needs of the patient and the system. Some interesting empirical work suggests it is more the length of time since starting therapy (and not the actual number of sessions) that is related to therapeutic outcome (Johnson & Gelso, 1980; Lorr, McNair, Michaux, & Raskin, 1962).

Therapist: If it is helping me?

Mrs. Follette: Yeah, right, to accomplish your goals.

Therapist: Hmm. What do you see as being my goal?

Mrs. Follette: Well, must be to become a—what—a psychiatrist or what? What? A psychiatrist?

Therapist: Uh huh.

Mrs. Follette: How is that coming?

Therapist: What did you say?

Mrs. Follette: How is that coming for you?

Therapist: It's interesting that you would view therapy as being something to help me [Yeah, it is . . .] in my goal.

Mrs. Follette: . . . isn't it?

Therapist: I suppose in general everything I'm doing is leading me towards that. Ah, but I wonder if you think of our meeting as being more for me than for you? It sounded like that is what you were suggesting.

Mrs. Follette: Hmm. Well, I think for both, really. You know, this is a dual-purpose situation. I come in here and this is to help you get, I guess your certification or whatever it is. And, ah, you're helping me, and I'm helping you—in a way.

Therapist: Does that, I wonder if that leaves any room for caring?

Mrs. Follette: Caring? [Uh huh] Um, I think so. Ah, ah, over the years I've had a number of, you know, therapists for different phases in my life. And, ah, I don't think I necessarily dealt with them differently. Ah, there may have been some areas that during that therapy session we didn't get to. And that could have been a couple reasons. One, ah, at that particular time that was not the issue that I was concerned with. And two, ah, you only let people know what you want them to know. But then, on the other hand, there are things that one do not verbalize that one can assume and know about a person.

Therapist: Do you think there are things that you're talking about, that there are things about you, I might assume that you don't need to verbalize?

Mrs. Follette: Uh huh, yeah, uh, well, yeah, right. 'Cuz we're talking about me now. Yeah.

[CLASSROOM]

LEVENSON: What do you see here?

TRAINEE: It's really kind of funny. It's hard to figure out at first who is the therapist and who is the patient.

TRAINEE: Yeah. It reminded me of this Mental Research Institute tape I heard once of two psychiatric residents interviewing each other. Each had been told that the other was a patient who had a delusion he was a resident.

TRAINEE: She is quite a challenge. She clearly doesn't want to talk about herself. She seems to be protecting herself.

TRAINEE: They don't seem to be getting into any deep material. It has a quality almost like a business meeting. That's how she came across. You give me this; I'll give you that. No one will owe anyone at the end of the meeting. It's all kind of even-Steven. It very much goes along with Dr. David's CMP.

TRAINEE: Yes. When she says that she's helping him get his certification, it reminds me of what Dr. David outlined under *acts of the self*—where others see her as being strong and independent and therefore not in need of their help or understanding.

LEVENSON: Although Dr. David came up with his understanding of Mrs. Follette's maladaptive interactional pattern some weeks before, this present interchange should give us increased confidence in his formulation. One can more readily understand the present interaction in light of the dynamic focus. Comparing present, in-session material to what one was hypothesizing in the formulation is one way of constantly refining the CMP.

TRAINEE: These first 5 minutes convey the tone of a business relationship to me also. A tug-of-war. She is very well defended.

TRAINEE: She was so distancing to me that I realize it was hard for me to listen to her. I drifted off. I felt left out. I wasn't engaged.

LEVENSON: This is part of your countertransferential reaction to her defensiveness. You are not engaged, and this woman often experiences others as not being there. It is as if you have confirmed her worst fear. How does Dr. David respond to Mrs. Follette's distancing, quid pro quo presentation? How is he handling her invitation to have the therapy maintain a businesslike quality?

TRAINEE: Overall, I think Dr. David is being very calm and gentle. He respects what she is presenting.

TRAINEE: He doesn't get flustered or defensive.

LEVENSON: What gives you that message? What is he doing that lets you know he respects her and doesn't get defensive?

TRAINEE: Well, when she implies that she is there in part to meet his needs for his training—his certification—he does not discount that she has a point.

TRAINEE: I liked the way he handled her direct question about how the therapy was helping him.

LEVENSON: What did he say?

TRAINEE: He acknowledged the reality of the situation, but then turned it right back to her.

LEVENSON: Right. Does anyone remember what he said?

TRAINEE: He said something like everything he's doing is helping him, and then he immediately said, "But it sounded like you think of the therapy as more for me than for you," or something like that.

TRAINEE: I really liked the way he responded to her. He didn't just shine her on and say, "Well, why do you ask that question?" There was an accuracy about her perception that her therapist is getting something out of the sessions. It *is* furthering his training.

TRAINEE: He answers her in a very matter-of-fact way with one sentence and then puts it back on her. He says there is a reality to what she is saying, but asks her if there isn't something more?

TRAINEE: I am so uncomfortable when patients ask me direct questions like this. I would have felt on the spot if she had asked me if I were, in essence, using her.

The trainees' comments about Dr. David's forthrightness illustrate two important therapeutic attitudes: therapist respect for the patient and clinical honesty with restrained self-disclosure. By Dr. David's responding to the realities of his being in training, he owns his portion of their relationship, which does have a quid pro quo component. She is there to get some help; he is there to further his training.

When Dr. David concedes that his work with her will help him in the grander scheme of things, he is confirming her perception. In this way he makes it safer for the patient to be in a relationship with him (new experience). I ask the trainees what else they notice about Dr. David's therapeutic stance.

[CLASSROOM]

TRAINEE: I got the impression Dr. David was trying to change the tone of the therapy session from this mutual business arrangement to something more affectively present. The patient feels more comfortable with this "you scratch my back, I'll scratch yours" type of interaction. Out of the blue, Dr. David introduces the concept of "Does that leave any room for caring." This directly challenges how the patient was setting up the relationship.

LEVENSON: Excellent observation. I think what you are alluding to illustrates another tenet of this model, which emphasizes trying to bring the therapist–patient interaction to an affective level.

TRAINEE: I would have said something like, "I think it is very difficult for you to be in a relationship where you are the one who is getting her needs met." My interpretation would have pointed out her difficulty in being needy or vulnerable.

LEVENSON: Your interpretation sounds valid, given her CMP. How do you think she would have responded?

TRAINEE: She probably would have denied it, or become more vociferous in her claim of Dr. David's gains.

TRAINEE: She might have heard your interpretation as blaming.

LEVENSON: Dr. David uses the phrasing of his question in a way to promote change—to see other possibilities—rather than to close down options and focus on present or past pathology. To say, "I wonder if that leaves any room for caring?" puts the listener in a position to move to a more affective (and hopefully more fruitful) level, rather than saying "Why aren't you more caring," which sounds blaming and focused on past inadequacy. The use of language, even in the simple phrasing of comments and questions, is critical. Solution-focused therapy [e.g., O'Hanlon & Weiner-Davis, 1988; Walter & Peller, 1992], using a different model of brief therapy, emphasizes the importance of the therapist's use of language in facilitating a different perspective, which increases the likelihood of change.

The trainees correctly point out the therapist's valiant efforts to introduce an affective tone into the therapy. The patient is implying that Dr. David is primarily interested in her because of his training needs; he tries to deepen their connection by pointing out there may be another basis for the relationship. In the patient's CMP, under *expectations of others' reactions,* we have observed that Mrs. Follette does not believe others will be there to provide closeness when needed. By suggesting that caring might be an important ingredient of the therapeutic relationship, Dr. David is providing another mini–new experience that runs counter to Mrs. Follette's expectation of how others behave.

Overall, Dr. David takes his time with Mrs. Follette. Even in a brief therapy where time is of the essence, there is the opportunity to let the pacing of the sessions evolve and not be unduly pressured or packaged. In addition to fostering an unrushed atmosphere, Dr. David keeps a respectful distance. He asks questions, but does not make a lot of interpretations or pronouncements. He is not defensive even when directly challenged.

[CLASSROOM]

TRAINEE: I wonder, though, if the patient's attitude like she had to be there to help her therapist has more to do with the fact that she is black and he is white.

This trainee is raising a critical issue concerning a factor that might influence the nature of the interaction between therapist and patient which has little or nothing to do with any maladaptive pattern of the patient. Mrs. Follette is a 59-year-old African-American woman; Dr. David is a Caucasian man young enough to be her son. Might not Mrs. Follette relate to her therapist in a certain manner because of his race, age, and gender—with such interactions having little or nothing to do with more chronic or pervasive interactional styles? And just as important, might not Dr. David relate to Mrs. Follette based on her race, age, and gender rather than his countertransferential response to her transference to him?

Clearly, the issues of race, gender, and age, just to mention a few, must be considered so that a dynamic focus is not derived which more appropriately has to do with specifics of a particular relationship rather than an overall pattern. For example, if Mrs. Follette's behavior and feelings (i.e., issues of trust, vulnerability, quid pro quo nature) have more to do with her attitudes toward Caucasians than a more general interpersonal pattern, then developing a TLDP dynamic focus based on her manner of relating to her (white) therapist will be detrimental to an understanding of her interactional life in general. Analogously, if Mrs. Follette has a unique interactional style with her son, and she views the therapist as her son, a similarly derived TLDP dynamic focus would not be an effective formulation for the case.

The best safeguard against such erroneous formulations is to gauge therapist–patient interactions in the here and now of the therapy sessions in light of what the patient says about her expectations of and behavior from other people in her life (who might be of the same race, gender, or age). In this case, Dr. David had noted that Mrs. Follette felt her female relatives were not dependable; she felt she needed to protect herself from family members and peers in her community by distancing herself. Thus when Dr. David experienced Mrs. Follette's keeping him at arm's length, it seemed like a piece of a larger picture rather than something idiosyncratic having to do with their particular relationship.

Following the discussion of Mrs. Follette's style as it was evidenced in the first 5 minutes of the fifth session, we next examine the middle 10 minutes of the same session.

MIDDLE 10 MINUTES

[VIDEOTAPE]

Therapist: The one thing that I'm thinking about, too, is what you brought up earlier in the session about therapy's ending and, you know, where the, ah, we sort of talked about the last week of this will be the first week of June [Uh huh], which is June 4th. I'm wondering how you feel about that and how that's affecting . . .

Mrs. Follette: I feel very fine about that because, ah, I don't have any burning issues, that, you know, when I came before, I was having problems with my supervisor on the job, and, you know, I was trying, ah, to feel better about, you know, that situation, so I had an issue that, you know, that, that was, you know, that was, you know, that we discussed that, you know, that was, that I had a lot of interest in. Ah, in this therapy session with you, I don't have any burning issues, you know, like, like, ah, my supervisor, you know. Like I wonder what's going on with me, this type of thing, the issue I originally came with. The fact that I thought that my memory was failing me, ah, however, ah, in a sense, coming here, talking to you, ah, I'm not feeling that way anymore, and ah, my memory is, you know, a lot better. [Uh huh] And I am not, where before I was, sort of gasping for things and I don't feel that way. So, ah, either with your help or with the other help or with my own help, you know, I feel a lot better about that particular situation. So June 4th, as far as I'm concerned, is a good time to, you know, to terminate, because I feel as though, over the next several weeks, that whatever other issues may come up that I can cope with them, and I can deal with them with your help, ah, or, you know, whatever. In other words, I come up with a lot of confidence about myself and not looking through, ah, dark glass.

Therapist: The one thing you said once, though, was, ah, you wanted to make sure that you didn't start to depend on 2:30 on Thursdays. [Uh huh] Because when that ends then you're left without, without that [Hmm] and that would be a very uncomfortable feeling. [Uh huh] So it just makes me wonder, ah, that your comfortable feeling about ending June 4th, ah, is OK because the feeling that, well, I'll just make sure that I don't get too dependent on this, and make sure that I hold back to a certain degree. Then we could end June 4th and it won't matter, because I never will have allowed myself to depend on this in the first place.

Mrs. Follette: Well, that's a form of protection, you know. If I don't protect me, who will, you know? And I'm not saying that's true, but it could be, you know, it could be. It could be that I have, you know, put up that wall that we talked about some time ago, and that it does exist. And I think it would be a valid reason for it to exist. [Uh huh] Ah, because things must come to an end, so you must either come to move along so you come to that conclusion so that when one walk out of this door, that one is all together. Ah (pause), some time ago I used to do, ah, ah, group sessions where we would talk about, ah, issues and stuff like that. And, ah, you know, sometimes people get so balled up in issues that when they walk out, they're no good. So you have to put the person back together before they left. [Uh huh] Because if you didn't, you know, they'd be devastated. And I'm sure, you know, in therapy, ah, in a day's session or whatever, you know, in an hour's session, you know, you have to try to come to some, not necessarily conclusions, you have to come to a point where when your client walks out the door, the client is not a babbling nut. You know, that you can [So you . . .] walk out and still be able to function until one get back to see you again. (chuckle)

Therapist: So if you got into it too, too deeply here and [Uh huh] pulled out too much of this old stuff, ah, you may sort of be this blathering, blithering basket case when you walked out.

Mrs. Follette: I don't think so. [And . . .] I, I, I don't think so, I don't think I would, ah, I don't think at this stage in my life that would, that would happen to me. I really don't. I really don't think so, because I have some other release valves [Uh huh], you know, in my life, and I don't think . . .

Therapist: And yet you said before that that's one of the things you might do for protection is to make sure you're not wanting to get too, ah, pulled apart—wanting to make sure that you were together when you walked out the door.

Mrs. Follette: Sure, right, that's important. You know, you know, you know it's important for, as a client, it's important for me because when I leave here, ah, usually I would go back to work [Uh huh] and I don't want to'go back to work and, you know, be sitting there look-ing into space trying to figure out, you know, all this stuff or what-ever. Ah, I can't afford to do that. And, ah, so, therefore, you know, I must know what my point is and hopefully that, as a therapist and as a client, that we're both on the same plane when it comes to that. And I, I know that you always have an agenda, and ah, you know, (pause) whatever. So, so we sit in here and we talk about the relationship between the therapist and the client. (laugh)

Therapist: What do you think about that?

Mrs. Follette: Huh?

Therapist: What do you think about that?

Mrs. Follette: (laugh) I think it's fun! I really do.

Therapist: Uh huh. What have you learned about that? Anything come to mind? What's coming up for you . . . talking about our relationship?

Mrs. Follette: Well, it certainly makes for a better ra . . . ah, feeling, you know, to come out here [Uh huh] and see and talk to you, you know, because we do have that type of relationship, ah, you know, it always helps. [Uh huh] Ah, you know, ah, you know, it help me. We won't talk about whether it helping you or not. But anyway, a dimension, ah, that, ah, that may be something else that we, I may need to throw out on the table, ah, for us to discuss.

Therapist: Something particular in mind that you were . . . [Huh?] Something particular in mind that you were thinking of when you said that?

Mrs. Follette: Uh huh, yeah, uh huh.

Therapist: What, what was that?

Mrs. Follette: (chuckle) It is funny, you know, ah, of all the therapy sessions I've been in, I've never brought up the fact that my stepfather, ah (pause), demanded, when I was about, what, 20, 21, whatever. Ah, my mother had, ah, gone to Chicago for the summer and ah, you know, we were there, and, ah, you know, and it's pretty hard to say he made me have sexual intercourse with him. But you know, it came down to that. And that didn't bother me until, oh, I guess about maybe 10 years ago, and then, you know, whatever, it came back very vividly. And, ah, out of all the therapists that I've been to and talked to, I've never brought that one little aspect up. And, you know, I was really curious about that. You know, I was wondering about that, ah, why I never, you know, brought that up as an issue, that it happened. Because I really think, ah, I really think, I think I told you I thought something else traumatic had happened, and maybe that's it. I don't know. But for some reason I just have a sense that something else happened, you know, to me, but I don't know what it is.

Therapist: (softly, in measured tones) That's a pretty heavy-duty [Uh huh] thing to have gone through. [Uh huh] This was not just a stepfather but he raised you like . . .

Mrs. Follette: Well, right, yeah. I always look at him as my father, right. And, ah, ah, you know, someone that you think of as your father, when they do one of those, you know, and what not, it make you very, ah, very distant, very distant.

Therapist: Very distant?

Mrs. Follette: Distant from, you know, with him and although, ah, I think I had graduated from college at that time and ah, ah, left home shortly after that, ah, you know, it's still something that, you know, that you, you never forget and you'd like to forget. But you can't forget that, ah, you know, a thing like that happened. And you know, I, I don't live in that city with my mother and father.

Therapist: Do you feel more distant from him ever since then?

Mrs. Follette: Oh, yeah. Right. Uh huh.

Therapist: Is he still alive?

Mrs. Follette: Yeah, uh huh.

Therapist: Still lives with your mother?

Mrs. Follette: Uh huh. Uh huh. And I never told my mother, but for some reason I think she knows. I get that sense someplace. That she probably knows.

Therapist: Uh huh. Uh huh. It must make you very, ah, first of all, it must have made it very difficult to have anybody that you could trust [Uh huh, right, yeah], if your own father [Uh huh, yeah] did this to you. [Uh huh]

[CLASSROOM]

Trainee: What a powerful segment! I'm struck by how she suddenly said that. And I'm trying to think back exactly when the turning point was.

Trainee: Yeah. I thought this was a major breakthrough. She had been closed and reserved, even vague. Now she makes a major disclosure about how she was forced to have intercourse by her stepfather.

Trainee: If you had told me that this was going to happen in the session before I saw this, I wouldn't have believed it. Why did it happen now?

Levenson: That is an excellent question. Why now? This woman had been in individual and group therapies before—even a women's group—but she had never discussed this rape. She does so with Dr. David in the fifth session. But why now?

Trainee: The first thing I think of is how this segment started, with Dr. David's talking about the fact that therapy will end soon. He asks her how she feels about therapy's ending. Perhaps in some way she realizes that there was a limited amount of time she would have to be able to work on this secret—a kind of now-or-never attitude.

Trainee: I was thinking that also. At one point she says that she has no "burning issues," like when she previously came to therapy. But then she hints around that she may have something else to put on the table, and I was wondering if she felt some impetus to discuss these other issues because they would only have a few sessions left. In other words, she would have to really make use of whatever time was left because it was running out.

TRAINEE: I had a somewhat different idea. Perhaps the idea of a time-limited therapy gave her a sense that there was a boundary to the therapy—that it would not go on interminably, with her becoming more and more enmeshed and dependent. She has quite a fear of becoming too dependent. A limited therapy might have been enough of a container to allow her to get into material that in an open-ended therapy would be too threatening.

These three trainees all point to the importance of the time-limited nature of a brief therapy in stimulating the patient to work. Two of the trainees emphasize the impetus time provides because of its existential aspects—being finite in quantity. James Mann (1973) has developed an entire theory and technique based on the notion that in order for people to get on with their lives, they need to grasp the existential issues associated with such concepts as limited time, independence, and even death. The reasoning of the third trainee underscores how a therapy that has at the outset a definite stopping point can offer a certain type of safety to some patients. In fact, one empirical study supports the notion that setting a time limit may actually encourage some patients to come to all the allotted sessions instead of dropping out earlier (Sledge et al., 1990).

[CLASSROOM]

TRAINEE: I thought time limits played a role, but perhaps in a boomerang fashion from what has already been mentioned. Maybe when Dr. David said that they would be ending soon, Mrs. Follette felt that she did not want to end the therapy, and so dropped this bombshell as a way of buying more time. How could her therapist end treatment now?

LEVENSON: You are developing an alternative hypothesis for why someone might reveal something disturbing about herself toward the end of a brief therapy—as a way of bargaining for more therapeutic time or attention. How can one decide between these alternatives? As a general rule, I give more weight to the hypothesis that is more consistent with the dynamic focus. Since Mrs. Follette's core issues involve fears of dependency and vulnerability, it seems more likely to me that she would have divulged her secret because the time-limited nature of the therapy gave her a sense of safety, protecting her from becoming too dependent on her therapist. Your hypothesis about bargaining for more time would seem more valid for a patient whose CMP included expectations of needing to be taken care of. This type of reasoning illustrates how each patient behavior must be evaluated against the backdrop of that particular patient's CMP.

In addition to the time-limited nature of the therapy, what else might have encouraged Mrs. Follette to share her secret? I should point out that Dr. David learns later that he is the first person, in or out of therapy, Mrs. Follette has ever told about the rape.

TRAINEE: I was wondering if perhaps Mrs. Follette felt like she had to share her secret with Dr. David after all the interest he had showed in her.

TRAINEE: You mean like she is continuing her quid pro quo behavior? Like this is what she owes him?

TRAINEE: Right. To be intimate and vulnerable and come across in the way Dr. David wants her to.

LEVENSON: That certainly is another alternative hypothesis. And a critical one, because it would mean that what we have been taking as an indication of positive change in Mrs. Follette's CMP is really only a variant of her maladaptive pattern. This kind of subtle substitution happens quite frequently in higher-functioning patients. Let's see if we can accept or reject this hypothesis as the session proceeds.

Stephen Mitchell (1994) speaks eloquently about the need for the therapist to be observant regarding repetitions of the old in the apparently new therapeutic relationship. He sees two advantages coming from such attentiveness. First, it helps the patient appreciate how subtly old patterns can be resurrected, and second, it conveys to a patient the therapist's willingness to question his or her own participation in the process.

[CLASSROOM]
TRAINEE: I think just before Mrs. Follette tells him her secret they are talking about the relationship between the two of them.

LEVENSON: Yes. Do you remember how this came up?

TRAINEE: I think the patient introduces it. She says something like, "So we talk about the relationship between the therapist and the patient."

LEVENSON: Yes. It's almost like she has read about TLDP. She knows over the past sessions that she and Dr. David have talked openly about their interaction. Do we know how she feels about discussing her relationship with him?

TRAINEE: He asks her, and she says "It's fun!"

TRAINEE: And then she laughs. It was the most spontaneous emotional expression we have heard from her. It seems quite genuine. And when she elaborates on what it feels like for her to talk to Dr. David in this way, she says something like it makes for a better feeling.

TRAINEE: She sounds lighter. Not guarded.

TRAINEE: She seems to be hearing herself talk and realizing that perhaps they do have a good relationship and perhaps she can trust this man.

LEVENSON: Yes. She does not seem to be using her distancing, cautious, intellectualized mode of responding here. She seems much more in the moment and more affectively connected to Dr. David. Talking about the relationship within the context of that relationship is a very intimate thing to do. The very process demands trust. Let's back up even further and see if we can hypothesize what led up to her feeling that talking about their relationship was fun and relating to him led to a good feeling.

The discussion turns to considering what transpired between Dr. David and Mrs. Follette earlier in this middle portion of the session. The trainees mention how when the therapist introduced the ending date, the patient said that was "fine" with her. However, Dr. David did not take her response at face value and accept that she was comfortable with ending soon. Nor did he contradict her. What he did do was question her nonchalance in terms of other things she has previously mentioned. He reminded her that she did not want to depend on their sessions ("The one thing you said once, though, was you wanted to make sure that you didn't start to depend on 2:30 on Thursdays"). He then wondered out loud whether she were feeling comfortable about ending soon because of her dependency fears. ("Then we could end June 4th and it won't matter, because [you] never will have allowed [yourself] to depend on this in the first place.")

Dr. David's confrontations reminded Mrs. Follette of what she herself had already said. These interventions led her to justify her "holding back" as a form of "protection," so that she does not become a "babbling nut." Here again, Dr. David explored her defensive strategy of how she avoids becoming a "blithering basket case."

The patient then disagreed that she had fears about becoming devastated should she get into this "old stuff" too deeply, because she has some other "release valves" in her life. Again, Dr. David reminded her of what she said earlier in the therapy; this confronted her with additional information and challenged her denial of her avoidant and distancing style. ("And yet you said before that that's one of the things you might do for protection [is never to get involved in the first place] as a way to make sure you were together when you walked out the door.")

Mrs. Follette was then able to agree with Dr. David's comment. She talked about how she and Dr. David needed to be on the "same plane." She told him she was aware that he always had an "agenda," and then she launched into an acknowledgment of how she and Dr. David talk about the "relationship between the therapist and the client."

[CLASSROOM]
TRAINEE: Dr. David was really skilled at bringing whatever she said back to the dynamic focus.
TRAINEE: And he was able to do that by using her own words—things she had said previously, which really must have made her feel heard and understood.
TRAINEE: Another mini–new experience!
TRAINEE: It isn't like he agreed with her by saying, "OK, ending June 4th is fine with you. I won't worry about it." But he also didn't tell her she was wrong—that ending June 4th was a bigger deal for her than she was admitting.
LEVENSON: Yes, I call what Dr. David did several times throughout the session "gentle confrontation." He stays very close to the material she is introducing, where she is psychologically, and uses this information in an empathic way to confront her rigid, distancing stance. So we have a combination of content and process. What he is saying to her is important in terms of her defensive pattern, but how he is saying it in the context of this relationship is even more significant. He is providing her with a series of new experiences in which she is being heard and responded to—he is helping her wrestle with facing her fears.
TRAINEE: I got this image of two fencers sparring. She's on guard with him, but he's not attacking—neither is he deflecting her blows. He's just moving with her. He contains her, but doesn't hurt her—she doesn't fall. He's always there with her, but he's never pushing her too hard.
TRAINEE: That's a great image. It helps me realize that what seems to be so helpful about Dr. David's behavior is that he doesn't push her like I imagine her stepfather did; he doesn't exploit her.
TRAINEE: He doesn't rape her.
TRAINEE: But he also doesn't back away and desert her like others have done. He's just there, and his active, present, but nonintrusive stance allows her the freedom to decide to come forward.
TRAINEE: It seems like a very respectful attitude.
LEVENSON: But very persistent. In the process of confronting her, he is inhibiting her from using her usual defensive style.
TRAINEE: Yeah. She shares and explores her feared consequences of what would happen to her should she fully enter into the therapy and trust Dr. David—she might become devastated. Now I can hear that also as her fears she might again be raped should she trust again. Dr. David's

interventions indicate to her he understands her fears even though she is being very oblique and vague.

I remind the trainees that Dr. David did not know about the rape when he derived his dynamic focus. He went by his own countertransference, the nature of the interaction between him and Mrs. Follette, and what she said about current others in her life. From this focus he knew he wanted to provide a new experience where she would not feel the need to be so defended—so withdrawn into her protective shell.

We have been trying to answer the "Why now?" question about Mrs. Follette's decision to reveal at this time her secret of 38 years. The ingredients that I consider contributory focus on factors involved in the therapist's stance, including: empathic listening, gentle confrontation, a respectful attitude, interest in affective connectedness, honest but not overindulgent self-disclosure, persistence but not heavy-handedness in the use of the dynamic focus, sensitivity to the patient's expression of fears and desires, and a readiness to engage with the patient in a series of new experiences embedded in the context of a human relationship. The imminent termination of therapy and an exploration of the patient's worst fears may also stimulate new material to be introduced or experiential risks to be taken, but I doubt these can be therapeutic without the foundation provided by a positive therapist stance.

Having considered what led up to the patient's uncharacteristic sharing, I now proceed to discuss with the trainees what happened afterward. How did Dr. David respond *after* hearing Mrs. Follette's secret? Mrs. Follette initially introduced the topic of the rape by her stepfather in a seemingly "TLDP-ish" sort of way. She began by saying that she was curious as to why, in all the therapy sessions she'd ever had, she had never brought up "that one little aspect" of being raped.

Mrs. Follette's comment *appears* consistent with TLDP because she is referring to the interaction between therapist and patient, raising the issue of something happening between them in the room, and wanting to explore the dynamics of this interaction, all within the context of the therapeutic relationship. And Dr. David could have responded in a seemingly TLDP-ish manner—something like, "You know, that really *is* curious. I too wonder what is going on here that you decided to share this now. Can we take a look at that?" This type of response would have received high marks on the VTSS—the TLDP adherence measure of how much a therapist is doing therapy according to TLDP theory and technique (see appendix A). Specifically, such an intervention would have seemed like a good example of TLDP strategy because it dealt specifically with transactions in the patient–therapist relationship, and encouraged the patient to explore the meaning and/or implications of a current transaction between patient and therapist that affects the therapeutic work. However, as the following discussion indicates, such an intervention can look appropriate on the surface, but actually undermine progress toward the overall goal.

[CLASSROOM]

LEVENSON: Does anyone recall how Dr. David responded to Mrs. Follette's revelation of her rape?

TRAINEE: He said something like, "That must have been horrible."

LEVENSON: He actually said, "That's a pretty heavy-duty thing to have gone through."

TRAINEE: And he says it very slowly and powerfully, as though he is modeling some affect for her. Her statement is without affect—like she is talking about some hypothetical situation far removed from her experience.

LEVENSON: I don't know if Dr. David's intention was to model affect for her, but I know he was greatly taken aback when he heard about her rape—although she never calls it that. So some of his response must be his natural reaction to hearing this disturbing news. When he says "heavy-duty," you can hear the anguish in his voice. The other reason for his emotional tone is that he has been trying to connect with this patient on an affective level for several sessions. I think his commenting on the "heavy-duty" nature of her experience is similar to his introducing the concept of "caring" earlier. He is trying to see if she can relate to him on a more feeling level. A third reason for his response, in addition to his natural reaction and trying to relate to Mrs. Follette on an emotional level, is that his emphasizing the "heavy-duty" consequences validates that she endured a truly traumatic incident when she was younger.

TRAINEE: So he is saying to her in essence, Forget about examining our interaction for the time being. Forget about our finding out why you are sharing this now. These questions are intriguing and interesting, but they pale in comparison to what you are telling me happened to you.

LEVENSON: Exactly. The answers to the issues she raises probably do contain important material. In essence, she herself is asking the "why now" question. "Why am I sharing this with you now when I haven't before?" But to engage with her on this level might have resulted in a very intellectualized discussion. Dr. David's "heavy-duty" response communicates to Mrs. Follette that he is interested in her emotional experience of the rape and of living with that secret for all of her adult life. His affect also underscores his empathic attunement to her and his understanding of the significance of her confiding in him.

This discussion with the trainees highlights one of the issues involved in using a manual to guide psychotherapy. On the positive side, such a manual provides concrete guidelines and parameters for conducting a therapy so that the process is not a mystery to be gleaned only after years of apprenticeship. On the negative side, a manual cannot replace the clinical judgment of the therapist as to the appropriateness of any particular "manualized" intervention at any one point in time, given the context.

In this case, Dr. David correctly ascertained that to engage with Mrs. Follette in a discussion about understanding the timing of her sharing her secret would be colluding with her avoidance of her need to be comforted and acknowledged, and would inhibit their connecting on a more affective level.

[CLASSROOM]

TRAINEE: I don't recall that her reply to his emotionally reflecting what had happened to her was all that emotional.

LEVENSON: Right. It wasn't, but she readily agreed with him. In fact, before he even finished his statement, she was concurring with him.

Sometimes trainees think that a total catharsis and a full emotional response are the ultimate goals in a psychodynamic therapy. In TLDP it is critical to stay mindful of the patient's CMP and the new experience. In this case, the patient is a woman who is afraid of coming unraveled, who has a need to preserve her outward control. She had already warned Dr. David that she did not want to be a babbling nut when she left the session. In fact, getting in touch with her long-warded-off emotions about this rape may have undermined any positive new experience of feeling safe and protected that was developing.

As a check on an overzealous attempt at catharsis, the therapist can ask himself or herself, How different is the patient being from his or her usual and customary reaction? The therapist can also ask the patient what he or she is experiencing at any particular moment. Although the magnitude of the response may appear minimal, objectively speaking, it may be experienced subjectively by the patient as an enormous risk. In Mrs. Follette's case, on the surface alone it does not look like she has had a major emotional breakthrough, but who can doubt that when she went home that evening she felt as though something quite significant had happened in her therapy that day?

After hearing the secret, experienced therapists can imagine several different therapeutically valid ways Dr. David could have gone. However, he chose to stay within the frame of the CMP and to continue focusing on her vulnerability, trust, and distance issues. It is interesting to note that the patient herself, after revealing her secret, talked about an interpersonal consequence consistent with Dr. David's conceptualization (pseuodoindependence vs. intimacy). "It make you very, very distant, very distant." Dr. David maintained the focus when he asked whether she had felt more distant from her stepfather. And then he expanded this specific behavior to the broader implications of her distancing style with other people: "It must have made it very difficult to have anybody that you could trust, if your own father did this to you." The patient readily agreed.

Sometime during our discussion of the middle 10 minutes of Mrs. Follette's fifth session, one of the trainees recalled that ironically the patient entered therapy because she was having a problem with her memory: she had initially framed her presenting complaint as difficulty remembering things. After her revelation to Dr. David in which she laments that she has experienced "something you never forget and you'd like to forget, but you can't forget," we realize that perhaps her real memory problem is not that she cannot remember, but that she cannot forget.

At this point we focus on the last 5 minutes of this fifth session.

LAST 5 MINUTES

[VIDEOTAPE]

Therapist: I just want to point something out. I've commented before about that feeling of there being a shell around you—that distance. I noticed when you came in today, there was very much that feeling again [Of what?], there being a shell around you. [Oh.] But that somewhere in the middle of the session it feels like that shifted. [Uh huh] I feel a lot more openness and warmth about you [Uh huh] now as opposed to early in the session. [Uh huh] Are you aware of that? Do you feel any difference?

Mrs. Follette: Um . . . (pause) Yeah, I think I do. I think so. I've reached some, I've reached some, ah, real, ah, decisions about, you know, about myself and about where I want to go. And the fact is, I can't move on if I'm holding all these things. You know, I can't move. [Yeah.] I mean, I can't be a part of, you know, be with other people and feel comfortable [Uh huh] as long as I'm keeping a whole lot of stuff. [Uh huh] And I think once I eliminate this stuff, and even when you verbalize it to one person—it's over and done with. You know, that's it. It's out there in the air. [Ah huh] Maybe someday if, ah, they make a machine and they can pick up the conversation that, that we had between 2:30 and 3:30 or 3:25, you know, that will be it. (pause) But you know, I feel a lot looser, and a lot more at ease, and a lot . . . You know, I want to let go of some of these things I've been holding. You can't hold something, what, ah, 37, 8 years and it not affect you. You have to let it go.

Therapist: Something of this magnitude especially.

Mrs. Follette: Yeah. So it's time.

Therapist: So, in other words, you think holding some of these things inside helps to create a distance between you and other people?

Mrs. Follette: Yeah. I guess so. I think so. Ah huh, I think so. You don't want someone to know I've gone through that too. Reading about it, discussing it. And how can I tell them that I've had the same thing happen to me? You don't do that. So you hold it and it's good to be able to be free of it, and be free and let it go and deal with it. It's something that's over and done with it. Ah, even with my aunt, you know, I feel a whole sense of relief or what have you. I'm going to Bakersfield Saturday. But I'm going to see an exhibit and afterwards I will go by and see her. Where before, first thing I would do would be go right there and sit there with her or go to lunch, shopping, and something, but I'm going to Bakersfield for another purpose. And I will see her after I've done what I want to do. (laugh) You know, it took a long time to hit that spot. And that's the way I feel. And, ah, even with my mother in Auburn. I have stopped in to see her. But, ah, where before I felt that if I had a spare moment I'd run down there [Hmm] and spend a couple of hours and run back. [Hmm] For what?

Therapist: It didn't feel like it was something you were getting anything out of. [Yeah.] It felt like it was for her.

Mrs. Follette: Yeah. So I've come a long way.

Therapist: Good. Good to hear. OK. (Softly) We have to stop.

Mrs. Follette: You know, I'm in a training session next week. And I was trying to figure out, ah, if I'm going to be able . . . I don't know what time the lunch period is going to be, it's at the corner of Pine and South. But I was trying to figure out if I would be able to break away to come out here. It's just real hard. I don't know.

[CLASSROOM]

TRAINEE: Wasn't this the woman who could only come to therapy every other week because she did these classes on alternate weeks?

LEVENSON: Right. They had an every-other-week contract, so this was her 5th session and 10th week of therapy.

TRAINEE: So, toward the end of this session, she is trying to see if she can come see him the very next week? Not to skip a week?

TRAINEE: That's great! So she feels she can trust Dr. David and wants to see him sooner.

TRAINEE: Yeah. I think that is a major advance for her. She's acknowledging that she wants to see him even if it's a hardship for her to work it out practically. This is a real switch from her quid pro quo, businesslike stance earlier in the session.

LEVENSON: I look at her introducing the possibility of seeing him next week as in-session evidence of a meaningful change. Earlier we were considering the possibility that Mrs. Follette might have told Dr. David her secret as another quid pro quo—as something she owed him because of his interest in her. A giving in to the stepfather, if you will. But if that hypothesis were true, that she felt subtly coerced by her therapist into "delivering the goods," then why would she want to see Dr. David more frequently? The alternative hypothesis, that she felt more trusting and safer with Dr. David because of his stance and specific interventions, seems more plausible, given this latest bit of clinical material.

TRAINEE: So what happened? Was she able to break away and see him?

LEVENSON: Yes, she was, although she was not able to manage to do that very often.

TRAINEE: It was curious that she said that after she talks about what she is going to do with her mother and aunt—how she is going to behave differently with them.

TRAINEE: Yeah. She is going to meet her own needs first.

TRAINEE: These are similar to her wanting to see Dr. David next week—because *she* is getting something out of it.

LEVENSON: Her stated intentions about how she was going to handle next week's interactions with her family could indicate out-of-session changes which would inform the therapist that he was on the right track. It would be of interest the following week to see if, in fact, Mrs. Follette was able to follow through with her plan to put herself first. These data, combined with the observed in-session changes, could provide Dr. David with sufficient process-outcome data to increase his comfort with ending as planned.

In many brief therapies, the therapist does not have the time to see such blossoming intentions result in a behavioral harvest. Usually the therapy is over before the therapist can have much of a chance to see the fruits of his or her labor. However, there are often minute changes that occur during the give-and-take of the therapy which, if attended to, can provide data indicating whether the therapy is on the right track. Just as the researcher must remain open to data that might confirm or disconfirm experiments, the therapist needs to be vigilant for clues in the sessions that portend the success or failure of his or her efforts.

[CLASSROOM]

TRAINEE: I like what Dr. David does at the beginning of this segment—sharing the positive changes he has observed in Mrs. Follette.

LEVENSON: That is a good observation. In brief therapy especially, we are trying to make the patients aware of what they are doing right. We need to build on their strengths and make their positive changes obvious to them. Quite often when patients begin relating in a more positive way, they are completely unaware of it. Therapists can be quite helpful to patients in pointing out these behavioral shifts. Unfortunately, often with a medical model, we become more accustomed to pointing out dysfunctions and deficits. Furthermore, when Dr. David introduces what Mrs. Follette is doing differently, he does so by examining its interpersonal effect on him. Do you remember what Dr. David said of a positive nature to Mrs. Follette?

TRAINEE: He said he felt a lot more openness and warmth about her after she shared her secret.

LEVENSON: Actually, he said that he felt a lot more openness and warmth somewhere in the middle of the session compared to the beginning of the session, when she felt like she had a shell around her. It was Mrs. Follette who made the connection between feeling more comfortable and the risk she took.

TRAINEE: There is one part I found very confusing. I didn't quite understand the image she had of a machine which could record the conversation between 2:30 and 3:30.

TRAINEE: Oh, right. I didn't get that part either. It was hard to follow her.

LEVENSON: Those places where usually coherent patients become unclear can indicate times of discomfort, anxiety, or conflict. What do you think was going on for Mrs. Follette here?

TRAINEE: Could you review exactly what she did say? It was hard to get it from the videotape.

LEVENSON: "Maybe someday if they make a machine and they can pick up the conversation that we had between 2:30 and 3:30 or 3:25, that will be it. But, you know, I feel a lot looser and a lot more at ease."

TRAINEE: I'm wondering if maybe on some unconscious level, she's recognized that not only has she told another person her secret, but it's also down on videotape.

TRAINEE: I agree. When she said she was looser, I thought she was in the sense of being cognitively looser.

LEVENSON: There certainly was a machine—the video camera—which was picking up the conversation.

TRAINEE: She has made a public record in a way. It's like documented—like the Zapruder film in the Kennedy assassination.

LEVENSON: And there may be some anxiety about telling her secret to so many faceless people, although consciously she does not express any concern. There may also be some relief in broadcasting her secret, so to speak. In any case, we might hypothesize that she has some strong feelings associated with the videotaping which get unconsciously expressed in a nonlogical, nonsyntactical manner.

TRAINEE: What about her statement that even verbalizing her secret to one person, "it's over and done with."

TRAINEE: I think this is more her wish. She hopes that she will not need to talk about this again. She tends to minimize things, and this would be consistent with her style.

TRAINEE: In Mrs. Follette's case, it seems that not sharing the secret made her feel very isolated. Sharing her secret with Dr. David and the team seems like sharing an intensely intimate aspect of herself. It is an important step toward being able to be close to somebody.

TRAINEE: The thought that strikes me is that she probably has a lot of feelings of shame and guilt associated with what happened to her. And to be able to share this traumatic experience with another person and have that other person remain calm and accepting, without being shocked and disapproving, must be a tremendous relief.

LEVENSON: The way you are framing what happened here is from an interpersonal vantage point. It is not the catharsis per se which is seen as helpful here—the expression of emotions attached to an experience— but rather the sharing of what happened to her with another person and that person's reaction. The former, catharsis, would be more in keeping with an intrapsychic view; the latter, sharing, would be consistent with an interpersonal framework.

TRAINEE: It is somewhat like a confession. Telling another person and receiving absolution.

LEVENSON: But Dr. David does not absolve her. In fact, he communicates to her that she has suffered, not perpetrated.

TRAINEE: About the "once it is out, it is over and done with" part, I have worked with a number of incest survivors, and one of the things I have learned from them is that once the secret is shared, even with one person, it is no longer a secret. For many of them, this talking about it with one other person was a turning point. I interpreted her statement about "it's over and done with" as reflecting what happened to her will never be a secret again.

TRAINEE: How much does the remaining therapy focus on her experience of the rape?

TRAINEE: Yes. Did they have an opportunity to work it through?

TRAINEE: I would refer her to a group of incest survivors. It seems she needs to work through the trauma of being raped, and I don't think that a brief therapy with only five more sessions is going to be enough.

The question about "working through," the suggestion that the patient receive more (and usually "long-term") treatment, and fears of the brief therapy's "not being enough" are common therapist responses in a time-limited treatment when unanticipated and/or traumatic issues are made known (such as this patient's rape). However, therapists need to be mindful that their concern about further treatment does not take precedence over the needs of the patient in terms of the new experience the therapist is trying to provide.

In Mrs. Follette's case, she is well aware of survivor-type therapy groups—in fact, she has already been in a women's group where incest issues were discussed by the other members. She felt unable to enter into the discussion at that time and share her experience. To make the decision about what would be appropriate at any juncture in the therapy, the therapist should consider that specific patient's dynamic focus and evaluate what would be the cost–benefit ratio of various interventions.

In this case, would such a referral for more (or different) therapy be helpful, or might this patient sense from the therapist that he had certain expectations of her—expectations that she might resent? Would the "suggestion" be heard as an exhortation? Would his mentioning the possibility of more therapy be seen as implying that she would not be OK without further treatment? Would the suggestion of more therapy be seen as a "caring" response by the therapist, or a paternalistic, "I-know-better-than-you-what's-best-for-you" attitude? Mrs. Follette already has a sense of herself as inferior; would Dr. David's recommendation for more therapy help reinforce this introject? Clearly, not all the answers to these questions are known, but the therapist must make his best guesses given the knowledge he does have.

Therapeutically, in the case of Mrs. Follette there could be several valid ways to proceed following her revelation of her rape 38 years earlier. From a brief-therapy point of view, however, I consider it preferable to stay within the frame of both the focus and the time limit whenever possible.

The critical point to keep in mind here is that in TLDP the emphasis is on the process. Therapists usually do not learn the specific content that might have originally encouraged a particular interpersonal style. In fact, most interactional patterns are so complexly intertwined (with other patterns and other people's patterns) that looking for first causes is a deceptive, unrewarding practice. Regardless of the content, the TLDP therapist is concerned with the *themes* that emerge. These themes are usually not tied to any one particular situation, but rather generalize across time, person, and place. In Mrs. Follette's case we may have been given a glimpse into content relevant to her distancing interpersonal style, but perhaps the rape was only the tip of the iceberg.

Although it is usually preferable to adhere to the established time frame and dynamic focus, in some cases this is not possible or advisable. For example, with only two more sessions to go another patient receiving TLDP learned his wife had just been killed in an accident. This unexpected trauma, combined with his clinical issues (he had been working on his ambivalence about staying in the marriage), made it unwise to terminate the therapy at that time. The patient remained in therapy for 10 more sessions, and then decided to join a bereavement group.

[CLASSROOM]

TRAINEE: At the present time, it doesn't seem like Mrs. Follette's at a point where she is emotionally struggling with her previous experience with her stepfather. Rather, she is still feeling distant from it. So I am not moved to intervene with referral suggestions. But what if the patient herself asked for more treatment?

LEVENSON: Here again the CMP can be used as a guide for discerning how to respond to special requests from the patient. Given Mrs. Follette's characteristic aloof style, if she asked for more treatment she would be taking another risk. Remember Dr. David was unsure for many weeks why this woman was coming for therapy; it was very difficult for her to ask for anything for herself. Even at the beginning of this fifth session, Mrs. Follette seemed more comfortable when she was helping her therapist rather than having the therapist help her. So for her to ask for more treatment would mean that she recognized she had needs and that she could reach out. In other words, Mrs. Follette would be attempting to create a new experience for herself.

I think you can see how asking for more treatment would be dramatically different from another patient with a more dependent style asking for more. For Mrs. Follette, I would want to interpret her request as a risk permitting more growth. If it were possible to continue to see her, I might do so.

Of course, in considering any therapeutic direction, the therapist must take into consideration the level of Mrs. Follette's distress. If discussing the rape reawakened memories and feelings that began causing her anguish, Dr. David should take an active stance to explore with her other vehicles she might use (friends, support group, therapy focused on incest survivors) to deal with her emotional pain.

Having a facilitative therapeutic stance doesn't include granting the patients' wishes in order to provide a new experience. Such a requirement would place an inordinate (and unrealistic) demand on therapists. What is necessary, however, is that patients experience their therapists as continuing to challenge their interpersonal schemata.

EPILOGUE

By the end of therapy, both patient and therapist thought it had been quite helpful. Mrs. Follette and Dr. David responded to several self-report measures to assess outcome in TLDP. Mrs. Follette's evaluation of her outcome from therapy was measured by a global rating on a seven-point scale. At termination, Mrs. Follette stated her problems were much better (a rating of seven). Dr. David likewise thought that she had made considerable progress (a rating of six).

Mrs. Follette also responded to two self-report inventories—one to measure symptom relief and the other to measure interpersonal change. Her symptomatic distress level dropped to a quarter of what it had been on intake. For example, at intake she indicated that a loss of sexual interest or pleasure was causing her moderate distress; at termination she reported this problem was not bothering her at all. Similarly, by termination Mrs. Follette's interpersonal distress level dropped in half. For example, at intake she responded that trusting other people too much was causing her quite a bit of distress; by termination this had ceased being a problem.

Six months after Mrs. Follette ended her brief therapy, I contacted her as part of a follow-up I try to do on all the trainees' patients. In a semi-structured interview, I asked some general questions about her therapy with Dr. David. I did not volunteer what I knew about her therapy or that I had seen excerpts of her sessions, but certainly would have told her had she asked. I show the following excerpt from my follow-up interview with her to the trainees. In the interview, Mrs. Follette never mentioned the rape and neither did I.

[VIDEOTAPE]

Mrs. Follette: So it was a real revealing session for me and I could better understand some of the things I had been doing over the years and why I was a, what I call a "paper chaser." In other words, when I said I chase paper, I chase certificates. I became a real estate broker and got my teaching credential. And doing all those things it was not an easy task. It was something I had to really work at. And in all of that, it came back to my relationship with my relatives and how they perceived me. And you know, it came out that this is maybe one of the reasons why I was chasing, what I call chasing paper. Because after I got the paper, it didn't mean that much. It didn't mean that I went out and tried to sell real estate.

Interviewer: It was like you were proving yourself.

Mrs. Follette: Right. Right. That I was proving myself. And all this came out with my, you know, in the session with him. And I was able to get a better handle on who I was. And it just was a really revealing part.

Interviewer: It sounds like it. And have you been able to use what you've experienced and learned in your therapy since then? Has it made a difference?

Mrs. Follette: Oh, yes. Oh, yes. Oh, yes. I think the amazing thing about it is that because I've come into my own, my relatives treat me differently. And I don't know if maybe instead of my being . . . Hmm. (pause) I don't know how to put it. But it seems as though they recognize the newness in me, and therefore things they said and did before, they did not do. And maybe because they felt like, I have not become defiant or anything, but I've become my own person.

Interviewer: And somehow you communicated that to them?

Mrs. Follette: Right. Right. Without saying that. Right.

Interviewer: Do you have any idea what they're picking up?

Mrs. Follette: I have no idea. I guess it's, ah (pause), I don't know. I have no idea. Maybe the video, one can see oneself. But insomuch as I cannot mentally see myself, I don't know what it is that I'm now throwing out to other people that they're getting. There is a new Joan Follette. It's not the old Joan Follette. And even people that I haven't seen in a long time, there's something about me that's different and they mention it.

Interviewer: They do?

Mrs. Follette: Either you've become prettier or something. They don't know what it is. And I know what it is. Because I have decided that, that ah, I guess I have a lot more confidence in myself. And I think that's the thing that maybe's coming out and they see. (pause) So it's been a real growing process. In other words, I've come of age.

[CLASSROOM]

TRAINEE: I can't get over how different she looks. She looks younger, softer in a way. She's more open with her body language.

TRAINEE: And I was surprised at how she related to you, given that you've never really met her before. She seems comfortable with you.

TRAINEE: It is striking to see how differently she presents. There is a real sense of authority and confidence about her.

TRAINEE: Also her use of language is less vague, a lot more use of "I" rather than "one." She is so much more exposed even in her language.

I like showing this portion of the follow-up tape because it nicely illustrates the chief principle whereby TLDP is thought to generalize. Ideally, a patient's experience in brief therapy helps disconfirm his or her ingrained dysfunctional interpersonal expectations and thereby encourages him or her to try out new, but shaky, behaviors with other people. In this particular case, Mrs. Follette was able to be more vulnerable, trusting, and self revealing (i.e., able to remove the "shell" surrounding her) in her sessions, encouraged by Dr. David's positive therapeutic stance (e.g., nonintrusiveness, empathic understanding, gentle confrontation) and adherence to the thematic interpersonal focus.

In this follow-up excerpt, Mrs. Follette talked about how she translated her in-session changes to out-of-session gains. She clearly evaluated the benefits from therapy in interpersonal terms. She gave evidence that she was trying out a more available, approachable attitude with her relatives who began seeing her as literally more attractive. She then related how her relatives in turn treated her differently. She was unsure ("I have no idea") exactly what she was communicating to them to elicit a different reaction but she knew they saw "something about me that's different." She acknowledged that the way she acted had an effect on people and vice versa.

It is interesting that Mrs. Follette's understanding of how she has changed involves what she sees as a growing confidence in herself. Dr. David's conceptualization as stated in his CMP, however, was somewhat different. He hypothesized that Mrs. Follette's difficulties with trust contributed to her relatives' feeling of being kept at arm's length, and therefore distanced, which in turn left Mrs. Follette feeling ignored and not cared about. Perhaps what is critical here is not the patient's precise understanding of some abstract principle about her CMP, but rather her experience of relating to Dr. David (feeling understood and having her worst fears disconfirmed), and generalizing this learning to others in her life.

Certainly, what is important to the significant others who interact with the patient also is not that they understand some abstract principle, but rather that they now find Mrs. Follette more approachable and receptive. Here, then, we have the beginnings of a cyclical adaptive pattern (CAP). Although the sessions had ended, Mrs. Follette was continuing the therapeutic work.

CHAPTER 8

Technique: Formulation as a Blueprint

AS A WAY OF ILLUSTRATING how one can use the dynamic focus as a blueprint for the therapy, I present to the trainees my initial session with the first patient with whom I decided to use TLDP formulation and intervention strategies. Like the trainees, I videotaped every session and reviewed the tapes prior to the next session. To prevent myself from ferreting out a particularly high functioning patient for this "test case," I told the social worker at the clinic that I would see whoever was referred next.

Mr. Johnson was a 74-year-old man who was about to be discharged from an inpatient psychiatry unit. He had been hospitalized for depression and binge drinking, and had been transferred back and forth between the Alcohol Inpatient Unit (AIU) and the Psychiatric Inpatient Unit (PIU). His therapist in the PIU arranged an outpatient appointment as part of his discharge plans.

I knew very little about Mr. Johnson prior to our first session. I had been told he was a widower, retired, with four grown children. The staff on the AIU believed that prior to hospitalization he had resumed his episodic drinking to cope with his depression and isolation. In addition, he had a tendency to experience his distress somatically (e.g., stomach aches, muscle pain). Mr. Johnson had cooperated with treatment during his one-month inpatient treatment, which consisted of individual sessions with a psychiatrist, antidepressant medications, an alcohol education group, and milieu therapy.

[CLASSROOM]

LEVENSON: I am going to show you the first 5 minutes of my initial session with Mr. Johnson. While you are listening to the tape, put yourself
in my shoes as the therapist and consider the following questions. First,
would Mr. Johnson be an appropriate candidate for TLDP? Second,
what are your countertransferential thoughts and feelings? How does
Mr. Johnson make you feel and think? How are you pushed or pulled to
behave?

Third, think about what might be Mr. Johnson's lifelong dysfunctional interpersonal problem. What is his CMP in terms of how he acts,
how he expects others to react, how he sees others behaving, and his
customary treatment and opinion of himself?

Fourth, what would be your therapeutic goals given this man's dysfunctional pattern? Specifically, what new experience would you want
him to have in the brief therapy? What new understanding?

And finally, consider how his maladaptive pattern might be reenacted
within the therapeutic relationship. What problems might I incur in
attempting to help this man? If you were my consultant as I began this
case, what words of wisdom or warning would you have regarding the
unfolding of the therapeutic process? What transference–countertransference interactions could I use as signals that the therapy might be
going awry?

I am encouraging the trainees here to begin to formulate the case immediately. After showing them just 5 minutes of the initial session, I am asking
them to make a selection decision, delineate their countertransference reactions, outline the CMP, define goals, and anticipate difficulties that are likely
to arise in Mr. Johnson's treatment. In other words, I am asking the trainees
to develop a blueprint for the entire therapy.

[VIDEOTAPE]

Therapist: Maybe the best way to get to know you is to have you tell me
what brought you into the hospital, what's been going on, and how I
can be of help.

Mr. Johnson: (with flat affect) Well, it started in June. We were living in
San Carlos, my daughter and I. We have four children. But Susan, the
youngest, lived with me the longest. We just got a notice from the
landlord one day that he was going to move into our apartment, and
we would have to get out and look for another place. So I started looking. We had a cat too. I started looking all over San Carlos and, ah,
down that whole area. My daughter was working down there. And,

ah, we just couldn't find a place at all who would take animals. So they decided somebody has to take care of our cat—a relative. But we still couldn't find a two-bedroom apartment for less than $700 or $800. It was just terrible. [Uh huh.] And, ah, I would go out every day. And go through the listings—the real estate listings. And go look. I got exhausted and got depressed and I started to drink a lot. I just couldn't find anything.

Therapist: When was this?

Mr. Johnson: Well, we got the notice in June that he wanted us out by July. But then . . .

Therapist: So just last month?

Mr. Johnson: No, no, no, a year ago.

Therapist: You are talking about a year ago? OK.

Mr. Johnson: What happened was I started getting depressed and nervous and exhausted and started drinking. We finally found a place that we could afford, you know, $700, which was way out in Tilton and it was at the end of a dead-end street—way up on a high place. It was very isolated. Anyway, I knew something was wrong—I was really behaving weirdly—so I came over here and they started taking me at the Day Treatment Center. I would come here every day to the Day Treatment Center. That was in October. Anyway, I was taking Librium and a sleeping pill (pause), but I was still drinking. And I . . . so my daughter complained to Betty, the nurse, down there about it, and Betty had me admitted to the Psychiatry Inpatient Unit. And I was there a couple of weeks. And then they convinced me I should go to the Alcoholic Inpatient Unit. So I spent a month in there and I quit drinking. Ah, but I was still depressed. So I came back one day for this depression to the admissions and they admitted me again.

Therapist: Back to the Alcohol Inpatient Unit?

Mr. Johnson: No, to Psychiatry. And I was there through June. Well, that's about it.

The trainees and I initially discussed Mr. Johnson's suitability for TLDP. We considered each of the five basic inclusionary criteria as applied to this case. First, was he in *emotional discomfort?* He appeared to be pain. He was depressed and anxious about being isolated. Second, did he have sufficient *basic trust* that he could be helped by coming to therapy? Although he did not seem particularly hopeful about anything at this point, on his inpatient stay he had been compliant with treatment. I felt he would come to sessions and talk, which are the minimal indicators of trust necessary. Third, did he exhibit a willingness to consider his conflicts in *interpersonal terms?* He gave some evidence that he could see his problems from an interactional point of view, but he certainly seemed to put more emphasis on external events. If only the landlord had not evicted them. If only housing were not so expensive. Fourth, was he willing to examine his *feelings?* Mr. Johnson was willing to talk about feelings, especially his depression. I was uncertain at this point, however, as to how open he would be to looking at the relationship between his feelings and his interpersonal problems. Fifth, with regard to his capacity for *mature relationships,* Mr. Johnson seemed able to interact with me. He could engage in the basics of an interchange, and he certainly knew he was a separate person from me. However, it was unclear at this juncture whether Mr. Johnson's dysfunctional style was so pervasive, rigid, and extreme that even my best efforts would be thwarted. We concluded that Mr. Johnson met (perhaps barely) the terms of the five basic inclusionary selection criteria. However, the issue of his alcoholism was problematical as a possible exclusionary criterion.

The exclusionary criteria presented in chapter 5 provide clinically relevant and helpful guidelines. I prefer to use these criteria as yellow lights cautioning me in my selection decision, rather than slavishly obeying them as if they were red lights stopping me from initiating treatment.

With regard to his alcohol use, Mr. Johnson had been drinking as recently as 2 months previously. His history was one of occasional binge drinking (once every several years) when under stress, particularly when threatened with potential loss. He would become acutely anxious and depressed when he feared others were rejecting or leaving him. At these times, he would turn to alcohol as a way of dealing with (self-medicating) his intense dysphoric states. Because TLDP does involve changing one's basic schemata of oneself, others, and interactions, it is somewhat of an anxiety-provoking therapy. We might be taking a risk in accepting Mr. Johnson into treatment in that he might resume drinking iatrogenically—as a way of handling any anxiety being aroused in the therapy.

I would not have accepted Mr. Johnson for TLDP if he had not had intensive inpatient alcohol treatment and had not agreed to abstinence as a precondition for treatment. Furthermore, he was involved in Alcoholics Anonymous, which he planned to continue. It was important, however, to gather additional information about Mr. Johnson's alcohol abuse (later in this first interview and from the inpatient records). It emerged that Mr. Johnson's problem drinking had begun later in life, usually in response to anxiety aroused by interpersonal issues. There was no indication of sociopathy or a conduct disorder. Recent research (e.g., Kadden, Cooney, Getter, & Litt, 1989; Litt, Barbor, Delboca, Kadden, & Cooney, 1992) on matching types of alcoholics to types of treatments indicates that alcoholics who are impulsive and insensitive to society's expectations do better in structured, task-oriented, coping-skills training, while less impaired alcoholics do better (and have lower relapse rates) in interactional therapies.

In addition to patient and treatment characteristics, TLDP chiefly emphasizes judging the usefulness of the approach by assessing what transpires within the therapy. With patients who turn to substances (e.g., drugs, food, alcohol, shopping) as a way of self-medicating their symptoms, I am continually appraising in the give-and-take of the sessions (and, ideally, gain the cooperation of the patient in evaluating with me) the appropriateness of this active approach. I gauge this by the patient's ability to handle anxiety within and outside the session. For example, if Mr. Johnson felt like he needed a drink to "settle himself down" before coming to a session, I could have modified my methods (to make them more supportive) and/or referred him elsewhere for more specific alcohol treatment.

So, all in all, I concluded that Mr. Johnson met the selection criteria, although he would be at the lower end of the acceptability continuum because of his recent alcohol history and a depression severe enough to require hospitalization. When I accepted Mr. Johnson for TLDP, I emphasized the importance of his continuing his involvement in AA, which had begun as part of his inpatient hospitalization.* Since Mr. Johnson kept returning to alcohol as a way to cope, it would be a mistake to assume that lessening his interpersonal fears alone (through TLDP) would automatically be sufficient to eradicate his addictive behavior (Khatzian, 1988; La Salvia, 1993). As Joan Zweben (1993) has noted, contrary to what many therapists have learned in training, there is little if any empirical evidence to support the idea that addictions can be "effectively treated by addressing the 'underlying' psychodynamic problems" (p. 260).

At this point I direct the trainees to consider their countertransferential reactions to Mr. Johnson as we begin to formulate this case.

[CLASSROOM]
TRAINEE: (cautiously) He really sees himself as a victim.
LEVENSON: And how do you *feel* being with this man who presents himself as a victim?
TRAINEE: Well, I guess you don't have to like your countertransference. He's a whiner. I want him to take some responsibility. So I didn't particularly like him. I didn't feel any sympathy for him.

---

*Stephanie Brown (1985) has discussed some of the difficulties that can emerge in the triangle created among patient, therapist, and a 12-step program. She offers suggestions for the therapist who is not an addiction specialist in working with a psychotherapy patient in recovery.

LEVENSON: Good, I like your forthrightness. Other reactions?

TRAINEE: I thought it would take an enormous amount of energy to move this man even a tiny step.

LEVENSON: So how were you feeling as you were thinking this?

TRAINEE: I was future-drained! Thinking about how depleted I would be working with this man.

TRAINEE: I saw a huge, gigantic sloth! Trying to push him and getting nowhere.

TRAINEE: I thought "Oh, great! A guy who needs Day Treatment. A guy you've got to take care of." I was feeling burdened and overwhelmed.

TRAINEE: I was also feeling fatigued. He wants other people to take care of him, and he is expecting maybe the therapist to do this. And I was thinking, "Oh, is this what every session is going to be like? Oh, no."

TRAINEE: It would not be your favorite hour.

TRAINEE: I couldn't connect. He was talking with no connection. So I was bored. People took him here and took him there.

TRAINEE: I wanted to step in and take over, because he was presenting himself as helpless.

TRAINEE: You tried to get him to clarify when this had all happened. As it turned out, it was a year ago, but he was telling you about the eviction like it had just happened to him. It shows the degree to which he hangs on to his victimization.

TRAINEE: I was feeling guilty I wasn't feeling more sorry for him. He was working really hard to get an apartment. He was trying and really got discouraged.

TRAINEE: My initial reaction was to feel sorry for him. I got sucked in by his explanations. All these awful things had happened to him and he just wasn't up to it. It took until the end of the segment before I began to feel frustrated with his externalization and his avoidance of responsibility.

LEVENSON: Let me summarize here. In terms of your reactions to him, you don't like him because he is a whiner, you feel irritated, frustrated, disconnected, bored and fatigued, some sympathy for him, yet also guilt at not feeling more positively toward him. Let's examine what there is in the content and process of what Mr. Johnson is saying that might engender these reactions in us.

TRAINEE: He's helpless, and he wants people to talk him into things. He used the words, "They convinced me to go to alcohol treatment."

LEVENSON: So you are affected by the way Mr. Johnson uses language.

TRAINEE: He's also very passive. People are always doing something to him.

TRAINEE: Yes, the nurse had him admitted to the inpatient unit, and the landlord had him evicted.

TRAINEE: And when he does do something, he literally ends up on a dead-end street.

TRAINEE: Not just *on* a dead-end street—at the *end* of a dead-end street.

LEVENSON: So he presents as helpless, and passive, and then other people convince him to do something or do something to him. What else?

TRAINEE: Nothing works out.

LEVENSON: And what do you mean by that, "Nothing works out"?

TRAINEE: He doesn't feel helped.

LEVENSON: He doesn't feel helped and that leaves him feeling how?

TRAINEE: Depressed and helpless. And more hopeless and passive.

TRAINEE: Back to the beginning.

LEVENSON: Yes, back to the beginning of this scenario. So we have created a rudimentary narrative which appears to be cyclic and maladaptive. And a pattern which appears to occur in a variety of settings. Thus we are beginning to uncover a cyclical maladaptive pattern. Anything else here?

TRAINEE: Yes, part of what I was thinking about is that he cannot be an agent for himself. No matter how much he tries to solve his problems, it won't work. So he ends up depending on the outside world.

TRAINEE: He's not an effective actor.

TRAINEE: What moves him are other people's actions.

TRAINEE: No matter how much he tries, he's not effective, so others jump in.

LEVENSON: How do these others end up feeling?

TRAINEE: Probably pretty frustrated because he doesn't take responsibility.

TRAINEE: Probably exhausted themselves.

LEVENSON: OK. If this is so, then what will they do eventually?

TRAINEE: They will give up on him, even though they might have felt sorry for him.

TRAINEE: Probably feel more guilty about not wanting to help him, which will only make them avoid him more.

LEVENSON: And how might that leave Mr. Johnson feeling?

TRAINEE: Even more ineffective and isolated than before.

TRAINEE: And with no one he can really depend on.

TRAINEE: Depressed.

TRAINEE: Drinking.

LEVENSON: Let's see what we have so far in terms of our CMP. We have this very isolated, depressed, dependent man who expects that others know best what he should do. He waits for them to assume responsibility for his life. Others do step in and direct him, perhaps because they feel sorry for him, or because they get worn down by his whiny passivity, or because they feel guilty for not wanting to do more. However, eventually they get frustrated and irritated by his hapless stance and defeatist attitude; they become angry and/or reject him. While Mr. Johnson may initially comply with others' directives and demands, he ends up not feeling helped, but rather, rejected, unloved, and worthless. Unable to feel effective and nurtured, he feels helpless and hopeless, leading to his increased drinking, isolation, and depression, completing the cycle. Let's see how this looks diagrammed on the board. [See figure 8.1.]

So let's say this is our working formulation—our 5-minute formulation. The next step is to generate goals based on this understanding of

Figure 8.1

Mr. Johnson's Cyclical Maladaptive Pattern

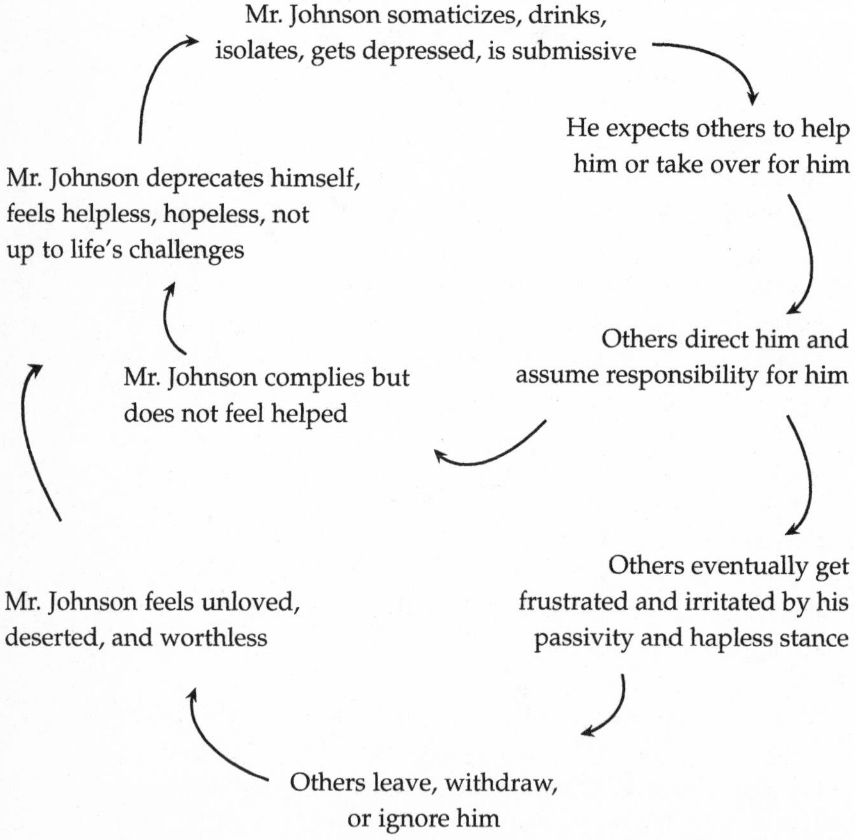

Mr. Johnson somaticizes, drinks, isolates, gets depressed, is submissive

He expects others to help him or take over for him

Mr. Johnson deprecates himself, feels helpless, hopeless, not up to life's challenges

Others direct him and assume responsibility for him

Mr. Johnson complies but does not feel helped

Others eventually get frustrated and irritated by his passivity and hapless stance

Mr. Johnson feels unloved, deserted, and worthless

Others leave, withdraw, or ignore him

his dynamics. What would you want him to get out of this brief therapy? What would be the new experience and what would be the new
understanding? Let's take the new experience first.

TRAINEE: I guess helping him to see the impact of his whining, or whatever you want to call it, on the willingness of other people to help him.

LEVENSON: Would that be the experience part or the understanding part?

TRAINEE: I guess that's the understanding part.

It is very difficult to get therapists, especially those trained psychoanalyt-
ically, to think of goals and interventions promoting a positive new experience as opposed to a new understanding. Therapists' previous dynamic
training usually emphasizes helping patients recognize and understand the
nature of their unconscious conflicts. One of the major psychoanalytic strategies used to accomplish this goal is interpretation: "the supreme agent in the
hierarchy of therapeutic principles" (Bibring, 1954, p. 763). However, understanding in the absence of experience is like knowing why one does not have
a good golf swing but never feeling what it is like to swing properly. Chapter
10 will deal with this issue in depth.

[CLASSROOM]

LEVENSON: So what would you want him to experience in the session that
would help him to interrupt his maladaptive pattern? It is helpful to
think of there being two facets to the new experience. One, how would
you want the patient to experience himself in the interchange, and two,
how would you want him to experience you, the other person, in the
interaction?

TRAINEE: Well, for himself, I'd want him to feel empowered.

TRAINEE: Yes, efficacy. I would somehow want to set it up where he gets
to demonstrate that he could make a choice. That things aren't necessarily being done to him, but that he has an opportunity to make a
choice, to take an action, as opposed to me doing things to or for him.

LEVENSON: So you are thinking about his taking some action, or having
the realization that he could take some action?

TRAINEE: For him to figure out what he wants to do, why he's there.

LEVENSON: So what you would like him to experience in the therapy, in
the session, is taking some kind of direction or action that he sees he has
initiated?

TRAINEE: Yes, he has a goal, rather than doing someone else's goal.

TRAINEE: He is more actively present.

TRAINEE: He can bring in an issue and work on it himself.

TRAINEE: I want him to shape up! Get a life!

LEVENSON: With this much affect, it sounds like your countertransference at work. Like part of you is responding to the pull from the patient for you, as the therapist, the authority, to be more directive, and even castigating.

TRAINEE: How do you know when it is a therapeutic goal or just your countertransference talking?

LEVENSON: In the way we are using countertransference—as the therapist's natural reaction to the patient's style—the two are not mutually exclusive. Your countertransference provides information about what would need to shift in the patient's presentation to alter your reaction. In the present case, you are rebuking him, taking control, and treating him like a recalcitrant child. In order for these countertransference behaviors to change, he would have to begin acting more like an adult and less like that whiny child. If he did take more control of his life, and made more of his decisions, your countertransference as expressed by your injunctive "Get a life!" would shift and be less condemning, directive, and harsh.

TRAINEE: I get it.

LEVENSON: Let's see where we are now. As far as the new experience of himself, you would like Mr. Johnson to feel more empowered and more in control of his life. We would want him to be more purposeful, active, and involved. He could take action; he's not just this passive pawn. What about the second part of the new experience? How would you like him to experience you?

TRAINEE: Not as a rescuer. That would be falling into the pattern. Just like his daughter and the nurse were responsible for his getting care at the hospital.

TRAINEE: And also not as rejecting him, because that would be part of the pattern too. Like the landlord's evicting him.

LEVENSON: So we know what we do not want to be a part of his new experience: rescuing or rejecting. These would only collude with his passive, victim stance, and provide fertile opportunities for him to continue his dysfunctional interactions. But how would you like for him to experience the therapist?

TRAINEE: As a partner, someone to work with, as opposed to a devil or a saint.

TRAINEE: As someone who will be there, even if he gets angry or remains listless.

LEVENSON: OK. And now what about the second goal—the new understanding? What new understanding would you like Mr. Johnson to have at the end of his time-limited therapy?

TRAINEE: I keep coming up with these trite things like, Alcohol will not solve your problems!

LEVENSON: It sounds like an accurate slogan. But it strikes me as too content-based, that is, focused solely on alcohol, for the more process-focused TLDP model. Let's examine what might be the rationale for your admonition. The way Mr. Johnson uses alcohol gives us a clue that he has difficulty experiencing or allowing himself to experience feelings, such as anxiety and anger. Also, we should remember from the inpatient records that Mr. Johnson somaticizes a great deal. Focusing on physical symptoms may also provide a way to avoid dealing with his feelings. Therefore, we can hypothesize that one reason Mr. Johnson may have difficulty coping with his emotions is he is not willing or able to entertain them long enough to understand what they are about and to see the consequences of having them. So your statement about Mr. Johnson's realizing that alcohol will not solve his problems implies that you would like for him to understand the importance and meaning of his various emotions.

TRAINEE: I would like him to understand that he can rely on himself instead of others!

TRAINEE: Yes, that he has strengths and the capacity to overcome obstacles.

TRAINEE: I am reminded of a poster on the wall of one of the community mental health clinics: "I was halfway through my life before I realized it was a do-it-yourself job!"

TRAINEE: And I want him to see the impact of his whining, or whatever you want to call it, on the willingness of other people to help him.

LEVENSON: So you would like him to understand the impact his behavior has on others.

TRAINEE: I'd like him to understand that he already is making decisions; he already is taking action. He doesn't see that he is; he views himself as inert and submissive to everyone else's wishes.

LEVENSON: So for the second goal, the new understanding you would like Mr. Johnson to have at the end of the brief therapy, it sounds as though you would like him to realize that he already is doing things, making decisions, and taking actions that impact people; he has capabilities and does not have to feel like an innocent bystander in his life; and that his feelings are important and trying to avoid them—through drinking, for example—will not work in the long run. An excellent beginning. Why don't we now turn to what you see as the transference–countertransference reenactments that might emerge in this therapy. If you were consulting with me on this case, how would you anticipate the therapy might go?

TRAINEE: He's really going to pull for you to tell him what to do, but if you do, he'll discount your help in some way. "I'm too weak."

TRAINEE: I will be curious to see how passive–aggressive he gets when you accept him and try to collaborate with him.

LEVENSON: Your comment raises an excellent point. Quite often when the therapist offers a new, and presumably healthier, experience for patients, they do not greet this new opportunity with open arms. Instead, it is quite common for patients, when presented with an unexpected attitude or behavior on the part of the therapist, to treat it with suspicion and anxiety, even when this very behavior fulfills a long-hoped-for wish.

TRAINEE: He might try to sabotage things because he is scared of change. He might not know how to deal with someone who expects him to act like an adult and is willing to stay receptive to his input.

LEVENSON: Yes, this is how he has lived for over 60 years. His way of interacting with people may not be fulfilling, but it is known to him and makes sense to him. Attempts to alter his perception of others might understandably be met with his becoming even more rigidly entrenched in his customary ways. There is the danger that we might, from our one-sided viewpoint, interpret his behavior as indicating he wants to sabotage the therapy or we might condemn him for being "passive–aggressive." Are there other thoughts about possible transference–countertransference patterns in which Mr. Johnson and I might engage?

TRAINEE: Initially, you might have a positive attitude, but then as he presents himself as more and more helpless, your response might be to withdraw because you feel helpless to effect any change.

TRAINEE: It would be real easy to be overwhelmed by him.

TRAINEE: Another possible pitfall would be your getting in there and wanting something to happen, thereby becoming very active, and if nothing happens, to become very impatient and even frustrated.

TRAINEE: Then there would be a danger for you to say things that might convey your frustration and then he would feel like a failure.

LEVENSON: So my frustration might come across as criticism and he would have reactions to that.

TRAINEE: I anticipate that anything you offer will not be enough, not quite right.

LEVENSON: How might that be a problem?

TRAINEE: He would not feel helped, and he would become more depressed and passive and you would feel drained and devalued. You might withdraw.

LEVENSON: So what is your advice? What if I came to you for a consultation and showed you this tape?

TRAINEE: I'd say don't try too hard, because the more you try, the more
he'll become entrenched.

TRAINEE: Be on the lookout for your feelings of anger.

TRAINEE: Remember he can do something. Expect things from him,
because if you don't, it will only confirm for him his feelings of being
helpless.

LEVENSON: We should note that this man did stop drinking after he was
in an alcohol program. Although he was "put" into the program, he
has been able to stay sober for 2 months now and tolerate more of his
feelings. So I think your point about expecting things from him is a
good one.

In brief therapy, in general, it is important to recognize and engage the
strengths of the patient. Since the sessions are limited in number, the therapist must learn to capitalize on the healthier capacities of the patient in order
to get sufficient movement and momentum in the therapy.

[CLASSROOM]

TRAINEE: If I were your consultant, I would warn you that as you try to
help him have a new experience, his anxiety would lead him to want
more medication. Or he might increase his drinking.

LEVENSON: Yes, both medication and, as we've already mentioned, drinking might be likely ways he would try to lessen his anxiety.

In doing TLDP, we want the patient to have a moderate but facilitative
level of anxiety. If our interventions do not arouse any anxiety, we would
have to question whether we were maintaining too much of the status quo.
The trainees have pointed out that there is a likelihood for Mr. Johnson and
me to get stuck in a reenactment of his dysfunctional style, which might
include my being impatient, angry, and frustrated; as a result I might become
too directive or critical, or withdraw. In addition, Mr. Johnson might perceive these behaviors and attitudes and respond by becoming even more
depressed and feeling more victimized in the room with me. The trainees'
advice is for me to monitor my desire to push him or distance myself, and to
remember he is not powerless and helpless.

The trainees were able to derive a working focus, delineate the two goals,
and anticipate transference–countertransference problems that might unfold
in the treatment. Not one trainee asked me for more history. No one said he
or she could not formulate the case because not enough was known about

Mr. Johnson. I am not so glib as to think formulation is just this easy. The trainees tuned in to their own reactions and observed how the patient behaved and what he said in the session. Having them encapsulate their reactions and observations within the CMP organizational structure provided them with invaluable data.

This 5-minute formulation can be modified, enhanced, discarded, or reinforced with information obtained in the next 5 minutes, and so on, until the clinical hour has passed. At the end of that first session, then, one should have a rudimentary formulation that will continue to evolve through refinements as more is learned in the therapy. This formulation at any one time can provide a working blueprint for the entire therapy.

The goal is not to learn how to formulate from 5 minutes of information, but rather, how to make maximal use of whatever data are available in a form that will foster a focus for the therapeutic work. Often mental health practitioners are distracted in the initial therapy session by the need to answer questions on a clinic form or to answer other standardized questions that have been externally imposed. No one can doubt the value of the categories in the typical psychiatric interview (e.g., presenting problem, previous psychiatric treatment, developmental history), or the diagnosis-and-treatment-plan approach of most managed care companies. However, while the content of such areas is usually quite significant in any particular clinical case, focusing solely on these questions typically inhibits the natural flow of dialogue between patient and therapist. And it is this dialogue or this narrative that can provide invaluable information concerning the patient's interpersonal style. It is, after all, a real-life example of how this patient interacts with others.

This "5-minute formulation" exercise is designed to highlight the necessity for clinicians to be exquisitely observant of themselves and their patients in the ebb and flow of the initial interaction. The exercise stresses the importance of readily discerning interactional patterns in the transference and in the outside world. These patterns become the focus of the therapeutic work. The more quickly they are recognized, the greater the potential for the therapist to work effectively as well as efficiently. The therapist must be able to differentiate significant clinical material from other, less relevant, but sometimes fascinating verbiage. The focus, therefore, becomes a filter that determines what is considered pertinent clinical material.

The focus also can be used as a signpost alerting the therapist to potential problems ahead. It is important to foresee transference–countertransference patterns that might cause problems in future sessions. By anticipating patient resistances, ruptures in the therapeutic alliance, and countertransferential acting out, the therapist is able to plan appropriately. Thus when therapeutic impasses occur, the therapist is not caught off guard, but rather is prepared to capitalize on the situation and maximize its clinical impact—a necessity when time is of the essence.

For example, in the case of Mr. Johnson, the trainees anticipated that if I did not take care of Mr. Johnson and instead treated him as an adult, he might become even more passive or perhaps even passively aggressive. Therefore, if Mr. Johnson becomes more helpless and hopeless as the therapy goes on, my first thoughts should not be that my interventions are inadequate or off-base and that he is decompensating and needs hospitalization. Rather, I should entertain the hypothesis that my approach is on target. Because Mr. Johnson's reaction was predicted from our understanding of his CMP, I can respond in turn with helpful interventions consistent with the focus (e.g., not to underestimate Mr. Johnson's capabilities). In this way, the therapist is empowered to use fully his or her knowledge and skill in navigating the therapeutic course; the waters have already been charted. The therapist is not left reeling when the interaction with the patient gets rough, because the therapist already has his or her sea legs.

I cannot tell you how many times I have been in team meetings or case conferences where a trainee presents a new case, giving the details of the patient's familial, social, developmental, and psychiatric history. This usually takes about 40 minutes. A short, dynamic formulation capped by a DSM-IV diagnosis might take another 10 minutes. As everyone is filing out the door, the despairing trainee asks in a plaintive voice, "But what am I supposed to do with the patient?" The trainee does not see how to derive the goals for the treatment or anticipate the process from the formulation. It is as though the presented formulation is a ritualized formality—a separate entity—which does not help the trainee figure out what is needed in the treatment to promote a more successful outcome. The TLDP formulation, by contrast, is structured to inform the therapist about the goals for the work and how the therapy might unfold. The TLDP formulation is integrally tied to the therapeutic process.

The 5-minute didactic formulation exercise contained in this chapter conveys the importance of quickly detecting patterns in the patient's narrative. However, we should note that there is a major danger involved in deriving a focus too early. A premature focus could result in filtering out critical data—data that needs to be incorporated lest one have a distorted or inaccurate understanding of the case.

This is a Scylla and Charybdis (rock and a hard place) dilemma for the brief therapist: If one does not formulate early enough, the therapy will be half over before one knows how to intervene; if one formulates the case too early, the therapy may proceed down a wrong or secondary path. (It is like the good news–bad news story of the airplane pilot who radios in to give the bad news he is lost and doesn't know where he is going; the good news is that he is breaking the world's speed record getting there!)

One way to solve the dilemma of deciding when one has enough data to formulate is by assessing the consistency and pervasiveness of the patient's relationship configurations. The more redundancy one can see in a variety of relationship patterns (across time and situation), the more confident a therapist can be in assessing a cyclical maladaptive pattern based on minimal data.

In my experience it is easier to derive CMPs for patients who have personality disorders. Their behavior is often so stereotypical and rigid that dysfunctional themes are readily discernible in their narratives, and transference patterns quickly become palpable in the therapy session. Dysfunctional interactional patterns that are more subtle or that depend on a particular state or situation to emerge are more difficult to formulate. More time is usually needed to gather data in these cases. Horowitz's (1987) theoretical ideas on states of mind provides a useful framework for thinking about patients who have major multiple role–relationship configurations.

Another suggestion regarding the when of formulation is to be open and flexible enough to steer one's understanding of the case in a different direction should new data of major import become known. For example, in the case of Mr. Johnson, what if we should learn in the next 5 minutes of the session that prior to retiring, he had been the CEO of a large firm and was considered to be an energetic and vibrant man of action? By seeing the CMP as a "work in progress" rather than as written in concrete, we will be in a better position to alter our formulation of him as having a lifelong, stylistically passive presentation.

Relevant to this point is the study by Larry Thompson and colleagues (1988), which found that older, depressed patients often reported symptoms that made them appear to have a personality disorder. They concluded that dependent and avoidant features often observed during a state of clinical depression in the elderly may actually reflect depressive processes rather than specific personality disorders. This research underscores the importance of obtaining data about personality functioning in a variety of situations both now and in the past, before concluding that a dysfunctional style exists.

[CLASSROOM]

LEVENSON: I have asked you to formulate the case of Mr. Johnson, including your countertransference, the dynamic focus, the goals for the therapy, and how the transference–countertransference patterns might play out in the therapy. Now I would like you to consider one more item: What do you think Mr. Johnson's family of origin was like?

TRAINEE: You mean his mother and father?

LEVENSON: Yes. What familial conditions might have promoted his view of himself and others? Remember, according to the TLDP model, the patient probably learned dysfunctional ways of interacting early in life—in the parental home.

TRAINEE: I would guess that Mr. Johnson's parents were highly critical. Parents for whom nothing was enough, and he would do things and it wouldn't be enough. It left him feeling ineffectual.

TRAINEE: Also, probably parents who had a history of alcoholism or depression. They were unavailable to him on some level.

TRAINEE: His father was alcoholic, probably violent.

TRAINEE: And his mother took care of his every need.

I like pushing the trainees to think about antecedents of Mr. Johnson's presentation. It fosters their thinking about how to use the past as confirmatory data to aid their understanding of the dynamic focus in the here and now. After soliciting more hypotheses about Mr. Johnson's early years, I inform the trainees about Mr. Johnson's history. At the outset of my treatment of Mr. Johnson I did not know a great deal about his past; much of his history was learned as our sessions progressed.

Mr. Johnson grew up in Oregon and Washington state. He was the second of four children. His father was an alcoholic and his mother was described as a "saint." Mr. Johnson said he felt love for his father until he saw him beat his mother when he was about 10 years old. He lived his early adult years as a loner and obtained a college degree in engineering. Following this, he married a woman who was referred to in the inpatient records as "a domineering alcoholic." There was continual marital stress and at one point they came close to divorcing. Shortly after this, Mr. Johnson was psychiatrically hospitalized. When his wife died suddenly of cancer, he was left to raise four children, the youngest of whom was his 10-year-old daughter, Susan. His older daughter left to get married, and his two sons ran away to work on a fishing boat.

Mr. Johnson lived with Susan in an interdependent relationship for 12 years until they were evicted. The search for a new apartment was stressful, and Susan left to find a place of her own. Mr. Johnson then moved into an apartment with his younger son and his son's girlfriend. About a year later he was again hospitalized and then referred to me for outpatient treatment.

I gleaned some of the patient's past history from the inpatient records. Significant portions of it, however, like Mr. Johnson's father's beating his

mother, did not emerge until the therapy was half over. While many therapists believe that taking a "good" history is a prerequisite for therapy, clinicians who do short-term work learn to formulate and begin therapy even
when they do not have all the "facts." Oftentimes, important genetic material emerges in the therapy as a consequence of therapeutic progress and a
working alliance and not as a precondition for it.

I tell the trainees that we will be viewing several more sessions of Mr.
Johnson and they will, therefore, have the opportunity to see the degree to
which their early formulation was on target.

CHAPTER 9

Technique: The Patient–Therapist Interaction

I~N THIS CHAPTER WE EXAMINE~ how the CMP derived for Mr. Johnson unfolds as a dynamic interaction between therapist and patient early in the second session.

[CLASSROOM]

LEVENSON: In the dynamic focus we developed after the first session, we hypothesized that Mr. Johnson was a passive man, who goes along with the program without saying how he feels or what he wants. What new experience did we hope Mr. Johnson would have in this therapy? What did we want to achieve in this brief therapy?

TRAINEE: Take on new things, be active, be empowered.

LEVENSON: You anticipated problems I, as the therapist, would get into. Remember that? Anything come to mind?

TRAINEE: You might get frustrated, angry.

TRAINEE: Because he was so passive.

TRAINEE: Nothing you did would be enough.

LEVENSON: OK. To continue with our series on technique, I now will show a portion from the beginning of session two. And afterwards, I will ask for your observations as to what is going on here.

[VIDEOTAPE]

Mr. Johnson: I just decided to tell you the two things that are really bothering me. I don't know why I didn't do this before. But it's been a point of pride with me to bear my own problems, my own troubles, and not tell them to someone else.

Therapist: So this is what has been gnawing away at you, has been Susan's leaving and the role you might have played in it?

Mr. Johnson: Yeah. And then our being used by real estate people over and over again. We've had to move. Not over and over again, but we've had to move. We're stranded out there. Now Susan pays too high rent for her salary, because she doesn't have anything left. And it's ... I don't know. We did have enough money and a pretty happy life. But all of a sudden we're up against it like all the street people almost.

Therapist: Do you think Susan's sorry she moved?

Mr. Johnson: I don't know. (plaintively) She still calls me Daddy. But then when she's gone, you know she's with her other friends. I guess she's forgetting me and it hurts. (emphatically) It hurts. I don't see her. She says, "Oh, Dad, I have other things to do." I ask her to come over—I say, "Let's meet and have an afternoon." (mimicking daughter) She says, "I have other things I have to do." One of her friends has a boat in College View. They go out on the bay—(pejoratively) baying it. And I just feel left out.

Therapist: (matter-of-factly) Well, you are!

Mr. Johnson: I am. (lamenting) Yeah, I'm really left out. So, I don't know ... (resigned tone, voice becomes plaintive and trails off)

Therapist: The least she could do after you went to all the trouble of raising her and giving her things was stick around for the rest of your life.

Mr. Johnson: Anyway, I guess these are the things, the fears ...

Therapist: (interrupting) How do you feel about what I just said?

Mr. Johnson: What did you say? (pause) At least she could have stuck around? (pause) I'm not that possessive. Really, I'm not that possessive to want her to stick around. I just want her in the same household. That's what I really want.

Therapist: (nodding) Yeah. How do you feel about the fact that I said the least she could do is not move out?

Mr. Johnson: I don't know. If I answer that it would seem like a selfish answer. If I just said, Well, I feel that she's unjust, or she's unfair, it would be a selfish answer on my part. Because I know kids have to grow up and go their own way.

Therapist: Well, you know that in your head, but I'm really asking how your gut feels.

Mr. Johnson: (begins crying) I don't want her to go! I want to be with her. She's my little kid. (pause) Oh, Christ. You know, my wife and I fought quite a bit and she always won. And she was able to domineer me completely. And we just withdrew from each other. So when she died, I turned all my love that I would normally have toward a wife toward this little kid who didn't leave me. My two sons left me and my older daughter left me. I never would have sold the house if they had all stuck together, but they started giving me all kinds of trouble. As I said. And I think all this frustrated feeling I had toward my wife because she was—she insisted on being boss. And it really bothered me. I was angry inside all the time at her. I turned on to this young girl all the feelings. So what it amounts to is I love Susan. I want her to be around. It's a fatherly love but it's a real close attachment. And I don't want it broken. (pause) If Susan goes, I don't really have anybody. (pause) Well, I'm feeling sorry for myself, but that's the truth of the matter. (sighs) Anger at myself for making (pause), you know, for getting rid of a house that could have kept us all together.

[CLASSROOM]

LEVENSON: What strikes you here? What is happening?

TRAINEE: He's vulnerable here. He starts off the session talking about a point of pride. This is messy stuff he's bringing up. He probably feels kind of ashamed.

TRAINEE: At first he wasn't able to tap in to his feelings, but you keep persisting with that interpretation. You keep asking him how he felt. Two or three times, you asked him how he felt.

TRAINEE: But what about that daring thing you said?

TRAINEE: Yeah, why did you say "The least she could have done is stick around for the rest of your life"?

LEVENSON: Why do you think I made that statement?

TRAINEE: I had a sense you were testing him. He is so passive. You were probably seeing if you could get a rise out of him.

TRAINEE: Yes. I thought you were trying to get him to see that he was being ridiculous in wanting his daughter to stay. By overstating what he was saying, you could get him to swing the other way and see that his daughter needed to be on her own. And it seemed to have worked, because next he says something like he knows kids have to grow up and go their own way.

This trainee seems to be alluding to the use of *paradoxical intent*, a technique used chiefly by strategic family therapists, whereby they might try to solve a problem or eliminate a symptom by suggesting that the patient maintain or even strengthen it (Brown & Slee, 1986; Watzlawick, 1967). Or he might be referring to the use of *reactance theory* to explain why a patient will resist the control of the therapist by doing the very opposite of the therapist's suggestion (Brehm, 1966). In these cases, the therapist's intent would be to get the patient to alter his or her behavior in a direction opposite from how the intervention appears. However, this was not my intent. Deciding on interventions based solely on obtaining a desired outcome regardless of the means would not be consistent with the TLDP therapist stance, which focuses on the development of a trusting relationship.

[CLASSROOM]

TRAINEE: I thought you were saying what the patient was really feeling. Just kind of stating it loud and clear and bringing it out in the open. I thought it was very empathic. I thought his unsaid message to his daughter was, "Don't leave me!" So you were just making it very apparent. That was my sense of what was going on.

TRAINEE: But it sounded sarcastic.

LEVENSON: Yes, it did sound sarcastic, didn't it?

TRAINEE: (relieved) Yeah.

TRAINEE: I thought it sounded sarcastic, too.

TRAINEE: Kind of harsh.

LEVENSON: What was there about my statement that gave you that feeling?

TRAINEE: Well, the tone of your comment made it seem sarcastic.

TRAINEE: I thought your phrasing, the content of what you said, sounded pejorative. "Well, the *least* she could have done . . . "

TRAINEE: It seems like there were many ways you could have said the same thing, such as, "I'm wondering if you felt that it was unfair of her to be out with her friends."

TRAINEE: Or "Did you feel like she was forgetting about you?"

TRAINEE: Or what about "How did you feel about her going off with her friends while you were alone?"

LEVENSON: All of those sound like excellent interventions, but what I hear you saying is that I sounded sarcastic in the phrasing and the tone.

TRAINEE: Maybe because you were seeing him as being kind of pathetic and helpless and you might have been feeling irritated with him.

TRAINEE: Yeah, I was wondering what was going on inside of you. You sounded angry with him. What about your reactions to him? What fueled that comment?

LEVENSON: Well, I made my comment about how Mr. Johnson's daughter owed it to him to stay with him because, as one of you already pointed out, I thought that was what he was really feeling. It was my attempt to be empathic—empathic in the sense of recognizing and feeling things from his perspective. It was a hunch, but a hunch based on what he had said and the way he had said it. He said that he felt alone; Susan was out with her "other" friends and this hurt him. It really got to him that she was out having a good time, and he was here in his old age, missing her, alone. I felt my hunch was confirmed a fewer seconds later on when he stated that he was not that possessive to want Susan to stick around— he "only wanted her in the same household"! But no matter how intended, it is likely my intervention came across as sarcastic or even baiting.

TRAINEE: So were you being sarcastic with Mr. Johnson because you were frustrated with him?

LEVENSON: Let's take a look at that. What do you think Mr. Johnson was pulling from me here in this second session?

TRAINEE: I think he was expecting you to be angry or disappointed in him. He might have wished for you to be supportive, but from his dynamic focus, I think he would be expecting you to reject him, to be disappointed in him.

TRAINEE: Well, he pulls for people to be frustrated with him because he is so passive and whiny.

LEVENSON: Yes, both of those comments seem pertinent. I like your use of the dynamic focus for understanding the process that might be going on between us—therapist and patient—in the session. If we check Mr. Johnson's CMP, we can see that we hypothesized Mr. Johnson would expect others to get tired, frustrated, and irritated with him.

TRAINEE: So are you saying that when you were responding to Mr. Johnson with that sarcastic comment, you didn't plan to say that?

LEVENSON: Well, it is not uncommon for me to say matter-of-factly to patients what I sense might be part of their underlying fantasies, wishes, censored feelings, or unconscious processes. But ideally I would try to frame my perceptions as that—only my perceptions and not as a corner on Reality with a capital R. In addition, I would hope that the tone in my voice would convey a sincere desire to understand things from their point of view. I would not want my tone to convey a mocking or condescending attitude. So, to answer your question, ordinarily I might have said something very similar to what I said to Mr. Johnson about his daughter's "sticking around," but I think the exact phrasing of the words and the tone in my voice would have been very different.

So, to return the question raised a while ago, what was going on with me when I made that provocative statement?

TRAINEE: You were reacting countertransferentially to the pull of the patient.

LEVENSON: Yes, I think so.

The assumption with TLDP is that by entering into a collaborative relationship with the patient, the therapist inevitably gets pushed and pulled consistent with the interactional pattern of the patient. The trainees initially exhibited some surprise that I as an experienced therapist would not be able to rise above my countertransferential feelings (or perhaps not have them at all). However, in TLDP the premise is not that only the incompetent, less experienced therapists act out their countertransferential feelings and behaviors.

According to TLDP, *all* therapists are initially expected to get hooked into playing out the cyclical maladaptive pattern with their patients. "If the [therapist] does not get emotionally involved sooner or later in a manner he had not intended, the analysis will not proceed to a successful conclusion" (Boesky, 1990, p. 573). However, differences occur between better and poorer therapists in the degree to which they can become aware of their countertransferential feelings and behavior, the time it takes them to become so aware, and their ability to extricate themselves from the roles into which they have been cast. So the goal is not to avoid becoming ensnared in the interactive web with the patient, but rather to learn how to make use of this entanglement to further the therapeutic process. In fact, some interactional theorists go so far as to say that one's awareness of countertransference must always be after the fact "in the sense that it is preceded by an enactment of which he has been unaware" (Renik, 1993, p. 141).

With regard to becoming aware, sometimes therapists have a model of what it means to be a good therapist that inhibits this awareness. Beginning therapists especially have an idealized and unidimensional model of the Good Therapist as one who can accept and like every patient, who is always ready, willing, and able to exude understanding and unconditional positive regard. This image is stultifying for a therapist, because it creates unattainable criteria that require the therapist, in order to feel good about his or her work, to shut off awareness of a whole range of feelings toward the patient—feelings such as animosity, jealousy, desire, or fright. The therapist can even label these feelings as "negative," and interpret them as signs of being an inadequate clinician, rather than seeing them as helpful information about the interactional process.

Sometimes therapists believe that even if they have these so-called negative feelings, they can and should keep them hidden from the patient. This is a curious perspective for a therapist to have, since therapists are usually in the business of helping create more awareness. Furthermore, there is a whole body of empirical literature in the area of experimenter expectancy effects which indicates that even experimenters conducting rigorous studies in controlled settings can convey to subjects their expectations as to the outcome of the experiment (Rosenthal, 1976). These expectancies are conveyed very subtly by tone of voice, minute changes in facial expressions, and other nonverbal and paralinguistic cues. Therefore, it is probably wishful thinking to assume we can always appear accepting and caring about our patients regardless of what is going on inside us.

[CLASSROOM]
TRAINEE: I was wondering what your relationship was like with your father?

This trainee's question raises an important issue having to do with countertransference in the more psychoanalytic sense of the un-worked-through conflicts of the therapist unwittingly and inappropriately interfering with the therapy (the classical view of countertransference). For example, if I saw Mr. Johnson as a father figure, and I felt conflicted about my anger toward my own father for his being too controlling, then I might erroneously infer that Mr. Johnson is being too controlling with his daughter or with me, and "act out" my anger inappropriately. Thus my perceptions and my behavior might have nothing to do with my developing relationship with Mr. Johnson, but have much more to do with my personal dynamics toward father figures. The remedy for this type of countertransference is to discuss my reactions in supervision or in my own therapy in order to deal with my own misperceptions and inappropriate behavior.

The question is invariably raised pertaining to how does one discriminate between the two types of countertransference—the classical and the interactional. This is a major issue because one would do very different things depending on which type of countertransference is at work. Several guidelines are helpful.

First, I would go back to the dynamic formulation. What responses does the patient expect to get from others? What did the patient say about how other people act with him? The therapist can use this CMP information to predict what dysfunctional interactions might develop between therapist and patient in the transference. As discussed previously, the formulation can be used as a rough map of the therapeutic territory the therapist and patient will cover. In fact, after listening to the opening portion of the first session with Mr. Johnson, the trainees predicted that I might become irritated and even angry with him as a response to his passive presentation. So this is a litmus test of sorts: Does my reaction make sense in terms of the dynamic formulation? If it does, then I can feel more confident that the patient and I are re-creating a dysfunctional interaction that has more to do with his style than with mine.

If, however, one's reactions do not make sense given the patient's CMP, then either the therapist must revise his or her understanding of the patient's CMP or analyze his or her reaction to see whether it has more to do with countertransference in the classical sense. It is helpful for therapists to think about their own patterns of relating to people. Do you have characteristic expectations of others? Are there ways you pull for a certain type of response from others? What about with patients? What is your introject? How do you typically treat yourself in the best of situations? In the worst of situations? Knowing one's own interactional scenarios will be of immense help in sensitizing the therapist to when individual issues might be interfering with the therapeutic process.

A second way to help therapists figure out what type of countertransference is occurring is to use patient feedback. When I feel unsure of whether my reaction (feeling, thoughts, or behavior) to the patient has more to do with my personal issues than with what the patient is putting out, I might ask the patient whether the way I am coming across feels familiar. When has he or she experienced this type of response before? Do I remind him or her of anyone in particular in my attitude or manner of interacting?

[CLASSROOM]

LEVENSON: In the group supervision, you are showing your own work in front of your colleagues. They have the opportunity via videotape to see you reacting toward your patient. To the extent everyone observing the tape has a reaction similar to yours, then most likely, this would be a strong indication that the patient is sending out signals, what Safran [1984, 1990] calls "interpersonal markers," which cause a complementary reaction in most other people.

TRAINEE: What about for our other cases which are not supervised in a group setting?

TRAINEE: Or what happens in private practice?

LEVENSON: Consultation is one of the most helpful antidotes for losing one's perspective. Since all forms of countertransference—the classical and the interactive—have components that are unconscious or not readily accessible for our pragmatic use, an independent clinician's assessment can give us a viewpoint not available to those within the interactive system.

Sometimes patients can tell us things indirectly as well as directly. For example, Mr. Johnson said something later on after my provocative statement which gave me a clue that my way of interacting with him was part of an overall pattern for him with significant people in his life. Anyone pick it up?

TRAINEE: He said something about his wife. I remember thinking at the time that perhaps he saw a parallel between you and his wife.

TRAINEE: I think he said that she was domineering.

LEVENSON: Yes, he said, "My wife and I fought quite a bit and she always won." As Mr. Johnson described what went on with his wife, I began thinking, Maybe I have fallen into the pattern he had with his wife. Perhaps I, too, was acting in a domineering way. Rather than tell me directly I was too overbearing, Mr. Johnson unconsciously related how he lost fights with his wife. Interactional psychoanalytic theorists such as Gill [1982] refer to this behavior as "allusion to the transference." In this way, the patient unconsciously communicates his views of the therapeutic interaction; he also avoids any anxiety he might have about the consequences of criticizing me. Furthermore, in his description of his relationship with his wife, Mr. Johnson gives us valuable information about what he characteristically did with his anger toward his wife. Does anyone recall?

TRAINEE: He says he kept his anger inside.

TRAINEE: He says, "I was angry inside all the time at her."

LEVENSON: Yes, this information about how he deals with his anger is consistent with the passive presentation we noted in the first session. Let's return to thinking about the videotaped segment and see if there are any parallels between Mr. Johnson's characteristic way of dealing with anger and what he did with me in our interaction in the session. How does Mr. Johnson respond to my statement about Susan's "sticking around for the rest of his life"?

TRAINEE: He claims that he's not that possessive.

LEVENSON: That's a bit later. What does he say before that?

TRAINEE: He doesn't respond to what you said; he just changes the subject.

LEVENSON: Yes. And then what do I say?

TRAINEE: You ask him how he felt about what you said.

While patients change the subject in therapy for a variety of reasons, the therapist should probe carefully when a patient changes the subject following an intervention that is likely to cause the patient some anxiety—anxiety brought about by fears of what would happen if certain thoughts and feelings were expressed.

After Mr. Johnson ignored my provocative statement about his daughter, I thought he must have had some internal reaction to it. While he was changing the subject, I reviewed what I had said and how I had said it, and began wondering, "Uh oh, I wonder how Mr. Johnson heard what I just said." Then I began thinking, "Just what did I say and how did I say it?" I therefore decided simply to ask him how he was feeling about what I had just said to gather more information about his internal state.

Mr. Johnson's changing the subject was so dramatic that it gave me a strong cue to make me reflect on what I had said. It was readily apparent to me that perhaps my remark had sounded short, clipped, and sarcastic. And I started thinking about the extent to which I might be countertransferentially expressing my frustration with Mr. Johnson.

[CLASSROOM]

LEVENSON: Now if you were a patient in therapy and at the beginning of your second session, your therapist had made a sarcastic remark about an issue of critical importance to you, how would you feel? What would you say?

TRAINEE: I would feel really angry.

TRAINEE: I would probably tell the therapist I wasn't coming back.

TRAINEE: I might be so taken aback, I might not have said anything, but I'd be very upset.

LEVENSON: Why wouldn't you have said anything?

TRAINEE: I would be afraid of angering the therapist—the person to whom I was coming for help.

TRAINEE: Yes, like not angering your surgeon before an operation.

LEVENSON: In our culture, a healthy reaction to being treated sarcastically might be anger and resentment. But Mr. Johnson doesn't become obviously angry; he changes the subject.

TRAINEE: Maybe he is afraid to be directly angry with you.

LEVENSON: Is not expressing anger typical interpersonal behavior from Mr. Johnson?

TRAINEE: Well, we know that he kept his anger at his wife inside.

LEVENSON: Yes, but we learn that later on in this session. What do we know at this point when I say, "The least she could have done is stick around," and he changes the subject?

TRAINEE: Well, we have the dynamic focus where we figured out that in the face of conflict or stressors he reacts in a passive way.

TRAINEE: He's dependent on others.

TRAINEE: He would be more likely to get depressed instead of getting angry.

This trainee's comment shows an appropriate and helpful use of the dynamic focus. From the rudimentary formulation of Mr. Johnson's interpersonal style, it is fair to expect that when confronted with hostility or even unpleasantness Mr. Johnson would react passively—withdrawing, changing the subject, not hearing, being ingratiating, and so on.

Using Mr. Johnson's CMP, I wondered whether Mr. Johnson were in fact angry at me for commenting in such a presumptuous manner about what his daughter should do. If that were the case, then I could see that the two of us might have reenacted an important dynamic for Mr. Johnson: his initially appearing helpless and indirectly angry causing the other person to be impatient and to respond in an insensitive way, which causes Mr. Johnson to feel criticized and to withdraw, which causes the other person to feel ignored.

Therefore, I asked Mr. Johnson how he was feeling about what I said, because I was attempting to talk to him about the pattern that had been re-created between us. This was an invitation on my part to metacommunicate about our relationship. It was a question I hoped would allow us to talk about the interaction and thereby momentarily break the dysfunctional pattern occurring between us. I wanted to give him the chance to have a new interactive experience—specifically, to be more assertive in expressing his negative feelings.

Could he avail himself of the opportunity to express his anger (either toward me or about his daughter) and then see whether there were dire consequences? Would I fire him from therapy? Would I get angry back? Would his anger mortally wound me? Would I think he is a selfish man? In this way, I take a small step toward trying to create the opportunity for Mr. Johnson to have the new experience that is one of the goals for this therapy.

In addition to trying to give him a new experience, I was also concerned that my sarcastic, provocative comment might have upset the developing working relationship between us—what Elizabeth Zetzel (1956) originally called the therapeutic alliance. One of the ways to try to repair a rupture in the therapeutic alliance is to address the patient's problematic feelings about the therapist. Steven Foreman and Charles Marmar (1985), who explored therapist actions in initially poor therapeutic alliances with patients, found that these alliances improved when therapists addressed negative interactions and defensive maneuvers as related to the patient–therapist relationship. I hoped by asking Mr. Johnson how he felt about my comment, I could begin to repair the breach in trust that might have occurred. In a brief therapy, in particular, it is critical to discuss in the here and now of the therapy anything that might contribute to a negative transference.

[CLASSROOM]

TRAINEE: So you asked him about his feelings toward you to give him the opportunity to express his negative feelings and to establish a trusting, working relationship?

LEVENSON: Exactly. In addition, this rupture in the therapeutic alliance provides what Jeremy Safran and Zindel Segal [1990] call a "useful window into the patient's subjective world" [p. 89]. It affords the therapist an opportunity to understand more fully the patient's CMP, and to learn how to provide the patient with a mini–new experience. So how does he respond to this question?

TRAINEE: He says that he knows kids have to grow up and separate.

LEVENSON: What does he say before that?

TRAINEE: Something about being selfish.

TRAINEE: He says, I think, that if he answered the question honestly, he would seem selfish.

TRAINEE: He says that his daughter has been unfair.

LEVENSON: Well, he doesn't quite come out and say it that directly. But he does allude to the fact that she might be. Now he still has not told me directly how he is feeling. However, he is letting me know that he is censoring his thoughts and feelings. He is indirectly conveying to me the inner workings of his interpersonal schemata—his understanding of why he keeps his feelings to himself in this particular instance. He assumes if he told me his censored thoughts and feelings, I would think he were being selfish. And probably, in his mind, my negative opinion of him would have deleterious consequences for how I might treat him. This is very valuable information for the elaboration of my understanding of his CMP.

   In addition, Mr. Johnson might have to acknowledge to himself that he had "selfish" wishes. Recognition of such a self-perception might lead to considerable anxiety for Mr. Johnson, because it could threaten his sense of relatedness to others. "How could anyone value me and how could I value myself if I had these selfish thoughts and feelings?" Therefore, Mr. Johnson's censorship might be motivated by a need to save both himself and me from concluding he was not deserving.

TRAINEE: But then you ask him how his gut feels. Is this an attempt to get him to uncensor himself?

This trainee has correctly surmised the intent of this intervention. I would like to give Mr. Johnson the opportunity to express his withheld thoughts and feelings. So I acknowledge that one part of him knows that kids have to grow up and go their own way, but then I ask him how his gut feels. In this way, I suggest that his feelings may be at variance with what he knows in his head. I am hoping that by giving him permission to have these feelings, I could get an unexpurgated version. This technique of positing other sides of a person can help patients recognize and express more warded-off feelings; it communicates to them that many feelings, some of them contradictory, can exist all within the same person.

When I asked Mr. Johnson how his gut felt, I relinquished questioning him about his feelings toward me. Ordinarily I would have pursued staying in the here and now of discussing our developing relationship. First of all, exploration of the therapist–patient relationship gives the patient the opportunity to do something differently—to test out in vivo his or her own interpersonal schemata and see what happens. Second, testing one's dysfunctional, interactional beliefs in the actual therapeutic relationship makes the learning affectively alive. One is not talking intellectually about something that happened years ago, but rather living it out in the present. And third, it allows therapist and patient to share and process what both experienced, providing the patient with the type of interactional feedback one rarely obtains in real life.

However, in this instance I do not stay with my question of how Mr. Johnson feels about my sarcastic comment. I do not examine the process between the two of us. I ask the trainees why not?

[LONG PAUSE IN THE CLASSROOM]

TRAINEE: (tentatively) It seems like Mr. Johnson started talking about some really important things—like his love for his daughter and his anger toward his wife.

LEVENSON: This is true. But sometimes patients talk about their relationships with others or historical material, even meaningful historical material, as a way of avoiding the heat of the moment. Here Mr. Johnson could have been talking about his anger toward his wife as a way of circumventing dealing with his anger toward me. Avoidance of examining what might be occurring in the transference–countertransference interplay could be depriving the patient of an experiential disconfirmation of his dysfunctional, interpersonal script.

How do you make decisions in your clinical work with patients about when to follow the patient and when the patient is taking you on a wild-goose chase—diverting you from important material?

TRAINEE: Truthfully, if I don't know what to say, I just let the patient talk.

LEVENSON: But even if you don't know what to say, my guess is that you still might have some clues as to when the patient is talking about something that will further the therapeutic work, and when the material is filler or is presented in a defensive manner.

TRAINEE: Oh, sure. When patients talk about what happened to them during the week—like they are reporting in—they just seem to be filling up the time.

TRAINEE: When it's filler, there is no emotional substance to what they are saying.

TRAINEE: They seem emotionally flat.

TRAINEE: I can usually tell because I feel bored.

LEVENSON: Good. So you are using the emotions of the patient and yourself to help guide you. Meaningful material is usually affectively laden—emotionally alive. So when Mr. Johnson starts talking about his attachment to Susan and his withdrawal from his wife, does he present this material in an affectively present way?

TRAINEE: Yeah, he really seems torn apart.

TRAINEE: Previously he seems very whiny and self-pitying. But after you ask him to talk about what's in his guts, he starts crying in a very real way.

TRAINEE: Yeah, this is the place where I feel sorry for him for the first time. I started thinking about how lonely it must be when all your kids grow up and leave, especially if you did not have a happy marriage.

LEVENSON: Yes, Mr. Johnson's behavior touches us perhaps for the first time. His words seem congruent with his affect. He conveyed this material in a highly affective way that increases our empathy for him; this is precisely why I did not go back to talking about the relationship between the therapist and the patient. I, too, felt that Mr. Johnson was experiencing some real sadness about the loss of his daughter here. It felt very genuine in the room. I felt moved. And I felt like I was truly beginning to understand what his world must have been like since Susan moved out. It would have seemed absurd to me, and I'm sure to him, at that point to have told him to stop focusing on losing the only meaningful person in his life and instead talk about how he felt about me!

TRAINEE: If he had responded to your question by saying your comment seemed sarcastic and he was angry with you, what would you have done?

LEVENSON: That's a really good question! First of all, if he had said that, I would have reevaluated my assessment of him. It would have indicated that he could recognize his own feelings. And, furthermore, from an interpersonal perspective, his reply would have demonstrated that he could tell me directly how he was feeling.

We have been working from a formulation that this is a very passive man, who presents his needs indirectly. We expected that he would be the last one to say he was angry. If he had been able to say he was angry with me in the second session, I would have changed my view of his CMP. I would have altered it to reflect that Mr. Johnson seems to take a passive stance in life, but when he is treated in a disrespectful manner, he knows his feelings and assertively expresses them.

Now to address your question of what I would have said if he had confronted me with his anger. I probably would have told him that he had some nerve and I couldn't possibly see him in therapy if he had that kind of attitude! (laughter from group) Only kidding. Just seeing if you were paying attention.

The first thing I would do would be to reflect on the remark I had made and see whether, upon examination, it did indeed sound sarcastic. My careful consideration of his reply would convey that I took his statement seriously, and might help repair the rupture in our therapeutic alliance. My taking the time to reflect on his opinion that the statement seemed sarcastic would model the manner in which our process can be examined—that I could receive his feedback as information about our relationship, not as a condemnation of me to which I needed to respond defensively.

Then it would be important to acknowledge the degree to which I too thought the remark was sarcastic. I might have simply said, "As I step back and listen to myself, it does sound sarcastic, and I can understand why you got angry." This owning of my interactive countertransference would give Mr. Johnson two new experiences: having his perceptions validated, and not being punished for being angry. In fact, I might tell Mr. Johnson that his letting me know how he felt about the things I said would be very helpful in our work together.

Next I might wonder aloud why I would be saying something in a sarcastic manner. I would invite Mr. Johnson to collaborate with me in discovering what might have been going on in our interaction that could have given rise to my chiding remark. In this way I would be conveying to Mr. Johnson that behaviors and feelings can be a product of interactions, and have causes and consequences which can be discovered by a dispassionate examination of the give-and-take of the interchange. I would also be communicating that we could work together to learn about such processes. In addition, my responding in this way would add to my being seen less as a detached and neutral observer of his pathology, and more as an active participant in the relationship—as one who influences and is influenced.

Finally, to facilitate Mr. Johnson's seeing our interchange as indicative of a larger interactional pattern, I might ask him whether he has ever noticed other people treating him sarcastically or disrespectfully, and to think about the conditions under which these reactions have occurred. I would prefer, however, to examine his interactions with others after his interaction with me had been thoroughly explored.

CHAPTER 10

Technique: Providing a New Experience

HELPING PATIENTS HAVE a new experience of themselves and others in the therapeutic context is not as simple as it might sound. Even with extensive training, such as that done as part of the Vanderbilt II studies (Strupp, 1993), therapists remain highly susceptible to being caught in negative transference reactions and countertransference enactments.

The therapist is invited repeatedly by the patient (albeit unconsciously) to become a partner in a well-rehearsed, maladaptive two-step. The therapist would like the patient to learn a new, less injurious, more fluid dance, but the patient's style creates a powerful force, often propelling the well-intentioned therapist into becoming an unwilling follower. If the therapist refuses to dance, the patient may feel rejected or humiliated. If the therapist attempts to be Arthur Murray (i.e., to instruct the patient) or points out how the patient is making a fool of himself on the dance floor (i.e., criticizes the patient), the patient may seek out a more obliging partner or stop dancing altogether.

I will use the case of Mr. Johnson to examine the perplexing and perennial problem of how to provide a new experience for the patient—a new experience that should establish the foundation for unlearning maladaptive ways of relating. I show the trainees a videotape of Mr. Johnson's third therapy session. Mr. Johnson begins by telling me that he has not eaten breakfast.

[VIDEOTAPE]

Mr. Johnson: I feel pretty low.

Therapist: Do you think it's more than not eating breakfast?

Mr. Johnson: Well, yeah, but I'm diabetic and if I could get some food.

Therapist: How come you didn't eat breakfast?

Mr. Johnson: I just hurried over here. I feel nervous.

Therapist: You feel nervous? Why is that?

Mr. Johnson: I should get some breakfast. I just felt nervous all week, you know. (pause) I take a stool softener and I had a little accident driving over and I'll have to clean it up, when I get back.

Therapist: Was that upsetting to you?

Mr. Johnson: (sighing) Yes, it was. It happened before.

Therapist: But that isn't why you've been nervous all week.

Mr. Johnson: No, it's because I'm not getting along with that girl, and . . .

Therapist: Your son's girlfriend?

Mr. Johnson: My son's mad at me and all that.

Therapist: Why is your son mad at you?

Mr. Johnson: Huh?

Therapist: Why is your son mad at you?

Mr. Johnson: I didn't hear you, Doctor.

Therapist: Sure. Why is your son mad at you?

Mr. Johnson: For not being friendly with his girlfriend.

Therapist: How do you feel when your son gets mad at you?

Mr. Johnson: I feel very sad, because we used to get along quite well.

Therapist: So you get sad when he gets mad.

Mr. Johnson: Yeah. (silence)

Therapist: Is that pretty typical for you, to get sad when anyone gets mad at you, or just your son?

Mr. Johnson: I get sad when someone gets mad at me. My kids are mad at me now because I'm not responding to treatment. I'm not doing anything. I'm just sitting around, so I feel pretty sad.

Therapist: What do they mean, you're not responding to treatment?

Mr. Johnson: They tell me I have to help myself, which is true.

Therapist: You're coming here.

Mr. Johnson: (deep sigh) Boy, I feel pretty weak.

[CLASSROOM]

LEVENSON: What do you see happening in this segment?

TRAINEE: He starts out talking about being a diabetic, which makes me wonder if he could pass out at any moment. I'm not sure what to do with this information.

LEVENSON: With regard to his being a diabetic, you raise an excellent point. It is important to determine whether Mr. Johnson's not eating has resulted in any untoward physiological effects that would render him incapable of having a therapy session. Specifically, are his alertness, judgment, attention, and comprehension impaired in any way? Assessing any physiological or organic condition or state must be an ongoing part of the therapist's task.

I had previously ascertained that Mr. Johnson was not on insulin and that he controlled his diabetes by diet. If I had observed that Mr. Johnson were not comprehending my questions, were not able to be redirected, displayed nonverbal signs of distress, or in any way seemed physically compromised, I would have interrupted our therapy session and switched from a therapeutic to a crisis-intervention mode. In this more directive, active, management role I would have taken whatever steps were necessary to attend to Mr. Johnson's worsening condition. For example, I might have offered to get him something to eat or insisted that he accompany me to the cafeteria.

However, at the time, it was my clinical judgment that Mr. Johnson was capable of sending and receiving messages. I observed he was able to respond to my questions, told me he had been nervous all week (not just that morning), and mentioned some upsetting incidents (like his son's anger toward him) that might be emotionally difficult for him to discuss.

It is important to have some guidelines for assessing how to judge whether someone is in a state preventing the effective use of psychotherapy. Is the patient in physiological distress, dangerous, intoxicated, or compromised in some other fashion? I had the opportunity several years ago to role-play this portion of Mr. Johnson's third session on two separate occasions for members of the Vanderbilt II research/training team. One of the more senior psychologists actually did assess that "Mr. Johnson" (as role-played by me) was too impaired to continue in therapy that day and reassuringly invited "Mr. Johnson" to accompany him to the cafeteria. It is just such a directive approach that therapists may need to take at times to maintain the safety of patients, staff, and themselves.

[CLASSROOM]
LEVENSON: Other observations?
TRAINEE: He's acting in a way to turn you off to him.
LEVENSON: Like how?
TRAINEE: It sounds like he has soiled himself because of the stool softener. He said he has to clean himself. What's happening to the chair he's sitting in?

TRAINEE: He's making himself a mess! Literally.

TRAINEE: He sounds like he is becoming regressed to the point of a 2-year-old. In terms of the transference, he is saying "Here I am, Mom. I'm a mess. Take care of me."

TRAINEE: Not only does he want you to change him, he wants you to feed him as well!

TRAINEE: He is so needy. He cannot even take care of his basic needs.

LEVENSON: So there is a baby in the room. And when I try to treat Mr. Johnson respectfully like an adult by saying "You are coming here," in response to his saying "I have to help myself," what does he do?

TRAINEE: He regresses.

TRAINEE: You confronted him with the fact that he was taking some responsibility for getting better, and his immediate response was to say he felt weak.

TRAINEE: And he sighed pitifully.

LEVENSON: Yes, he sighs and says he's feeling weak; especially when I am trying to support him and treat him as an adult with capabilities who is taking appropriate action to get help. Because Mr. Johnson's dynamic focus is one where he sees himself as stuck and passive, anything that goes counter to that self-perception (and potentially threatens his sense of security or integrity) will be met with resistance.

It can sometimes be surprising or disappointing for therapists to have their supportive comments met with unenthusiastic or even hostile responses. This seemingly negative reaction can be understood more easily if we remember that while patients come to therapy hoping to learn more fulfilling ways of interacting with others, the more dysfunctional ways (in this case, Mr. Johnson's feelings of inadequacy and his expectations that others might take care of him if he is helpless) are overlearned and familiar. This is the only reality that Mr. Johnson knows and he interprets his world accordingly. Going with the known reduces anxiety, but at the price of short-circuiting growth. Mr. Johnson has made an unconscious decision that his indirect and passive stance (which makes him feel childlike and weak) is preferable to taking the direct and active risk of stating his needs and showing his anger (which may result in physical or emotional abandonment). Part of the therapist's function is to provide a bridge between the familiar but damaging and the unknown but potentially more rewarding.

[CLASSROOM]

TRAINEE: He's talking about a series of things that are going wrong and he's not doing anything about them.

LEVENSON: Yes, here in the third session Mr. Johnson presents almost as a caricature of himself. Feed me. Clean me. Take care of me. As we've discussed previously, for patients with serious character pathology, the presentation will be as blatant and obvious as here. When the dysfunctional behavior is less severe, the cyclical maladaptive pattern is more subtle and varied in its presentation in the therapeutic setting.

Let's return to the session and see how it proceeds. I will play another several minutes of videotape, and then I will stop the tape and ask what you, as the therapist, would have said or done at that moment.

[VIDEOTAPE]

Mr. Johnson: I need something to eat.

Therapist: Do you think it would be hard for you to have a session today?

Mr. Johnson: I think so, yeah. Until I get something in me.

Therapist: How do you feel when you are weak?

Mr. Johnson: I just feel weak all over.

Therapist: Like where . . . do you feel weak?

Mr. Johnson: In my stomach, and arms, and my hands are weak.

Therapist: Do you think it would keep you from talking with me? Even though you feel weak, could we still have a session?

Mr. Johnson: Yeah. I'm having trouble concentrating.

Therapist: And you think it's just because you missed breakfast?

Mr. Johnson: Because I'm upset about a lot of things. Everything's going wrong. I'm not doing the dishes or helping take care of the house, and her cat is mad at me because I chase him out of my room where he goes in and sprays.

Therapist: And that makes you sad, that the cat is mad at you.

Mr. Johnson: (halfhearted laugh) Yeah.

Therapist: (in disbelief) And that makes you sad that the cat . . .

Mr. Johnson: Yeah, I really like the cat.

Therapist: You like the cat. [Yeah.] So the cat's mad at you and your reaction is to get sad, because the cat is mad at you.

Mr. Johnson: Well, I guess so. Yeah.

Therapist: So if someone wants to make you sad, all they have to do is get mad at you.

Mr. Johnson: Yeah. (silence)

Therapist: Well, that sounds pretty simple.

Mr. Johnson: (halfhearted laugh) (pause) There isn't a place in here where I could get a tomato juice or anything?

Therapist: No, not here.

Mr. Johnson: (distressed) Oh, boy.

Therapist: Mr. Johnson, you are saying two different things. You're saying you would have trouble sitting here continuing with our session because you haven't had breakfast; then you say it's more than that. You would have trouble sitting here talking because you're upset about the things that have gone on this week and it would make this session hard anyway.

Mr. Johnson: Well, they decided to go up to Vancouver to visit some people and they just left and I've been alone for three days in the house and I haven't been going out.

Therapist: But right here, sitting here now, do you feel talking with me is difficult because we'll be talking about some upsetting things, or do you think sitting here talking with me is difficult because you didn't have breakfast this morning?

Mr. Johnson: I think it's because I didn't have breakfast.

THERAPISTS' INTERVENTIONS

[CLASSROOM]

LEVENSON: What I would like you all to do now is to pretend you are Mr. Johnson's therapist. And he has just told you that it is difficult to talk in the session because he hasn't had breakfast. Think of the actual words you would say to Mr. Johnson at this point. I'll write your responses on the board.

TRAINEE 1: I'd say, "Here's my lunch!" (laughter) He is tying the therapist's hands. Trying to make you feel helpless. (pause) Actually, I don't know what to say. I'd probably say nothing.

LEVENSON: OK. (writing response on the board). Anyone else want to respond to Mr. Johnson?

TRAINEE 2: "I wonder if you might really be distressed because of what is going on in your family, and not because you haven't eaten."

TRAINEE 3: "What are your concerns about what might happen if you stayed here and talked about what was bothering you this week?"

TRAINEE 4: "Does this remind you of types of interactions you get into with your children?"

TRAINEE 5: "It seems hard for you to focus on the work."

TRAINEE 6: "Mr. Johnson, we've been talking for so many minutes about the issue of your wanting to leave. You feel like breakfast and I am thinking you should stay—so how do you think I am feeling?"

TRAINEE 7: I might say, "So what would you like to do?"

THERAPISTS' INTENTIONS

LEVENSON: Now I would like for each of you to think about your choice of what to say next, and tell me what you were hoping your particular intervention would accomplish. I'll write your intentions in a column next to your respective interventions. [See table 10.1.]

In all therapies, the therapist needs to be mindful about the purpose of any particular communication and how it will be received. In brief therapy, interventions need to be especially on target in order to be both effective and efficient. What is critical in a brief therapy is for the therapist to assess at all times what he or she would like to accomplish with a particular intervention. The therapist should be thinking about how each verbal and nonverbal message might affect the patient.

Let's see what the trainees say were the reasons behind their responses. The first trainee was ready to give Mr. Johnson her lunch!

Table 10.1

Trainee Comments and Reasons	
Interventions	Intentions
(1) "Here's my lunch!" Silence.	No intent. Feeling awkward. Not knowing what to say.
(2) "You might really be distressed because of what is going on in your family."	Refocus on his feelings toward his family to get him to understand he is angry with them.
(3) "What are your concerns about what might happen if you stayed here and talked?"	Create an opening for him to talk about his fears and need to divert attention.
(4) "Does this remind you of interactions with your children?"	Help him see how the same pattern occurs with others.
(5) "It seems hard for you to focus on the work."	Have him understand his pattern of avoidance.
(6) "How do you think I am feeling?"	Point out the effect he has on others.
(7) "So what would you like to do?"	Put the responsibility for the decision on him.

TRAINEE 1: I really wouldn't say "Here's my lunch" but I am pulled to take care of him. I feel I don't have many options, because he is so needy and unable to take care of himself. I really didn't know what to say. I'd probably say nothing and wait.

This trainee's reactions are excellent illustrations of how Mr. Johnson's presentation results in a countertransferential reaction of helplessness in the therapist. She is also responding to his regressed and whiny stance by being pulled to give him what he wants, partly out of concern that he really is incapable of taking care of himself and partly out of frustration at not knowing what else to do with his passive, annoying behavior other than give in.

Here we see this trainee reacting to the pitiful and pleading behavior of the patient in much the same way as Mr. Johnson's children are pulled to do. The trainee is trying to appease Mr. Johnson by assuming a caretaker role, even to the point of wanting to feed him. Although this trainee "knows better" than to actually give Mr. Johnson her lunch, she may interact with him in other, more subtle, caretaking ways. Her awareness of this countertransferential pull may discourage her tendency to take care of the patient, and thus limit her reenactment of the patient's dysfunctional interpersonal scenario.

This same trainee went on to state that since she did not know what to say, she would say nothing. In a time-limited therapy, however, an overuse of silence keeps the therapy from moving along. The failure to make necessary interventions (such as focusing the session or addressing maladaptive behaviors) will result in less progress toward the goal. And the inappropriate use of silence (to the extent that it unduly raises the patient's anxiety or makes it difficult for the patient to resume the therapeutic work) can lead to irreparable ruptures in the working alliance.

Silence is as much an intervention as any other, and should not automatically be considered a fall-back position. In brief therapy, it is usually necessary for the therapist to be active and directive. Increased therapist activity is not without its own risks, however. Results from the Vanderbilt II studies indicate that negative behavior on the part of therapists (e.g., blaming) was partly due to the fact that the therapists stepped up their own verbal participation after training (Henry et al., 1993b). As the therapists' output increased so did the opportunities to make mistakes. In sum, silence and activity can both be used with positive or negative consequences. The judicious use of silence can be most therapeutic. But one must know how, why, and when to use it as much as any other intervention.

Returning to the classroom, the stated intent of the trainee who said that Mr. Johnson might really be distressed not because of lack of food, but because of what was going on in his family, was as follows:

[CLASSROOM]

TRAINEE 2: He says he's uncomfortable not having had breakfast, but I think he is denying the role his family plays in his distress. So I said this as a way to help him get back to the interpersonal factors causing his discomfort. I wanted to make some sort of interpretation that would help him see how he feels toward his family.

LEVENSON: So you have considered that it would be more therapeutic for him to focus on his feelings toward his family than on his hunger?

TRAINEE 2: Yes. He is unwilling to talk about his anger toward his family. The business about being hungry is a diversion—a resistance to examining his own conflicts.

LEVENSON: If he responded in the best possible way to your intervention, what would happen?

TRAINEE 2: He would say, "I see what you mean. I think you're right. I am angry with my family for deserting me."

LEVENSON: You would be hoping to provide him with some insight, then, into a better understanding of his behavior and how he avoids anger?

TRAINEE 2: Yes.

This trainee's intervention was an attempt to get the patient to understand that he is angry with his family, and that his focusing on food is a resistance to the therapeutic work. Traditionally conceived, resistance is in the service of keeping what is unconscious unconscious. Usually it is experienced by beginning therapists as the patient's almost willful and obstinate refusal to get to the real material. Sometimes in the therapist's zeal to uncover conflictual material, a contest of wills results, with the therapist attempting to break through the patient's resistances. It has been my experience that this is met with an even greater "resistance" on the part of the patient, often leaving the patient feeling confused, misunderstood, or threatened. Frequently the neophyte therapist tries to cut through the patient's defensive posture, as illustrated by this trainee. The hope is that the patient will "see the light" and "the error of his ways" and confess to some destructive or libidinous wish, much as the guilty perpetrator in a Perry Mason courtroom.

Resistance from the perspective of TLDP is viewed within the interpersonal sphere—as one of a number of transactions between therapist and patient. The patient is attempting to retain personal integrity and ingrained perceptions of himself or herself and others. The patient's perceptions support his or her understanding of what is required to maintain interpersonal connectedness. Resistance in this light is the patient's attempt to do the best he or she can with how he or she construes the world (Kelly, 1955).

The next trainee's intervention, rather than confronting the patient's resistance, seeks to understand it.

TRAINEE 3: I asked Mr. Johnson what might be his concerns about what might happen if he stayed and talked about what was bothering him. I was hoping to create an opening for him to talk about his fears and thereby help him understand why he had difficulty talking about his feelings.

This trainee's intent, consistent with classic psychoanalytic technique, was to examine the defensive posture used to minimize conflict. In the case of Mr. Johnson, we could hypothesize that he probably fears his anger will become uncontrollable and result in some disastrous behavior and that this expression of his anger will cause his loved ones to desert him. He is less anxious, in the short run, with his passive, one-down entreaty to others to meet his needs or to feel sorry for him.

We proceed to consider the intervention of the trainee who asks Mr. Johnson whether the type of interaction he is having with the therapist is reminiscent of how he interacts with his children.

TRAINEE 4: My reason for saying this was to help him see how the same pattern gets repeated.

The intent of this intervention is quite consistent with the approach of TLDP: helping the patient see how his actions and reactions with the therapist are mini-replications of how he interacts with other significant people in his life. The hope ultimately would be to have Mr. Johnson begin to understand how he is partly responsible for inviting certain behaviors from others.

Often this type of intervention of drawing parallels between transference behaviors and behaviors with other significant people in the patient's life is worthwhile. It is one of the cornerstones in a psychodynamic therapist's armamentarium. However, early in treatment this type of interpretation is generally met with confusion and disavowal by patients because it is so far afield from where they are experientially. Mr. Johnson has just stated that he is having difficulty talking in the session because he did not eat breakfast. To suggest to him then that there are other things more important to discuss (e.g., interactions with others) is not to take the patient seriously. In this particular case, not meeting Mr. Johnson "where he is at" can be a subtle form of abandonment by the therapist.

To take a patient seriously does not mean believing him. I, too, regard Mr. Johnson's focus on food as both a diversion away from more conflictual material (e.g., feelings about being abandoned by his family for 3 days) and a derivative of his feeling needy and dependent (e.g., wanting to be fed). However, if I do not empathically acknowledge that he has said he needs food, I run the risk of having Mr. Johnson either submit to me in his characteristically dependent manner or become even more helpless and immutable.

A colleague of mine said that the first rule she learned in her social work practicums was "Start where the patient is." After 30 years of professional work, she now believes the second rule is "Stay where the patient is." The rule of thumb here is *Take the patient seriously.*

The fifth trainee, who said he would simply say to Mr. Johnson that it seemed hard for him to focus on the work, appears to be attempting to intervene without making major inferences, more at a descriptive level. This is usually a good place to begin for highly resistant patients, such as Mr. Johnson. The statement describes what is going on without pathologizing the patient. If agreement can be obtained here, and Mr. Johnson can feel heard, it might create a foundation to permit more anxiety-provoking interventions.

The sixth trainee's intervention introduces her own feelings.

TRAINEE 6: I told Mr. Johnson that we were in a bit of a tug-of-war, and asked him how he thought I (as the therapist) was feeling. I remembered that people felt frustrated when dealing with him. So I thought I could have him see the effect he has on people by asking him what the therapist might be feeling. I wanted him to realize how irritating he is.

This trainee has considered an important aspect of this man's cyclical maladaptive pattern: the effect he has on others. Her intervention also is focused on the therapeutic relationship in the here and now, and she has introduced their interaction as a topic for discussion.

From a TLDP perspective, this therapist appears to be right on target. It is important to discuss the interaction between therapist and patient, whether in terms of how the patient seems to be coming across to the therapist, how the therapist might be experienced by the patient, how the patient might expect the therapist to react, or self-involving disclosure by the therapist concerning how he or she is affected by the patient.

This therapist's intent is to examine the patient's view of how she, as the therapist, might be feeling. My only misgiving about this therapist's saying "How do you think I am feeling?" is that Mr. Johnson might hear her question as blaming him (i.e., "See how *you* make me feel?"). Since Mr. Johnson is already quite self-punitive and self-effacing, he might all too readily agree that he is doing a poor job in therapy, and his therapist is, therefore, justifiably disappointed or angry with him.

Rather than engaging in a discussion of Mr. Johnson's perceptions of this trainee's negative view of him or even self-disclosing her negative reactions to him, the therapist could first wonder out loud how it is that the two of them repeatedly seem to end up in a tug-of-war. The decision of which way to proceed should always be based on what will be helpful for a particular patient, given a particular CMP, at a particular therapeutic juncture, and not on some abstract TLDP technique.

Last, but not least, the seventh trainee asked Mr. Johnson, "What would you like to do?" Here is his justification:

TRAINEE 7: I asked him what he would like to do because this would leave the decision for his behavior in his hands. He could decide to stay or go—but he would have to make the decision, not defer to what he thought were my needs.

LEVENSON: And if he decided to leave the session because he needed to get something to eat?

TRAINEE 7: That would be fine with me.

TRAINEE: But it wouldn't make sense to have him leave the session, because then he wouldn't talk about his feelings. You would be colluding with the patient to act out his avoidance of talking about his feelings. I suspect he's feeling depressed about being alone and angry at his family's treatment of him; having him stay and talk would be a way to get to it.

LEVENSON: (to the entire trainee group) OK. I have now written your interventions on the board and you have given the reasons behind them. There is a quite a variety. Now I would like you to select the best intervention.

The trainees are astonished at my request. In all their years of training they have never put their interventions to a vote. The purpose of this exercise is to demonstrate that all interventions are not equal—that there should be a rationale for just about everything one says and does in a brief-therapy session. I encourage the trainees to think about which intervention seems preferable to them and why.

LEVENSON: Do you have your favorite picked out?

TRAINEE: I like number three.

LEVENSON: Why?

TRAINEE: Because it gets at the fears behind his avoidance—the reasons why he is focusing on the food instead of his feelings. It would be helpful for him to understand his motivations.

TRAINEE: I prefer number five, because it would help him understand his pattern of avoiding.

TRAINEE: And I like number four, because it examines interpersonal patterns with others as well as with the therapist.

TRAINEE: I think number seven is best. It focuses on his taking responsibility for his life.

LEVENSON: So there is some divergence of opinion. How are we going to decide which intervention is best?

TRAINEE: Well, we could see which intervention gets him closer to the idea of the new experience.

TRAINEE: In that case, number seven is the most likely to empower him.

TRAINEE: Yes. I change my vote to number seven. It will put the control back in his lap.

LEVENSON: The way we formulated this case was to see Mr. Johnson's main problem as that of passivity and dependency. If this is our focus, then helping him become more proactive instead of reactive—to be more in charge of his own life—would be accomplishing our first goal. Of course, there is the second goal of giving him a new understanding of his own dynamics and how he re-creates his disappointing relationships with others. But first and foremost we want him to have a new experience. Therefore, anything we communicate should help him take one step closer toward feeling more responsible, more activated, more empowered. Which of your interventions would help him take that step?

TRAINEE 6: My intervention of asking him how he thought I was feeling would only make him feel worse, because it conveys I am feeling negatively about him.

TRAINEE 2: And mine would actually make him feel not heard. I heard him say he was hungry, but I was discounting it as an excuse. I think he might feel ignored or even controlled by my remark.

TRAINEE 1: I think my silence would be received by him as disapproval or lack of help. Perhaps he would get sad, if he thought I were mad. I think the question of "What would you like to do?" is the best one.

TRAINEE: Yes. Tell him its OK to get something to eat if this is what he feels he must do.

TRAINEE: But there's a danger in saying it that way. You don't want to say, "It's OK for you to get something to eat," because this would be giving him permission, like he was a kid. If the therapist did give permission, she would be reenacting the role of his domineering wife who calls the shots, and would be like everyone else who takes control.

LEVENSON: As you can see, not getting pulled into colluding with the patient, being a partner in the dysfunctional dance, is extremely difficult. But the therapist can figure out what the countertransferential pull is by relying on the dynamic focus. In Mr. Johnson's case, the behavior of others was described as others' taking care of him and making decisions for him. This knowledge should facilitate the therapist's awareness in the sessions and, therefore, make him or her more likely to recognize them as they are being reenacted. Giving permission to Mr. Johnson to go get some food would not only recapitulate his CMP; it would also dilute the new experience of his making a decision on his own behalf. Mr. Johnson's decision to get something to eat, knowing he has his therapist's approval, would be easier than the decision to go not knowing whether his therapist might be angry or disapproving. In the former case his decision would be less risky because it requires less of a shift from his usual and customary style, that is, he had explicit permission, even urging.

TRAINEE: But I am still uncomfortable about what happens if he decides to leave the session. If he retreats and this is where he has a problem, I can't see where replicating this will be of help. Especially if there is no time to examine what is going on with him.

LEVENSON: Have we identified Mr. Johnson's central problem as one of repeatedly leaving the field?

TRAINEE: No, not physically. But emotionally he avoids conflict with others.

LEVENSON: Well, let's talk about that. What would happen if he left the session?

TRAINEE: Well, he would be retreating from dealing with his upset in the session. We would be letting him off the hook.

TRAINEE: But he would be the one calling the shots of what to talk about or not. Not someone else.

LEVENSON: Yes, exactly. Our goal is for him to become active and empowered. What if his decision were to avoid my brilliant interpretations? What if he actively chose to avoid the therapy and the emotional discomfort that morning?

TRAINEE: He could be very assertive and leave therapy altogether!

LEVENSON: But how have we been conceptualizing this case? Leaving relationships is not Mr. Johnson's major dysfunction. In fact, he is the one who is afraid relationships will end. Another patient with a prominent commitment problem would have a different CMP; that patient's leaving would be a reenactment of his dysfunctional pattern and, therefore, would not be a desirable outcome in the session. However, leaving relationships is not a well-worn path for Mr. Johnson.

If you still believe that Mr. Johnson's central issue is abdicating responsibility and leaving decisions up to others without saying what he wants, then choose your goals and interventions accordingly. Once you have formulated a dynamic focus, you have to repeatedly reevaluate it in light of new information coming forth in the therapy. The dynamic focus is not written in concrete; its usefulness is heuristic. But before changing the focus (and correspondingly your goals), you would want substantial new data about the content and process of the patient's past relationships or about a different type of dysfunctional interaction occurring between the two of you. Sticking with a reasonable focus in brief therapy is perhaps one of the most difficult, but crucial, requirements for a successful outcome.

TRAINEE: Are you suggesting that it might be therapeutic for Mr. Johnson to leave the session?

LEVENSON: Yes. First of all, I see that Mr. Johnson is quite dependent on me as his therapist as he is on his family, so the chances are quite high that he would not leave therapy permanently at this stage. He would come back next week. Second, he would have an experience of himself as making a decision, with its accompanying anxiety and sense of risk-taking. And third, he would have the experience of the therapist as accepting his decision without becoming punitive or deserting him, or conversely, pressuring him to stay and talk about it.

TRAINEE: If the therapist takes either side, trying to get him to stay or suggesting he leave to get something to eat, she is taking responsibility, and colluding with the cyclical maladaptive pattern.

LEVENSON: True. If we say to him, "Oh, Mr. Johnson, you need something to eat, why don't you go get something," we are making a decision for him. If on the other hand we say to him, "Well, I know you say you are in distress because you haven't had something to eat, but let's talk about it because I think there are some other, more important, issues going on," the message is that the therapist knows what is best for him and does not believe or does not care that he is hungry. But if one asks, "What would you like to do?" Mr. Johnson is empowered to make his own decision.

TRAINEE: But you said you didn't believe that Mr. Johnson really needs something to eat; you think that his claiming he is hungry is a way for him to avoid talking about his feelings.

LEVENSON: Yes, I think that talking about how angry he feels toward his family for leaving him is extremely difficult for him. But if I as the therapist start arguing with him about whether or not he is *really* hungry, I end up getting hooked in to a power struggle. Again, the main goal is to provide a new experience that will make him feel more like an adult than a child.

We usually don't think of "good therapy" as involving the patient's leaving the session. But why not? If you have a dynamic focus with a clearly defined new experience, then you can judge what interventions will keep the two of you on target. Does this make sense?

TRAINEE: So if you only have a split second to think about what is happening in the session, you can run the focus through your mind, and then that would guide you?

LEVENSON: Exactly.

TRAINEE: Can we see what happened with the rest of the session?

LEVENSON: Sure.

[VIDEOTAPE]

Mr. Johnson: If I just got something in my stomach I would feel better.

Therapist: Uh huh. And what keeps you from getting something in your stomach right now?

Mr. Johnson: I'd have to go over to the restaurant, cafeteria over there. (points to next building)

Therapist: That's right.

Mr. Johnson: (sigh)

Therapist: And what would keep you from deciding to do that?

Mr. Johnson: (sigh) Well, the fact we're having a session, and I don't want to be rude.

Therapist: So rather than be rude, you'll sit there and be uncomfortable for the remainder of the hour.

Mr. Johnson: Well, I don't know. I guess so. Unless you'd let me go.

Therapist: Unless I'd let you go?

Mr. Johnson: (taken aback) Well, I feel obligated to come and see you, because you're helping me.

Therapist: (pause) Mr. Johnson, it seems you're faced with a dilemma. Right here, right now, with me in this room. And the dilemma is, Can you concentrate and really make use of the time, or do you need some food in you to be able to do that? Your dilemma is whether to take care of you or to take care of me.

[CLASSROOM]

LEVENSON: I didn't quite think that was his dilemma, but I thought that he could relate to the conflict better by phrasing it in this way. What I really thought was his struggle was that he thinks the only way to take care of himself is indirectly through taking care of others. Perhaps if he is submissive enough, people will tolerate him and might meet his needs somewhat. He sees his deference as the price he must pay to maintain a relationship.

TRAINEE: Yeah. He would not leave the session because he didn't want you to think he was rude.

TRAINEE: And if you thought he was rude, you'd be mad.

TRAINEE: And if you were mad, he'd be sad.

LEVENSON: Probably because it was a signal he was not going to get his needs met, and I might abandon him.

TRAINEE: I keep thinking of what it must have been like as a boy in a home with an unpredictable alcoholic father.

TRAINEE: You wouldn't want a drunk, violent father mad at you!

LEVENSON: So we can certainly begin to see how Mr. Johnson's passive, placating, but depressed, hopeless stance in life gets played out in the session. And you can appreciate the difficulties I am having in creating a new experience for him in this context.

TRAINEE: I notice that you still seem to be sarcastic several times during this session. Are you still frustrated with him?

LEVENSON: Yes. I am still immersed in reenacting my countertransference and, with growing awareness, trying to work my way out even as I attempt to move us toward a new experience of each other.

TRAINEE: So what happened? Did he stay in the session?

LEVENSON: Well, after the segment I just showed, Mr. Johnson just kept talking. He tried to avoid making an active decision in the room by simply continuing to talk. After listening to him for a couple of minutes, I interrupted him and said that I was not clear as to what his decision was—whether he had decided to stay or to get something to eat. Mr. Johnson said that he was feeling better and could stay, so we were able to finish the session.

I would have felt more secure in Mr. Johnson's truly having had a new experience if he had chosen to leave the session and taken a chance I would be displeased. This would have clearly been the riskier choice and a significant break with his familiar pattern. Nonetheless, he voiced a decision, and our interaction around the breakfast issue had raised the saliency of his customary way of denying his own needs in favor of what he thinks others want.

CHAPTER 11

Technique: Microanalysis of a Session

THE PRECEDING chapters concentrated on the major TLDP techniques of finding a focus and using that focus as a guide for creating a new experience and a new understanding. Now our attention turns to how to incorporate this time-limited, focused approach in an ongoing way as each session proceeds. To illustrate the use of TLDP in this manner, I show the opening of the fourth session with Mr. Johnson to the trainees. By microanalyzing this segment, I will demonstrate how to translate overall goals into specific interventions and formulations. Microanalysis has been used chiefly by researchers to discern what happens in the therapeutic process in a sentence-by-sentence, phrase-by-phrase fashion; it can also be an invaluable method of honing one's clinical skills.

[VIDEOTAPE]

Mr. Johnson: Julia, I mean Susan, told me that a couple of days ago, the restaurant where she was doing the night work closed up. They didn't have any business, so she asked me if she could borrow money to tide her over. And I said yes. Which I will do. I'll give her the money. But that means she's up against it. She has to pay pretty high rent for that share space she's in, $285. And I hate to see her without money.

Therapist: How do you feel about lending her the money?

This is one in a series of questions that I will ask Mr. Johnson about how he feels. We have already established that Mr. Johnson has considerable difficultly expressing his angry feelings. We have hypothesized that suppression of these feelings contributes to his depression. Therefore, while it might be important in any dynamically based therapy to inquire about the patient's feelings, it is particularly useful to do so here. I ask the trainees to anticipate how Mr. Johnson might reply.

Anticipation of what the patient might say or do allows the therapist to evaluate the appropriateness of the intervention (i.e., did it "work"?) and to assess one's understanding of the patient (i.e., could I predict what the patient will do?). A therapist who is able to predict the range of responses given by the patient gains confidence in the accuracy of the dynamic focus he or she has derived. As the therapist acquires a better understanding of the CMP, he or she can be thinking ahead about the next set of interventions. This planning and anticipation make the therapy more efficient and directed.

[CLASSROOM]

LEVENSON: Here I ask him how he feels about lending Susan the money. Any guesses as to what he is going to say?

TRAINEE: Well, he won't answer the question. I don't know how, but he will not answer. He'll avoid it.

LEVENSON: Well, that's a really good guess, given what we have seen with him so far.

TRAINEE: I think he'll say, "She really needs the money." He'll focus it on what his daughter needs. Her needs, not his.

LEVENSON: That certainly would fit with his dynamic focus—his attempting to get his needs met by meeting the needs of others around him.

TRAINEE: I think he'll say, "I feel like I have to do it." But I think deep down he'll be furious, because two sessions ago he talked about how he wanted his daughter to live with him. Not only is she borrowing money from him, but she's using it to live with someone else. She is taking his money for her independence.

This trainee has made an excellent observation. The trainee describes not only what Mr. Johnson might say, but also what he might be feeling. The trainee suggests that Mr. Johnson might be angry about Susan's taking his money for her independence, but that he would not share those feelings with the therapist.

[VIDEOTAPE]

Mr. Johnson: I don't mind lending her the money.

Therapist: Uh huh. But how do you feel about it?

[CLASSROOM]

LEVENSON: So he says he "doesn't mind." Your guesses as to what he might say were in the ball park. He doesn't directly say how he does feel—only how he doesn't feel. Although you have only seen snippets of this man's therapy, you are already predicting by the fourth session with more or less accuracy the range of responses you might get back. Because I still do not know what his feelings are, I ask him again for the second time.

[VIDEOTAPE]
Mr. Johnson: I just feel that I'll do it. That is, I'm willing to do it.
Therapist: I hear you're willing to, but I'm not sure how you feel about it.
Mr. Johnson: I hate to see her in a position where she needs money.

[CLASSROOM]
LEVENSON: OK, that's the third time I have tried to find out about his feelings. I have said to him, "How do you feel; but how do you feel; but I'm not sure how you feel." My rule of thumb concerning interventions is three tries and do something else. I have made no headway learning about Mr. Johnson's feelings directly, but I have considerable information about what he is willing or able to communicate to others. Now what I as the therapist can do is to examine the process that has evolved between us as I have attempted to learn about and understand his feelings.

TRAINEE: You have a guideline that you ask someone something three times and then you make a comment about the process? How did you come up with that?

Obviously there is nothing magical about three times, although the number 3 does appear frequently in mythology and religion, not to mention baseball. Three times gives a patient ample opportunity to respond. If you have asked something three times to no avail, you probably do not want to ask yet a fourth time. In this instance, I have asked him three times in pretty much the same way each time. Sometimes I vary the way I ask the question if I think a different phrasing would be helpful.

While I am still interested in Mr. Johnson's feelings, I am *more* interested in his manner of interacting with me—in this case, how he does not communicate his feelings.* In TLDP, the patient's manner of resisting usually has more implications for how that patient interacts with others than the origi-

---

*I am making the assumption here, based on my previous interactions with Mr. Johnson, that he is capable of relating his feelings but is afraid of doing so because of what he fears will be untoward consequences. The therapist, however, should be alert to the possibility that there are some patients who do not have affective and symbolic function available to them. This condition has been called *alexithymia* (Sifneos, 1973). "Although the alexithymic patient is able to be aware of emotions and to think, he seems unable to connect any

nal content he or she was avoiding expressing. The patient's way of resist-ing, to a large extent, determines his or her personality style. To escape what is feared, what is being defended against, becomes that person's characteris-tic mode of relating, which often leads to the dysfunctional interchanges with others.

What I am suggesting to the trainees is that after attempting to get at some affect directly several times, comment on the process. This procedure is very much in keeping with the TLDP approach. If you have asked a patient a number of times how he or she is feeling and you still do not know, you might share your observations with the patient—and try to collaborate with the patient in understanding his or her process in interacting with you.

> [VIDEOTAPE]
> *Therapist:* It's interesting when I ask you how you're feeling, it seems like, uh, that's a hard question for you to answer.

Here I make a very simple process statement. "When I ask you how you are feeling, you have a hard time answering." Now I am no longer asking how *he* feels, but rather commenting on *our* process—the interaction that is occurring between therapist and patient.

> [VIDEOTAPE]
> *Mr. Johnson:* Yeah, because I don't know what my feelings are most of the time. It's just I can't sift my feelings out. They are all mixed up.

[CLASSROOM]
LEVENSON: What would you do here?
TRAINEE: You don't want to wait and let him try? There might be some feelings he could talk about.
LEVENSON: So you might wait? What happens if he kind of sighs, takes off his glasses and looks forlorn? [Trainees acknowledge that these behaviors are likely.]
TRAINEE: You might suggest that maybe he could take a look at what some of the feelings are.
LEVENSON: And if he says, "But I don't know what they are"?

---

thoughts with his emotions. Thus he has an inability to experience feelings—a *feeling* being defined as 'biological emotion *plus* the thoughts which accompany it'" (Sifneos, 1987, p. 38). Because such patients have an impaired ability to recognize their feeling states, uncov-ering or anxiety-producing psychotherapies are usually contraindicated (Krystal, 1988; Taylor, Bagby, & Parker, 1991).

TRAINEE: You could say, "How do you think we could sift them out?" It would be collaborative.

LEVENSON: I think that using his language, "sift," and the introduction of "we" are excellent suggestions. Also your asking him the question of how this could be accomplished encourages him to be more active, which is our ultimate goal for him. Your intervention would encourage Mr. Johnson's having a new experience. The other thing I really like about your intervention is that you are taking him at face value.

This taking the patient at face value is part of taking the patient seriously. In the vignette on tape, Mr. Johnson has just said that he can't sift his feelings out. The trainee suggests saying, "How do you think we could sift them out?" The question implies, through the use of the patient's own words, that the therapist believes that the patient is having difficulties sifting out his feelings.

Sometimes therapists are uncomfortable with taking the patient seriously, because they feel like they will be seen as implicitly agreeing with the patient. In the case of Ms. Ludlow (chapter 5), for example, Dr. Ellison responded to a very critical comment by the patient ("Sometimes your questions, I can't believe you're that dumb!") by simply asking the patient what there was about her questions that seemed dumb. Dr. Ellison took the patient seriously; being dumb could be examined. There is a major difference between agreeing with patients' perceptions and communicating to them that you are going to work with their reality, or at least the level of reality they wish to put forth at that point.

[VIDEOTAPE, BACKING UP THE TAPE SLIGHTLY]

Mr. Johnson: Yeah, because I don't know what my feelings are most of the time. It's just I can't sift my feelings out. They are all mixed up.

Therapist: So why don't we clear away a little space so that maybe you could do a little sifting and unmixing.

[CLASSROOM]

TRAINEE: What about priming the pump? What about saying, "Some people might be upset or angry about lending money"? This might allow him to start talking about his feelings.

LEVENSON: For some patients, paving the road in this way might be necessary. It is particularly helpful for patients who have never made good connections between their feelings and ways to describe them to others. However, it can be risky to suggest feelings so directly to patients—especially passive ones like Mr. Johnson. Later on in the session I will do something very similar to what you suggest, though, because my more open-ended approaches were not succeeding.

Instead, at this point I suggest to Mr. Johnson that he might need "a little space" to figure out how he is feeling. In keeping with the goals of the therapy, I am trying to put the responsibility back on him. "Why don't you give yourself time to see how you are feeling?" I think he is conscious of his angry feelings, and is more censoring them in our interaction than unconsciously repressing them. But in any case, I am going to take him seriously that, for whatever reason, he is communicating that he does not know what he is feeling.

In this fourth session with Mr. Johnson I do struggle with a situation that is very common for therapists, when you know, feel, or intuit that there is something more going on than is being openly discussed. This differential between what is consciously acknowledged and unconscious dynamics or censored material is usually the focus for the therapeutic work. How can the patient have a new experience and come to realize what motivates his or her behaviors? From a TLDP perspective, Mr. Johnson is not being uncooperative or difficult. His presentation is not getting in the way of the clinical work—it *is* the work.

In my present situation with Mr. Johnson, I take his saying his feelings are "mixed up" seriously and my reply, I hope, conveys that I am prepared for us to devote some time and attention to "unmixing" his feelings. I use his words. I try to understand what he is saying. And I am willing to play it out with him.

Mr. Johnson could respond by becoming curious about these mixed-up feelings, and afford us the time to delve deeper into them. Or if he is quite fearful, my saying we could take some time to sift his feelings might make him feel even more anxious.

> [VIDEOTAPE]
> *Therapist:* You just seem to rush on, and maybe what you need is a little time to see what you're feeling. Could that be?
> *Mr. Johnson:* I really don't know. (sigh) All I know is that I'm mixed up.

> [CLASSROOM]
> LEVENSON: How does Mr. Johnson respond to my saying "Take your time"?
> TRAINEE: "I don't know. I'm mixed up."
> TRAINEE: It's not going to be possible.
> LEVENSON: And the tone of his voice?
> TRAINEE: He's subdued, defeated.

TRAINEE: More whiny.

LEVENSON: Yes. His voice gets weaker and more distressed. Here I said something, which some patients would feel as supportive, "Take your time," but he responds in a more pathetic and defensive manner. As a way to help him tune into what he does feel, I ask him to concentrate on his bodily sensations. Given that he often somaticizes his emotional pain, I am asking him to communicate in a way that is familiar to him.

[VIDEOTAPE]

Therapist: Mr. Johnson, you might want to just give yourself time to just shut off your mind, and see what your body feels like. How do you feel about lending Susan the money?

Mr. Johnson: Oh, I don't really know. I want her to earn a job, but she's working such long hours. That daytime job and that nighttime job. I don't see how she does it. (long pause) Right now, I just feel constipated.

[CLASSROOM]

TRAINEE: (laughing) It's a feeling!

LEVENSON: Yes, it's a feeling.

TRAINEE: That's amazing. It's so symbolic. He's stuck! He can't get his feelings out.

TRAINEE: Yeah, he is emotionally constipated. It's a great association!

TRAINEE: A 180-degree turn from where he was last week, when he came in after soiling himself because of the stool softener.

TRAINEE: This may be the indirect route to his emotions—his physical sensations.

TRAINEE: You asked him to see how his body is feeling and he gives you a bodily feeling.

LEVENSON: Yes. And we know already from the previous session, in which he wanted to be fed because he was hungry, that his physical feelings can provide striking metaphors for what is happening with him psychologically. So when he says to me here "I am constipated," I hear that on at least two levels—he is physiologically constipated, and psychologically, he is blocked also.

[VIDEOTAPE]

Mr. Johnson: I'm constipated most of the time and I have to take a stool softener.

Therapist: So it is easier for you to talk about your physical feelings [Yeah] than your emotional ones?

Here I acknowledge that he is letting me know how he does feel. And I make the interpretation that he is more comfortable talking about his bodily sensations than his emotional feelings, and he concedes this is so.

Mr. Johnson: Yeah, because I don't know my emotional feelings.
Therapist: Why do you suppose that is?

I have dropped the subject of how Mr. Johnson feels about lending Susan the money. Here when he says he does not know what his emotional feelings are, I ask him how he understands that—"Why do you suppose that is?" I have expressed some curiosity about the "whys" of his behavior. And so here we have a beginning inquiry into both his internal and interpersonal process; why he does not know his emotional feelings and, if he knows his feelings, why he does not tell me.

This technique of learning about what the patient is defending against involves exploration of defenses. At the beginning of this therapy segment, I was confronting his defenses by asking him three times how he was feeling. When such confrontational attempts are frustrated, the therapist often has the experience of hitting a wall. This wall often demarcates the patient's defensive maneuvers and defines the patient's cyclical maladaptive pattern.

Rather than continue to hit the wall in an attempt to break through it, the therapist can stand back, recognize the wall, and invite the patient to look at the wall also. What usually happens is that a different therapeutic scenario gets created—one with both patient and therapist standing on the same side of the wall, observing, and wondering why this structure exists. Such an intervention often avoids power plays and passive–aggressive behavior on the part of both therapist and patient, and can promote empathy and collaboration.

In addition, a therapist's exploration of the defense can often reduce a patient's anxiety. Since anxiety can inhibit one's awareness and flexibility, reducing a patient's anxiety may facilitate recognition of feelings that were previously unavailable for conscious report.

[REWINDING THE VIDEOTAPE SLIGHTLY]
Mr. Johnson: Yeah, because I don't know my emotional feelings.
Therapist: Why do you suppose that is?
Mr. Johnson: Because they've been hidden so long, they're deep down.

[CLASSROOM]

TRAINEE: That's interesting.

TRAINEE: He's aware of that!

TRAINEE: He starts off by saying, "I don't know," and then gives you an answer as to why he doesn't know. Why it is that he isn't aware, because his feelings have been stuffed way down.

LEVENSON: So there has been a shift; the situation gets clearer. He has used the word *hidden*, which takes it out of the realm of some kind of mysterious haze and into an area that is defined, but private. OK, so what would you do here? He's said his feelings have been hidden.

TRAINEE: I might ask him why they've been hidden.

TRAINEE: I think that is a good direction. If someone has hidden feelings, they are hidden for a reason.

TRAINEE: You could ask him how come, or you could ask him what feelings might be hidden.

[VIDEOTAPE]

Therapist: So they are down there, but they're hidden. Even from you. Do you think maybe there's a good reason to keep them hidden, from your point of view?

I decided to raise the issue of "a good reason" because often patients believe that keeping something hidden is bad; that being unconscious of something or withholding something is a sign of being uncooperative. They fear that their therapists will be displeased, condemning, or incited to delve deeper.

Instead, the therapist can be curious about the "why" of a behavior. The therapist can exhibit an interested attitude about understanding a particular feeling or behavior. "Let's take a look at why this might be just the thing you should do, before we attempt to change it." "Perhaps there is a good reason from your point of view why your feelings should stay buried." "In my experience most people do not behave irrationally."

Also, inquiring about a good reason for a patient's behavior conveys a supportive stance: "You have not been acting ineptly." "Perhaps what you are doing made sense at some point in the past." Usually patients are very surprised to hear that there might be a good adaptive reason for what they have assumed are their negative and stupid behaviors or attitudes. Patients often feel supported by their therapists' seeking to understand the complexity of their motivations. Since Mr. Johnson is so ready to condemn himself for being wrong, I thought that this approach of respecting his internal wisdom could help curb his own self-critical attitude.

[CLASSROOM]

TRAINEE: It also puts an element of choice and control back into his life. I had a patient who felt he was self-destructive because he did not study for his college exams and consequently failed them. When we tried to figure out what he might be gaining from failing his classes, he felt more in control. He said other therapists had tried to come up with techniques for dealing with his procrastination, rather than understanding what psychological function it served.

TRAINEE: Also it seems that this refocusing is a way for Mr. Johnson to have some empathy for himself.

LEVENSON: I think those are very important points. As I have said, in a brief therapy, supporting the strengths of the patient is critical. Let's return to our video. I have asked him whether there is a good reason for keeping his feelings hidden—what I hope will be seen as a positive, supportive intervention.

TRAINEE: I think he'll respond passively.

[VIDEOTAPE]

Mr. Johnson: (pathetically and immediately) I don't know.

[CLASSROOM]

LEVENSON: Listen to the tone of his voice. So here we hear him as being even *more* doleful. "I don't know," said in a meek, plaintive voice. I feel like I have lost ground. He almost sounds like he is on the verge of tears.

TRAINEE: He responded so quickly to your question. He hasn't taken the time to even think about what you have said.

LEVENSON: That also is an excellent point. Often patients will tell us something reflexively, almost automatically. That they are not giving themselves time to even consider what we are saying can be a clue to understanding their defensive stance.

I am beginning to see my interaction with Mr. Johnson as one in which I am pulled to say something supportive with the intent of bolstering his feeble self-esteem, but in response to my support he becomes even more helpless and woeful-sounding. However, I do not want to respond to the opposite pull, prodding him or browbeating him into becoming more assertive. This is often how others end up responding to him, out of their frustration with his passivity. So I am in a bind. Realizing that my interventions thus far were not giving Mr. Johnson a new experience or a new understanding, I decided to try something educative as a way to give him permission to go further.

[VIDEOTAPE]

Therapist: Sometimes people keep feelings hidden, from even themselves, because the feelings might be disturbing to them, frightening
to them, make them feel anxious. Do you think you could be having
some feelings about lending Susan the money that might make you
feel uncomfortable if you got in touch with them?

[CLASSROOM]

LEVENSON: I am attempting to educate Mr. Johnson and perhaps invite
him to explore his feelings. Here I do supply a range of possible feelings
for him.

TRAINEE: At this point are you doing what he wanted you to do—sup-
plying him with feelings?

LEVENSON: I don't know. That's a danger here—colluding with his dysfunctional pull to get me to be his caretaker—to fill in the blanks for him.
Let's see how he responds to this educative intervention.

[VIDEOTAPE]

Mr. Johnson: (barely audible, head hung) I don't know.

[CLASSROOM]

[Much head nodding and talk from the trainees as Mr. Johnson responds
in the dejected manner they had predicted, and they identify with my
frustration as the therapist]

LEVENSON: So when I make another supportive intervention, this time in
an educative fashion, he becomes even more forlorn.

TRAINEE: Well, even before you got to the final part of it when you were
putting out the proposition that he could be feeling something because
his daughter wants the money from him, his head dropped down and a
half-mumbled "I don't know" came out.

TRAINEE: There is something withholding about him in this interaction
with you. You would like him to reveal some of his emotions, and he is
not doing that.

TRAINEE: He is not able to tell you about his feelings about giving something to someone else, but in the transaction you are saying, "Give me
something. Give me something to work with."

LEVENSON: I think that is an interesting point. So you see there might be
some parallel process going on here, where he does not want to give to
me what I am asking for, any more than he wants to give his daughter
what she is asking for. In fact, if he could say to me, "You know, I don't
want to talk about this," in an up-front way, rather than in this passive,

withholding manner, I would see that as a positive step. I would then try to respond to such a statement in a manner to acknowledge that forthrightness, that assertiveness. On the surface, this might look like a very strange therapy, where in essence I would be reinforcing Mr. Johnson for telling me he doesn't want to talk about these conflicts. However, since our goal is for him to be able to say what he needs and run the risk that the other person might not like what he has to say, this would be an important step forward.

TRAINEE: You would be trying to give him another new experience.

LEVENSON: Yes. I have been trying to give him new experiences all the way throughout this transaction. So I am running out of things to do here. What would you do as his therapist?

TRAINEE: You've been carrying the ball and have come up with the agenda to help him figure out his feelings. I would want to have him take more of the lead.

TRAINEE: You could comment on the process, pointing out that the more the two of you proceed on this topic, the weaker he becomes.

LEVENSON: Yes, I like your suggestion of returning to the process between us. When stuck, you always have the process to talk about.

There are different ways of talking about the process, just as there are different levels of interpretation. In making process statements there is a range of possibilities, from the very descriptive to the very inferential.

At this point in my work with Mr. Johnson I want to make an observation about the process at the most surface level, because if I start using words like *weak* or *helpless*, they will reinforce his negative self-evaluation. He will hear me as ridiculing him or finding fault with him. So my process comment will be at a descriptive level—just observing externally what I see. In this way I hope to avert his supersensitivity to being blamed.

[VIDEOTAPE]

Therapist: Mr. Johnson, I notice that when I ask you these kinds of questions, you tear up and your voice gets a little quivery. Do you notice that, too?

Mr. Johnson: Mm hmm.

[CLASSROOM]

LEVENSON: Here I did not give him a feeling. Instead, I described his behaviors which conveyed to me how he was feeling. "You tear up and your voice gets a little quivery." I'm not putting any labels on that. I am not calling him resistant or avoidant or passive–aggressive. I am not saying what his behavior means, just here is what I see. I am bending over backwards at this point not to say anything that could be interpreted as blaming, because I have become very aware of my proclivity to do so.

In addition, I am hoping that if I could comment on something very obvious, Mr. Johnson would be able to agree with me, and we would have a foundation on which to go further. I ask Mr. Johnson whether he notices these small behaviors. He murmurs he does, allowing us to take the next small step. If he were unaware of how he were responding, then I would need to retreat from my present goal and work on helping him become a better observer of his own behavior. I would need to do this before I could link his behaviors to something else.

Perhaps one of the more common mistakes I see therapists make in trying to use TLDP is putting forth major interpretations concerning the transference relationship before sufficient groundwork has been laid. Such groundwork includes illuminating for the patient the details of the give-and-take nature of the patient–therapist interaction. This is illustrated by my drawing a link between my supportive interventions and Mr. Johnson's woebegone behavior.

[VIDEOTAPE]

Therapist: What are you feeling at those moments when your voice gets quivery and you tear up when I ask you these questions?

[CLASSROOM]

Levenson: It is true I am asking about feelings again, but now I am asking about feelings associated with particular behaviors of his in the here-and-now. Specifically, I am asking him what he feels when he is being resistant—only I frame it in terms of his behavior. I would like him to become more curious about his own behaviors as markers for understanding his own feelings and the effect he has on others.

[VIDEOTAPE]

Mr. Johnson: I can't really explain it. I just wanna keep them, keep them h-h-hidden, and not talk about them.

[CLASSROOM]

Levenson: What is Mr. Johnson saying here?

Trainee: He said the feelings are hidden.

Levenson: But how did he say this?

TRAINEE: He kind of stuttered.

LEVENSON: Yes, I noted that in the session. This is a man who usually doesn't stutter, but for this fleeting moment there is a dysfluency. Let me play this segment over one more time. There is a key word in his reply. What would be that word?

[I REPLAY THE SAME SEGMENT OF VIDEOTAPE]

Mr. Johnson: I can't really explain it. I just wanna keep them, keep them h-h-hidden, and not talk about them.

[CLASSROOM]

TRAINEE: Want?

TRAINEE: He said it very quietly.

TRAINEE: Yeah, but he said it.

TRAINEE: He's saying something active for a change! It's the first time he's said what he wants.

LEVENSON: Yes. It is critical for the therapist to hear that Mr. Johnson used the word *want*, because this is a man who usually does not say "I want." When you initially recalled what he said, you heard his statement as he usually might say it—in the passive voice—"the feelings are hidden." But in actuality, he makes his statement in the active voice, "I *want* to keep the feelings hidden, and not talk about them." So he has just made this statement, albeit a bit hesitatingly. Now what might you say?

TRAINEE: To acknowledge—"Well, you're saying you want to keep them hidden and here I am asking you what they are; I wonder if you have some mixed feelings about that."

LEVENSON: So bring it into the interpersonal, here-and-now dialogue between therapist and patient. Sounds good.

TRAINEE: I would acknowledge the confusion. "You said something I didn't quite understand; it got kind of mixed up. Can you step back and try to say it again and figure out what you were trying to say?"

LEVENSON: I might not do that, because I liked what he said from a new-experience point of view. He was being assertive. And I would want to capitalize on it, and not give him the chance of taking it back so quickly.

I am constantly judging what goes on in the therapy in terms of the goals for the therapy. What is the new experience we would like Mr. Johnson to have? What is the new understanding? In developing Mr. Johnson's CMP, I formulated that Mr. Johnson's new experience should include his taking steps to be more active, decisive, and assertive—to take risks in letting people know his wants and needs. Mr. Johnson's CMP served as a focus that sensitized me to hearing such assertive remarks. I was, therefore, primed and ready to capitalize on this statement when I heard it.

In the fourth session, he has let me, his therapist, know that he wants to keep his feelings hidden. While the patient's manner was faltering, and certainly not forceful or definitive, the therapist should appreciate the change from his baseline style. It is a step in the right direction, and in TLDP these steps, and not some finished product, are our target. Let's return to the classroom and see how the trainees would handle the remainder of this vignette.

[CLASSROOM]

TRAINEE: I might try to make an empathic statement to kind of hold him here, because he is having more affect than before.

LEVENSON: Yes, I too would want to hold him here. I don't want him to slide away to the point where he might forget what he just said. So holding him here might allow him to hear what he said and help him to wrestle with his own competing fears and wishes—the wish to be his own person and the fear he will be punished for doing so.

TRAINEE: If he could go a little further, you might ask him what bothers him so much about what he has said.

LEVENSON: What I do is much simpler. But maybe I would get to that place eventually.

[VIDEOTAPE]

Mr. Johnson: I can't really explain it. I just wanna keep them, keep them h-h-hidden, and not talk about them. (pause) I don't know what my feelings are.

Therapist: I think you are saying something very important. You're saying you *want* to keep the feelings hidden.

[CLASSROOM]

LEVENSON: What I do is underline that part of what he has said which represents his shift toward a more assertive stance.

In this excerpt from the fourth session, we have heard Mr. Johnson go from "I don't know what my feelings are" to "They're hidden" to "I want to keep them hidden." This last statement is very different for him, since it involves his saying what he wants. I would like for him to recognize what he has said: he "wants"—no longer this vague, beyond-his-grasp situation in which he is a helpless victim. He *wants* to keep his feelings hidden.

Even more important than realizing what he has said is that Mr. Johnson experience the aftermath of his direct statement to another person. He does not want to talk about his feelings. Will I chastise him? Isn't he, after all, in therapy to discuss his feelings? Will I declare him uncooperative and terminate the therapy? Will my feelings be hurt?

To learn how to maximize their therapeutic impact within specific time limits, therapists can profit greatly from analyzing their own sessions phrase by phrase. Therapists who do not have access to videotape equipment can audiotape their own sessions. Another useful endeavor is to microprocess colleagues' tapes. Transcripts of actual therapy sessions that have been published in various journals and books can be very useful. Fortunately, with disciplined practice, this kind of acute line-by-line awareness becomes more automatic, and therapists are able to take in larger gestalts to understand where they are in the process and where they need to go.

Toward the end of this same fourth session, Mr. Johnson again complained that he was constipated. He mentioned that he had a stool softener in his car and broached the subject of terminating the session early to take it. Objectively speaking, in terms of Mr. Johnson's comfort level, it would not have made much difference if he took the stool softener immediately or when our session ended in 15 minutes. But subjectively, this seemed like a big step for Mr. Johnson—to suggest that his needs might come before what he might see as my needs to have him remain in the session.

In the third session, described in chapter 10, Mr. Johnson decided not to leave the session to get something to eat. In the fourth session, Mr. Johnson's saying that he wanted to leave the session to take the stool softener appeared to be a test to see whether I really would let him go early. I was encouraged by Mr. Johnson's direct statement of what he wanted to do. Here was another opportunity in the therapy for him to make a decision that might go counter to the wants and needs of others (namely, his therapist). I told Mr. Johnson that since he had decided to leave the session early, I would see him at our usual time next week. For readers who wish to see the contextual flow of the microanalyzed transcript, it is reproduced in its entirety as follows:

[VIDEOTAPE]

Mr. Johnson: Julia, I mean Susan, told me that a couple of days ago, the restaurant where she was doing the night work closed up. They didn't have any business, so she asked me if she could borrow money to tide her over. And I said yes. Which I will do. I'll give her the money. But that means she's up against it. She has to pay pretty high rent for that share space she's in, $285. And I hate to see her without money.

Therapist: How do you feel about lending her the money?

Mr. Johnson: I don't mind lending her the money.

Therapist: Uh huh. But how do you feel about it?

Mr. Johnson: I just feel that I'll do it. That is, I'm willing to do it.

Therapist: I hear you're willing to, but I'm not sure how you feel about it.

Mr. Johnson: I hate to see her in a position where she needs money.

Therapist: It's interesting when I ask you how you're feeling, it seems like, uh, that's a hard question for you to answer.

Mr. Johnson: Yeah, because I don't know what my feelings are most of the time. It's just I can't sift my feelings out. They are all mixed up.

Therapist: So why don't we clear away a little space so that maybe you could do a little sifting and unmixing. You just seem to rush on, and maybe what you need is a little time to see what you're feeling. Could that be?

Mr. Johnson: I really don't know. (sigh) All I know is that I'm mixed up.

Therapist: Mr. Johnson, you might want to just give yourself time to just shut off your mind, and see what your body feels like. How do you feel about lending Susan the money?

Mr. Johnson: Oh, I don't really know. I want her to earn a job, but she's working such long hours. That daytime job and that nighttime job. I don't see how she does it. (long pause) Right now, I just feel constipated. I'm constipated most of the time and I have to take a stool softener.

Therapist: So it is easier for you to talk about your physical feelings [Yeah] than your emotional ones?

Mr. Johnson: Yeah, because I don't know my emotional feelings.

Therapist: Why do you suppose that is?

Mr. Johnson: Because they've been hidden so long, they're deep down.

Therapist: So they are down there, but they're hidden. Even from you. Do you think maybe there's a good reason to keep them hidden, from your point of view?

Mr. Johnson: (pathetically and immediately) I don't know.

Therapist: Sometimes people keep feelings hidden, from even themselves, because the feelings might be disturbing to them, frightening to them, make them feel anxious. Do you think you could be having some feelings about lending Susan the money that might make you feel uncomfortable if you got in touch with them?

Mr. Johnson: (barely audible, head hung) I don't know.

Therapist: Mr. Johnson, I notice that when I ask you these kinds of questions, you tear up and your voice gets a little quivery. Do you notice that, too?

Mr. Johnson: Mm hmm.

Therapist: What are you feeling at those moments when your voice gets quivery and you tear up when I ask you these questions?

Mr. Johnson: I can't really explain it. I just wanna keep them, keep them h-h-hidden, and not talk about them. (pause) I don't know what my feelings are.

Therapist: I think you are saying something very important. You're saying you *want* to keep the feelings hidden.

CHAPTER 12

Termination Issues

TERMINATION IN BRIEF THERAPY can be a particularly difficult time for both patient and therapist. If termination is handled poorly, the previous therapeutic work can be undone. Thus it is quite dismaying that so little emphasis is placed on helping trainees recognize and deal with termination issues. Numerous training experiences related to the initial session abound (e.g., intakes, evaluations, triage); however, I have yet to hear of a clinic termination-team meeting where last sessions with patients are discussed. Similarly, I am no longer surprised to hear that many trainees (even those almost finished with their education) have never seen the beginning, middle, and planned ending of one case. Several writers have commented on the dearth of clinical literature and empirical research concerning the termination phase of treatment (Levinson, 1977; Weddington & Cavenar, 1979).

Since TLDP is based on an interpersonal model, with roots in attachment theory and object relations, issues of loss are interwoven through the therapy and do not appear just in the termination phase. As termination approaches, one can expect to see the patient's anxiety handled in ways characteristic for that particular patient's CMP. The best advice for the TLDP therapist is to stay with the dynamic focus and the goals for treatment, while examining how these patterns are evidenced when loss and separation issues are most salient.

Mr. Johnson was seen for 20 sessions. The number of sessions was set in advance, and Mr. Johnson was told of the termination date in his second session. In this chapter I present several segments from my last session with him to illustrate some of the issues that emerge in the termination phase of a brief treatment.

I had formulated that Mr. Johnson was a very passive man, in part due to the inhibition of his feelings, especially anger. According to his CMP (see chapter 8), Mr. Johnson feared that if he expressed his anger toward people, they would reject or hurt him. Since such rejection would be devastating for Mr. Johnson, he learned to be placating—swallowing his anger instead of expressing it. In the treatment, my goal was to provide a new experience in which Mr. Johnson could become more active and begin to take some control over his life. I had reasoned that one way to encourage Mr. Johnson's sense of empowerment was to be receptive to his expressing his feelings in general, and his anger in particular.

In order to place the last session in context, it is particularly important to know what transpired in the sixth session and 2 weeks prior to our last session. In the sixth session, Mr. Johnson began by talking once again about being constipated. He had deduced that his constipation was caused by the antidepressant medication he was taking—a reasonable conclusion, since constipation *is* a common side effect of tricyclic antidepressants. He claimed he had never been informed that he had to take a stool softener every day to cope with this problem. Since his medications were being managed by a consulting psychiatrist, I could have easily said, "Well, look, I'm not responsible for your medication. You'll have to speak to the psychiatrist and let him know."

I did not do that, however, because I noted Mr. Johnson was somewhat irritated about having been kept on a constipating medication. When I heard his annoyed tone emerge, I did everything possible not to close off his anger, consistent with my goal for the therapy. Could Mr. Johnson get angry with me and experience my not retaliating nor being destroyed as he feared significant other people in his life would?

Therefore, when Mr. Johnson complained about being kept on a constipating antidepressant, I asked him, "What is it like having me, who is managing your case, keeping you in discomfort?" With further inquiry, Mr. Johnson was able to express some anger toward me. He did not become rageful or even irate, but he was able to maintain an irritated stance for most of the session. Given his difficulty even being mildly annoyed with someone directly, I considered his being openly displeased with me as quite a significant step for him.

In evaluating what is an adequate new experience for a particular patient, the therapist needs to take into account the patient's baseline level of responding and the context of the therapy situation. For Mr. Johnson's inhibited, passive–dependent style, his expressing his upset concerning the medication regimen was a major step in the therapy. Later in the therapy, Mr. Johnson and I processed that sixth session. He confided that he really thought I was going to throw him out of therapy at that time, because I would not be able to tolerate his complaints. He was feeling very dependent on me, since his children were becoming quite frustrated with him and he was relying on me for understanding and attention. The idea that he might get angry with me, a person on whom he was becoming increasingly reliant, was very frightening. The fact that he could be upset with me and I did not dismiss him from therapy truly created a new experience for him.

However, I do not want to give the impression that in TLDP the therapist tries to create that *one* new experience which realigns the patient's affective and cognitive world. Rather, new experiences should be encountered throughout the therapy—sometimes as almost imperceptible nuances embedded in the relationship context. In our long-term follow-up study of patients who have received TLDP (Bein et al., 1994), many patients talked about their therapies as having provided opportunities for them to relate in new and healthier ways to their therapists. Rarely do they mention just one critical new experience. It should be noted that our research has indicated that patients feel they benefit more from their therapies the more the therapist has provided such opportunities for them.

During most of the time I had been seeing Mr. Johnson, he had been living with his son Ward, Ward's girlfriend, Jean, and the cat who sprayed in his bedroom. He found living there difficult. A search for a new living situation, with help from inpatient placement services, resulted in Mr. Johnson's moving into a house owned by two elderly women. These women were interested in having an older man live with them—a man who could drive, shop for groceries, mow the lawn, and do other assorted tasks. Two weeks prior to our last session, Mr. Johnson had moved to his new home.

Mr. Johnson and I had an unplanned tapering of our sessions toward the end of the therapy. He was on vacation for a week, and then I was. In our last session I had a four-part agenda. First, I wanted to catch up on what had happened to him in the time since I had last seen him, especially his new living situation. Second, we needed to say our good-byes and process our affective reactions to ending. Third, we continued our work together to make every session count, even the last. And fourth, since this was my first case that followed the TLDP model, I was interested in Mr. Johnson's feedback as to what was helpful about the therapy and what was not; what he got out of it; and what meaning it had for him.

[VIDEOTAPE]

Mr. Johnson: I'm fine, and I know that I'm going to be there, you know, to stay.

Therapist: Right.

Mr. Johnson: It's the uncertainty about things.

Therapist: Now, this feels like home.

Mr. Johnson: Yeah, it does. It really does. Susan came down to visit me the other day, and I was mowing the lawn, and she had to mow—she wanted to mow. So she pushed the lawn mower for a while.

Therapist: How's she doing?

Mr. Johnson: She's doing OK. She's working. She got a raise at the store. So she plans to stay. Although they don't have a pension plan, and she's not worried about that right now. As long as she got that raise.

Therapist: Uh huh. She's kind of young to worry about a pension plan.

Mr. Johnson: Yeah, she was a little bit concerned, though. And Julia [older daughter] is fine. She's installing alarm systems around the area. She's working for a different company now.

Therapist: Oh.

Mr. Johnson: And she's actually doing better, she says, than she did with Western Alarm.

Therapist: Uh huh.

Mr. Johnson: So she's doing fine, and Ward moved to St. Clair, and he's close to his job.

Therapist: Uh huh.

Mr. Johnson: And I'm not around Jean.

Therapist: Uh huh. Uh huh.

Mr. Johnson: Because . . . (pause) well, you know about that. So it's going OK.

Therapist: And Henry [younger son]?

Mr. Johnson: Henry's fine—he drives to Easton to the university. And I see the kids. I just took a trip with Henry and Dawn and the kids down near Margate.

Therapist: Uh huh.

Mr. Johnson: Then Henry and his friend went hunting. It's a hunting area, but it was at a real nice campsite down there. And we just sat around the swimming pool, playing with the kids, and his wife, Dawn, and I played with the kids in the swimming pool. And they went hunting. Things are just—my life feels so much better.

This segment succinctly shows how when one person in the system (Mr. Johnson) changes, the other people (in this case, his children) shift also. Now that Mr. Johnson was feeling less depressed and anxious, his children were more eager to get involved with him. Their increased interest further reinforced the positive changes Mr. Johnson was already making. For a brief therapy to be successful, such a ripple effect is essential. The therapeutic work needs to continue after the sessions have ended.

[VIDEOTAPE]

Therapist: Yes. I'm glad to hear that you're doing so well.

Mr. Johnson: Oh, I just feel . . . (drifts off, choking back tears).

Therapist: You got a little teary there.

Mr. Johnson: (tearful) Well, I'm . . . (takes a deep breath). I'm back in the good graces of my kids and all that and that's fine. (pause)

Therapist: But?

Mr. Johnson: (swallows deeply, and pauses)

Therapist: (softly) It's OK. Take your time.

Mr. Johnson: (takes a deep breath, and then sobbing) I just feel very grateful to . . . to you.

Therapist: Hard to think about saying good-bye?

Mr. Johnson: Huh?

Therapist: Hard to think about saying good-bye?

Mr. Johnson: (brightening) Yeah. You've helped me so much.

Therapist: Seems like you've also helped yourself a whole lot. You really took a lot of risks in here.

Mr. Johnson: (smiling) Yeah, I think I have. But I said the very same thing to Julia, how grateful I was for her help.

Therapist: Mmmhhh.

Mr. Johnson: And she said just what you just said, that she knows that I helped myself a whole lot.

Therapist: Uh huh. There would have been no way I could have helped you unless you let me.

Mr. Johnson: Yeah.

Therapist: Unless you took a chance on me. And on your own feelings. Remember how angry you got [Uh huh] at me, and you let it out here.

Mr. Johnson: Yeah. I'm really . . . I'm very grateful to the nurses in the inpatient unit also. And the nurse, Wally, he was a wonderful guy. He usually was very patient with me. And the doctors too, you know.

Therapist: Uh huh.

Mr. Johnson: I'm grateful to everybody. Now I'm sure I've got the strength now to go on by myself.

Therapist: (nodding) I'm sure you do.

Mr. Johnson: You feel that way, too. Don't you?

Therapist: Yes, I do. You can tell? Yeah?

Mr. Johnson: Yeah.

[A bit later in the same session]

Therapist: Do you have any idea what went on in here with the two of us that helped?

Mr. Johnson: You understood me. You were very patient. You are very patient. I used to leave meetings with you, and for an hour or two, I'd be thinking about exactly what we talked about.

Therapist: Uh huh.

Mr. Johnson: And I realized you were always trying to get me to assert myself.

Therapist: Uh huh.

Mr. Johnson: Not withdraw, but assert myself, because it was the honest thing to do, in the therapy, and I had that right to do that.

Therapist: Uh huh.

Mr. Johnson: But I always withdrew from that right to do it. [Uh huh] I had this kind of subservient attitude about myself, but I'm gettin' over that. (smiles broadly) And that's what you gave me. You certainly are perceptive, because you saw what my fault was, and I didn't know. Over there at the hospital, Dr. Samuelson and everyone—they're very busy all the time. And so they had meetings with me like once a week, but it isn't the same as seeing you.

Therapist: So there's something about my being patient that seemed to help?

Mr. Johnson: Yeah, that and the fact that you knew what was wrong with me. And I knew that you knew.

Therapist: Uh huh. You came in with a certain understanding.

Mr. Johnson: Well, I never really knew it was anger. I used to think it was self-pity, you know, when I'd get into trouble before.

Therapist: I see.

Mr. Johnson: And I used to think I was indulging in self-pity. And then you started drawing out of me the fact that for years I'd been angry at my father, especially on weekends when he'd stay drunk. You know, sittin' down at the dinner table and I had to go through this thing of trying to ignore his drunkenness. And I know now that I just got in this habit of getting very angry inside and then keeping it in.

In this passage, we see a good illustration of how Mr. Johnson has learned a new narrative about his life. He commented on his previous way of understanding his behavior ("indulging in self-pity") and contrasted this with his present understanding ("getting very angry inside and then keeping it in"). Helping someone to have a different understanding of his or her life is a critical factor in a successful dynamic therapy.

This segment also shows how important the family-of-origin work is in enabling this patient to view his present interactional style as stemming from a childhood adaptation to a difficult and threatening home life. Although TLDP puts much emphasis on current interpersonal relationships, it is crucial that patients come to understand the important function such styles served in the past. In this way they can avoid pathologizing their present behavior (e.g., Mr. Johnson's seeing his dysfunctional pattern as "this habit"), and appreciate how anachronistic it is, given present circumstances and potentials.

[VIDEOTAPE]

Mr. Johnson: And the anger against the landlord, who evicted me. And the anger against Jean for being there in place of Susan. All those things, all those angers.

Therapist: Not to mention your wife.

Mr. Johnson: Yeah. Anger against my wife.

Therapist: And me, too. For having you on that medication [Yeah, right] that gave you constipation.

Mr. Johnson: That wasn't a big anger. That was . . .

Therapist: It was an important anger between us.

Mr. Johnson: Yeah, I know.

Therapist: Because you took a risk that I might throw you out of therapy, right?

Mr. Johnson: Uh huh.

Therapist: You didn't know what was going to happen when we got into it.

Mr. Johnson: No, I didn't. But I knew either you or the doctor or maybe Wally, the nurse, told me that one of the side effects was constipation.

Therapist: Uh huh.

Mr. Johnson: I knew that. But he didn't say anything about it's very necessary that you take this stool softener every day.

Therapist: Uh huh.

Mr. Johnson: I was taking a stool softener, but I got so loose from it, you know, that I just, I said to the nurse that "I don't think I'll take it today, because it makes me awfully loose." And he didn't say anything about that I should stay on it. But I was getting awfully loose, and so I cut it out for 2 or 3 days, and, all of a sudden, I find myself unable to go. You know, it's that kind of thing.

We can see that Mr. Johnson still gets preoccupied with his somatic symptoms. Clearly, this brief therapy did not result in a total personality transformation. In fact, in this TLDP I did not focus at all on Mr. Johnson's proclivity to express distress somatically. It was one of the many specific areas I "benignly neglected." Most likely in a longer-term therapy his psychological use of physical symptoms would have been addressed more thoroughly.

Despite the side effect of constipation, Mr. Johnson clearly did receive symptomatic benefit from the antidepressant medication that was begun in the inpatient unit. In brief therapy, as in long-term therapy, the most common approach to treating patients with major mental illness is therapy with a nonmedical therapist combined with medications prescribed and monitored by a physician (Beitman & Maxim, 1984; Chiles, Carlin, Benjamin, & Beitman, 1991). This parallel treatment, or treatment triangle, as it is called, is becoming more common for a variety of reasons, such as the increasing demand for mental health services, advances in the effectiveness of certain psychoactive medications, and the growth of managed health care plans that usually seek the least expensive provider for psychotherapy (Kelly, 1992).

In TLDP there is no theoretical reason not to use appropriate psychotropic medication when warranted. In my supervision of the TLDP therapies of hundreds of patients, over half were receiving some type of pharmacotherapy, usually prescribed by a psychiatrist in the context of a medication clinic. My experience of the synergistic effects of medication is similar to that reported by Myrna Weissman and Gerald Klerman (1991) for the effectiveness of another model of brief interpersonal psychotherapy for depression. Looking at a number of studies, they concluded that medication (usually tricyclic antidepressants) had a positive effect on patients' likelihood and capacity to benefit from their short-term therapies.

The interested reader is referred to Beitman and Klerman (1991) on the issues involved in the integration of pharmacotherapy and psychotherapy in general, and to Kisch (1991) and Sovner (1991) for descriptions of various collaborative models within HMOs specifically. Unfortunately, there is an absence of theoretical and empirical studies examining what happens when a brief psychotherapy ends and the medication monitoring continues.

[VIDEOTAPE]

Therapist: Well, I know you said it was a little anger, but I really saw it as a turning point in our work together.

Mr. Johnson: I think it was. I think it was. But I mean, it's a little anger compared to all the other big angers I've had.

Therapist: But it was important as far as we were concerned.

Mr. Johnson: Yeah.

Therapist: Not as big an anger as toward your father or toward your wife. I understand that. I understand that.

Mr. Johnson: (smiling) Well, I'm a little amused, because you're not the kind of a person people get angry at, really. I mean really angry, because you're too patient and understanding.

Therapist: Mmmhh. Well, I wasn't at the beginning of our work.

Mr. Johnson: Huh?

Therapist: I wasn't at the beginning of our work. Do you remember?

Mr. Johnson: Uh huh.

Therapist: I was pretty much on your case. You know, I've looked back at some of the videotapes [Uh huh] that we've done, and I see myself as kind of—it surprises me to see myself like that, to tell you the truth—but it seemed like I was talking to you like you were a child at times. [Yeah.] Kind of pushing you here, pushing you there. I don't know if you felt that.

Mr. Johnson: I felt that. I felt those things happening, but I knew that you were trying to make me see a point.

Therapist: Uh huh?

Mr. Johnson: And that was that I better stand up and get angry.

Therapist: Uh huh.

Mr. Johnson: Learn to get angry.

Therapist: Uh huh.

Mr. Johnson: I knew that's what you were doing was teaching me to learn to get angry.

Therapist: Uh huh.

Mr. Johnson: An honest anger.

Therapist: So that by my coming across like that, it gave you permission [Yeah] to get angry with me? It was easier to be angry with me [Yeah] if I was gonna be pushy?

Mr. Johnson: Yeah. Uh huh. I remember you being impatient with me several times.

Therapist: (nodding) Uh huh. Uh huh.

In this segment we see Mr. Johnson's tendency to be placating and ingratiating emerge in the context of a sincere appreciation of my patience and understanding. The brief therapy has not eradicated his proclivity to avoid conflict. However, with my mentioning my brusque, take-charge behavior, Mr. Johnson was able to acknowledge my impatience. Nonetheless, he framed it in a helpful, well-intentioned context—that I was trying to make him see a point, that he was entitled to "honest anger."

[VIDEOTAPE]

Mr. Johnson: And, you know, you didn't say this, but you said, "Frank, get off the . . . get off the . . . ca . . . . Stop feeling sorry for yourself and sitting back!"

Therapist: Uh huh.

Mr. Johnson: I remember the whiny voice that I used a lot.

Therapist: So my kind of coming across like I were impatient or something like that made it easier [Yeah.] for you to get angry?

Mr. Johnson: Yeah. For me to respond. You know, in the same way.

Therapist: That's interesting.

Mr. Johnson: Yeah.

Therapist: That's interesting. There's a lot to think about how this whole
therapy thing works.

Mr. Johnson: Yeah. I just feel very grateful to you, and (pause), you
know, I feel like a father to you.

Therapist: Mmmhh.

Mr. Johnson: (smiling and with a chuckle) I feel very good about being
free of myself, my inhibitions.

Therapist: I appreciate your caring feelings.

Mr. Johnson and I then say our good-byes. When I showed these portions
of the last session to the training class, they responded as follows:

[CLASSROOM]

TRAINEE: It's exciting. Not only can he tell you how much he appreciated
the work, but he just looks so much better.

TRAINEE: It's really neat to see that dramatic change. And it really is dramatic. He looks 10 years younger. He's looking at you squarely in the
face. He's relating to you in a thoughtful, give-and-take way.

TRAINEE: Yeah. The last time we saw him was the 4th session, and now 16
sessions later, he seems to have made gains I never would have thought
possible after seeing him those first few times.

TRAINEE: It's really impressive how he can verbalize those things about
his father.

TRAINEE: It's quite clear that his kids' perceptions of him have also
changed.

TRAINEE: I think the thing that I was most impressed with was not what
he was saying, but his nonverbal communication. He looked—he just
looked better. I mean, he looked more put-together. He just physically
presented much better.

TRAINEE: Yeah. Even his posture was better.

TRAINEE: He didn't look or act pathetic.

TRAINEE: He didn't have that hangdog expression.

LEVENSON: What do you make of how he understood what went on in his
therapy?

TRAINEE: He really seemed to get the focus. He thought that the purpose of the therapy was to assert himself instead of feeling subservient. That was very close to your goal of having him be more active and less passive.

TRAINEE: He emphasized your patience and understanding.

TRAINEE: And that you knew what was wrong with him and that he knew you knew.

LEVENSON: Yes. Quite often in a brief, focused therapy, patients will comment on how they get a sense that the therapist has an overall understanding, a focus, or even an agenda for the therapy. This realization that there is a working plan can be quite reassuring to patients in establishing hope and a forward momentum.

TRAINEE: What did you think about his saying it was hard to imagine anyone being angry with you?

LEVENSON: I thought a couple of things. First of all, his anger toward me did pale in comparison to the anger he had toward his father and wife, for example. Secondly, however, I thought it was part of his idealization of me as someone who had helped him and therefore could not have made any mistakes. Nonetheless, when I told him that I did not feel very patient at the beginning of our work, he was able to agree.

TRAINEE: But he puts it in terms of something you did on purpose to help him realize he'd better get angry.

LEVENSON: Yes. I was very curious about that. He does justify my impatience as in the service of his seeing that he had better get righteously angry—to stand up for himself. He goes on to elaborate that there was something about my behavior that gave him permission to get angry. He seems to be saying that I modeled an angry way of being for him. This certainly isn't our understanding of the process. We were trying to provide a new experience in which people did not respond angrily when he tried to meet his own needs. There may be a difference here between what Mr. Johnson is able to consciously acknowledge at our termination (gratitude) and what he experienced from time to time during the therapy (my impatience). It is also possible that my impatience was experienced by Mr. Johnson as coming from my perception that he could make changes and was entitled to do so. Thus my impatience might have provided some sense of hope and positive regard. I did not treat him as a fragile old man.

TRAINEE: Yes. And in terms of hope, Mr. Johnson asks if you think he can go on by himself.

One of the indirect benefits of a brief therapy is the sense of confidence the patient assumes from knowing that his or her therapist feels comfortable terminating the therapy. Patients often take cues about their progress from their therapists' view of the advisability of continuing therapy. In addition, patients are curious about how they will know when they are "done." Brief therapists maintain the perspective that patients, like other people, are never "done"—that the developmental process continues until death. With such an outlook, cure is not seen as a necessary precondition for ending therapy. The assumption is, from the short-term therapist's point of view, that growth will continue after the sessions end.

[CLASSROOM]

TRAINEE: What would you have done if Mr. Johnson had said, "I'm doing pretty well, but I think another 10 sessions would really help?"

LEVENSON: I would hope that such a request for more sessions would not come as a complete surprise to me in the last session. A brief therapist wants such termination anxiety to emerge as part of the therapeutic dialogue well before the end of the therapy. While it is difficult to say precisely when termination issues should be discussed (because to a large degree it depends on the individual patient's CMP), I suggest that if feelings or thoughts about termination have not come up by the last third of the therapy, the therapist should introduce the topic. Sometimes simply saying, "We have six more sessions before we end our work together" can promote a discussion of the patient's reactions.

James Mann (1973) has a 12-session model of time-limited therapy that focuses almost entirely on termination. Mann encourages the therapist to count down the sessions as they go by to convey to the patient that time is passing and can never be recaptured. TLDP, on the other hand, does not put such a strong emphasis on termination per se; rather, it is the backdrop against which the dysfunctional patterns can get played out. If a particular patient becomes anxious or depressed during times of separation, the therapist can explore how this gets manifested in the reenactment of the CMP. The TLDP therapist continues working on the goals of a new experience and a new understanding during the termination phase. Exploration of previous endings and losses can help put the patient's reactions into perspective.

To return to the question of what to say if Mr. Johnson had stated that another 10 sessions would help, I would first explore the reasons for his request (e.g., fear of relapse, pain of ending). I then might have replied with one or several of the following:

(1) "I can understand that. I think we have worked well together and you have made considerable progress." My intent with this response would be to

acknowledge that I think his request is reasonable and understandable. It does not mean, however, that continuing is possible or even preferable.

(2) "While our therapy is finished, your growth and development are not. Hopefully, they will continue for as long as you are alive." My intent here is to suggest to the patient that while the therapy will end, his personal growth will continue. Ideally, such an intervention will encourage the patient to have a less dependent and more optimistic view of what he can accomplish outside of therapy.

(3) "Is it hard for you to say good-bye?" With this question I validate that seeing something good come to an end is sad and somewhat anxiety-provoking. However, since endings are a part of life, the termination of the therapy does not have to be postponed or avoided. We can face the sadness and apprehension together and survive unscathed.

(4) "I have confidence that you can continue to make progress." With statements such as this, the patient can gain from the therapist's faith and trust. As Jerome Frank (1974) put forth in *Persuasion and Healing*, the therapist's expectation for therapeutic gains can exert a powerful influence on outcome. Unfortunately, this also happens in reverse: the therapist's doubts about what can be accomplished in a brief period of time can get subtly or overtly communicated to the patient and foster insecurity and demoralization.

(5) "In the future if you get stuck in your efforts to further your growth, I will be glad to work with you again." The intent of this comment is to send the message that I will not view additional therapy an indication of failure. TLDP should not automatically be considered a one-time occurrence, but rather as a helpful intervention that can and should be used repeatedly as needed. There are ample data that later on many patients return for more treatment following a brief therapy (e.g., Bein et al., 1994; Budman & Gurman, 1988; Patterson, Levene, & Breger, 1977), and that therapists and institutions remain available to the patient through continuing (though discontinuous) relationships (Bennett, 1983).

[CLASSROOM]
TRAINEE: What would you do if toward the end of therapy Mr. Johnson started getting depressed and passive again?

Brief therapists encounter this type of situation all the time. Termination can be an emotionally difficult part of the treatment. It may involve leaving someone who has, ideally, been empathic, respectful, and helpful; the process might rekindle memories of other losses and separations the patient has endured. It is no wonder that some patients have a return of symptoms

(Sansone, Fine, & Dennis, 1991), or express disappointment over the inadequacy of treatment length. Sometimes they may even introduce new problems as a way of trying to maintain the relationship.

However, one should not automatically assume termination is solely a painful process. Often patients also experience a sense of pride and hope (Fortune, 1987; Marx & Gelso, 1987). Clearly Mr. Johnson evidenced pleasure in his accomplishments and hope for his future successes.

What often happens, though, is that an inexperienced brief therapist, because of his or her own issues with termination, finds patients' direct and indirect pleas for continued therapy difficult to handle. Ending a therapy earlier than one is accustomed to usually creates psychological dilemmas for the neophyte brief therapist; the therapist can avoid or postpone these dilemmas by finding "good reasons" for extending the length of the therapy. Because of therapists' tendencies to lengthen brief therapies, I suggest that clinicians or trainees who are learning how to do brief therapy initially employ a time-limited approach with a definite ending date (as apposed to a specific number of sessions, or a focused therapy approach). By having an explicit ending date, therapists are compelled to confront their resistances to terminating in a timely fashion, and this can be a very important part of the learning experience.

The inexperienced brief therapist can profit from becoming aware of his or her possible resistances to termination. These can include:

1. Dependency issues—obtaining vicarious nurturance while offering help
2. The need to be needed
3. Conflicts around separation and loss (saying good-bye)
4. Conflicts around attachment and intimacy (saying hello to new patients)
5. Loss of an intimate and meaningful relationship
6. Therapeutic "perfectionism"—overinvestment in therapeutic results
7. Fear of being seen as sadistic, withholding, rejecting
8. Difficulties accepting the limits of therapeutic intervention
9. Insecurities regarding one's own skill
10. Economic pressures to hold on to that which is profitable and dependable
11. Anxiety over loss of one's professional role
12. Guilt over failing the patient
13. Overconcern for the "successful" termination

Some of this material from Bauer & Kobos, 1987; Hoyt, 1985; Martin & Schurtman, 1985.

[CLASSROOM]

TRAINEE: I was impressed that even in the last session you are still doing a lot of therapy.

TRAINEE: Yeah. It is not just a rehash of previous sessions, but further work on challenging his passivity and promoting his assertiveness.

TRAINEE: And in this session you continue to explore your own behaviors as a part of the interaction with him.

TRAINEE: What about the last part of the videotape you showed, where he says he feels like a father to you? How were you feeling about that?

TRAINEE: I was wondering why he said that too.

LEVENSON: But what about that? Would you feel good about Mr. Johnson's saying that, if *you* were his therapist? Or would you feel uncomfortable? These are almost our last words together.

TRAINEE: Well, he expects his children to take care of him, so maybe it's a statement asking you to be there for him like his kids.

TRAINEE: I don't think so. It seems like he is taking back his power. He's been like a needy child in the past, but now he is able to be more like a father. Maybe *he* can give to *you*.

TRAINEE: And it also seems to be a statement that he feels OK to leave now. Because if he still felt like a child he might not feel strong enough to leave you.

LEVENSON: Well, I was reassured to hear that he felt like a father to me. I interpreted it back to him in my last remark you heard on the tape, when I said I appreciated his caring feelings. I thought he was in part communicating about how close he felt toward me—like a father. In addition, I was glad to hear he felt more like an adult than the whiny child he appeared to be at the start of the therapy. This is the same man who came in and said, "Feed me, change me, take care of me." His feeling like a father to me is much more appropriate age-wise. In actuality, he *was* old enough to be my father.

My response to the trainee raises the issue of what evidence is there by the time of termination that Mr. Johnson was on his way to achieving the two goals of the therapy: increased self-efficacy with an active involvement in his life, and an understanding of his role in re-creating a passive–dependent interactional stance. Throughout this termination session, Mr. Johnson provides ample indications that his life is more active, with more pleasant interactions with his children. It seems his children are now more eager to involve him in their lives: he is invited on a vacation with his son and his grandchildren; his daughter comes to visit. This type of feedback about changes in the outside world is reassuring for the brief therapist.

Often, however, a brief therapy ends without a clear, visible, positive outcome, since the patient is still in the midst of changing. How does the therapist know when the patient has had "enough" therapy? What should the therapist use as a guidepost for knowing when to terminate? In doing TLDP, I use five criteria, presented here in approximate order of reassurance to the therapist.

First and foremost, has the patient evidenced interactional changes with significant others in his or her life? Does the patient report more rewarding transactions?

Second, has the patient had a new experience (or a series of new experiences) of himself or herself and the therapist within the therapy?

Third, has there been a change in the level on which the therapist and patient are relating (from parent–child to adult–adult)?

Fourth, has the therapist's countertransferential reaction to the patient shifted (usually from negative to positive)?

And fifth, does the patient manifest some understanding about his or her dynamics and the role he or she was playing to maintain them?

If the answer to most of these questions is no, then I do not consider that the patient has had an adequate course of TLDP. The therapist should consider why this has been the case and weigh the possible benefits of alternative therapies, another course of TLDP, a different therapist, nonprofessional interventions, and so on.

EPILOGUE

One year after Mr. Johnson's therapy was concluded, he was invited back for a videotaped follow-up session with another therapist in the clinic. He apparently was doing quite well. He was not drinking and was still living with the same two elderly women. He was not depressed, and had not sought out more therapy. He described his children as doing well and his relationship with them as improved. With a psychiatrist's monitoring, he had discontinued his antidepressant medication some 5 months prior to the follow-up interview.

Mr. Johnson related how he had made several impressive changes in his life. He and his two housemates had devised a direct way to handle their anger. They decided that if any of them were feeling angry with anyone else in the household, they would all sit around the dining room table after the dinner dishes were cleared away, and talk about it. Furthermore, Mr. Johnson was volunteering 2 days a week at a halfway house near his home.

Thus he clearly had not only been able to maintain the therapeutic gains evidenced at termination, he had even furthered his splendid progress.

Some 6 years after my therapy with Mr. Johnson had ended, I unexpectedly obtained some informal, unsolicited, long-term follow-up data. I had presented a videotape of Mr. Johnson as part of a professional training workshop, and a therapist in the audience asked me whether Mr. Johnson (pseudonym) were really Mr. So-and-So. She elaborated that she did not know the patient personally, but as a clinician who led a group for older people interested in meeting members of the opposite sex for friendship and possible romance. Two weeks previously, Mr. Johnson had come to her group. She said he appeared to be doing quite well, was apparently still living with the same two women, but wanted to expand his social network.

Obviously, not all brief psychotherapies turn out as well as Mr. Johnson's. But Mr. Johnson is an example of what can be achieved in a brief therapy despite "negative selection indicators." Mr. Johnson was an elderly widower, presenting with somatic complaints, depression, and a drinking problem serious enough to warrant inpatient hospitalization. Nonetheless, we were able to discern a clear dynamic focus concerning his dysfunctional way of relating to others that contributed to his being well suited to TLDP.

CHAPTER 13

Patients Presenting with Specific Problems

THIS CHAPTER SERVES as a model for the treatment of any type of specific presenting problem (e.g., adjustment reaction following a move, post-traumatic stress reaction caused by a natural disaster, major depression brought on by retirement) when those symptoms are superimposed on an underlying dysfunctional personality style.

The directive of many managed care companies is to "just treat the Axis I symptomatology" and to disregard long-standing dysfunctional personality styles. Ah, were this possible! Even neophyte clinicians know that the successful treatment of reactions to truly very discrete stressors (e.g., loss of a spouse) depends on whether or not one is dealing with a hysterical, obsessive, or narcissistic personality style (Horowitz et al., 1984).

The clinically sophisticated yet time-sensitive brief therapist attends to the specific problems within the broader interpersonal context. By comprehending the patient's interpersonal style, the therapist has a greater likelihood of discerning how to intervene to ameliorate the immediate presenting problem. Furthermore, since the TLDP therapist is interested in providing a fundamental change in the patient's manner of dealing with problems, an in-depth understanding of this coping style is critical.

To demonstrate the TLDP treatment of specific issues, I will discuss two patients with medical problems. Psychologically, patients with medical illnesses are in a prime position to benefit from time-limited interventions (Levenson & Hales, 1993). Because those who are ill are trying to cope with issues of loss (e.g., of actual body parts or function, self-esteem, status, or even life itself), a brief therapy can be a good choice for their treatment. Time-sensitive therapies echo the issues of loss in their emphasis on time limits and termination. Furthermore, patients with medical problems are usually not interested in delving into ancient history. They are often in pain, frightened, hopeless, or confused and want immediate help with their present situation. Consequently, formulations and techniques that focus on the here and now are particularly relevant and satisfying to the patient with medical problems.*

The first case involves a young man who was dealing with the death of his lover as well as his own infection with the human immunodeficiency virus (HIV). This case will serve to illustrate how a therapist can address a presenting problem that is *superimposed* on a preexisting dysfunctional interpersonal style. The second case, of an older man chronically incapacitated by his diabetes and kidney failure, highlights how long-lasting, persistent medical conditions can actually *promote* a dysfunctional interpersonal style.

PRESENTING PROBLEM SUPERIMPOSED ON PATIENT'S CMP

Arthur Allen was a 32-year-old, white, openly gay man who had learned he was HIV-positive one year prior to beginning TLDP. His lover had died the previous year from AIDS. Since that loss, he had been depressed, with anhedonia, tearful episodes, and chronic suicidal ideation, but asymptomatic with regard to his HIV status.

Mr. Allen had originally come to the outpatient clinic to participate in an HIV support group. After attending one group session, however, he said he decided not to continue, because the group leaders were not HIV-positive and he disliked the group's format of adding new members in an ongoing way. The group therapists' perspective was that Mr. Allen had difficulties tolerating being in a group where he was not the center of attention, and that the other group members were put off by Mr. Allen's entitled, condescending, and arrogant manner. As a consequence, they referred Mr. Allen for individual TLDP, with the hope that he might learn enough about his off-putting effect on others to be able to reenter the group. Some investigators (Perry &

---

*Similarly, a TLDP formulation about the patient's interpersonal style can provide a jargon-free conceptualization for any medical staff treating the patient, which can help them understand what previously may have been a confusing and frustrating set of patient behaviors and attitudes.

Markowitz, 1986) have commented on how the premature referral of gay patients may be an indication of a therapist's countertransference. In Mr. Allen's case, it may be that the group leaders' referral of him to the Brief Psychotherapy Program may have been a part of their countertransferential reenactment, exacerbating the patient's feelings of rejection.

Mr. Allen began TLDP with a 30-year-old psychology predoctoral intern, Vickey Morris. Ms. Morris had never known anyone with HIV or AIDS. As part of her work with this patient, the Brief Psychotherapy team consulted with a clinician who specialized in the psychiatric treatment of patients with HIV/AIDS.

In formulating this case, Ms. Morris identified several present issues that were traumatic for the patient. He was clearly grieving the loss of his lover of 6 years. Such grief was complicated by feelings of survivor guilt (Horowitz, 1976) and Mr. Allen's unrealistic perception that if he had only been home when his lover died, he could have prevented it. Furthermore, Mr. Allen was coping with his adjustment to learning of his own fatal diagnosis. Another factor adding to the complexity of the case was that it was the anniversary of both Mr. Allen's lover's death and his own positive HIV test.

Apart from these acute situations, it became clear to Ms. Morris that Mr. Allen had a lifelong pattern of relating to others in a manipulative, nonempathic, entitled fashion. How could this narcissistic man resolve his grief, deal effectively with his own present and future, and develop healthier relationships in which he could feel loved and supported, within the context of a brief therapy?

Undoubtedly such goals would be daunting and discouraging for any therapist. Ms. Morris decided to focus on Mr. Allen's issues of grief and loss (actual and anticipated), while also providing him with a new experience of relating to a real person with her own thoughts and feelings; someone who could be there for him as a collaborative partner, not as an adoring audience nor as a convenient target for his rage. This goal is consistent with Lorna Benjamin's (1993) focus on having narcissistic patients learn to be empathic as part of their interpersonal therapy.

The new understanding Ms. Morris wanted to encourage was for Mr. Allen to begin to realize how his demeaning way of treating others actually kept him from receiving the nurturance he craved. In addition, it was hoped that the time-limited format of the therapy might provide him with a healing experience of a loss which would not be perceived as rejection, punishment, or abandonment.

The following is an excerpt from the fifth session. The patient is talking about a new relationship with a younger man.

[VIDEOTAPE]

Mr. Allen: What I have found in Andy is a transformation of my body. In other words, if a barrel of apples is rotting, you start taking the good ones out because they can be given to someone else and they will not rot. This is what me and Andy have done. We have not stopped talking. Every time we turn around I've been explaining something to him. Why we do this, why we do that. It's not doing me any good with me any more. Because I'm slowly but surely decaying. But I can give this to him. It's like Andy wants to go to the gym. He wants me to push him. I have something in my life to work for. I can develop him, if not mentally, like a teacher would, I want to push him to develop his body.

Therapist: How do you see yourself decaying?

Mr. Allen: See myself what?

Therapist: Decaying.

Mr. Allen: Well, it's the same when I was told that I was positive. That was the day they put the three nails in and crucified me. And basically I am on the cross right now. And eventually I'll go . . .

Therapist: You saw the HIV findings as . . .

Mr. Allen: As a crucifixion. That's why I don't read the papers no more. "Oh, we think we've found some cure for AIDS." Yeah, you read it cures the rats. But I'm no damn rat!

In this vignette we see how the therapist ignored the patient's grandiose statements of what he will do for Andy—that Andy will be his creation, so to speak. Rather, she brought the patient back to themes of loss—to his perceptions that he was decaying. Mr. Allen's rather tangential mention of a barrel of rotting apples suggested how pervasive the patient's sense of being "rotten" might be.

Mr. Allen told the therapist that his HIV-positive status represented a crucifixion—that others put him on this cross. This view illustrates his sense of his special status (comparing himself to Jesus Christ) and his belief that it was done to him by others (external locus of control). The therapist was very put off by the patient's grandiosity, a countertransference reaction that is common for therapists working with patients with narcissistic styles. In this therapy, the countertransference issues are even more complicated because the patient's terminal medical condition and sexual orientation provide further obstacles.

The therapist may have profound countertransference reactions to the illness itself; . . . the therapist who believes that homosexuality or intravenous drug use led to the infection may have an impaired capacity to listen noncritically and with empathy. Fears of contamination may result in a reluctance to accept the patient and can manifest themselves in the treatment, e.g., by undue caution in demonstrating simple courtesies, such as a handshake . . . (Adler & Beckett, 1989, pp. 203–204).

In addition, Ms. Morris felt guilty for being healthy and for the stigmatization that the patient's sexual orientation and HIV infection had caused him. Nonetheless, with the dynamic focus serving as anchor for treatment, Ms. Morris was able to pursue her goal of introducing a collaborative relationship into the therapy, as illustrated by the following excerpt from the ninth session. The patient had just described how he was used by others in his life.

[VIDEOTAPE]

Therapist: How would that work in here? How would I use you? Or how do you see me as using you?

Mr. Allen: I'm using you as a whipping post.

Therapist: You said that before. [Yeah.] What does that mean?

Mr. Allen: A whipping post is . . . We use our friends as whipping posts most. In the olden days, Caesar would send out a slave and whip him—getting the anger out. Or somebody just going out with a whip and hitting a post. Talking to somebody. Getting it out—like cleansing the mind. Not bottling it up, like throwing shit at a fan. You know sometimes some of it will come back at you, but at least you've gotten it in the right direction.

Therapist: That makes me sound not human.

Mr. Allen: Yes, it is, because you're feeling what I'm feeling. Like what I said about throwing shit at a fan and sometimes it comes back at you. I'm getting feedback, which makes me start to think. Makes me start to wonder what am I doing to cause this buildup of shit (laugh). What part am I playing? What responsibility do I have to myself, to either go through with what I'm doing or not to do it at all? I could go home and say to everybody, "Get out of my house! Leave me alone!" I don't want to live all by myself. I don't want to be in my own shell. I don't care what it costs. But I don't want to be used in the sense of what is most valuable to me, which is time.

Therapist: You're saying two different things about our relationship. On the one hand, you see me as the nonhuman fan or a whipping post. On the other hand, you want feedback from me. You want for us to work together. And helping you to look at the things going on in your life and seeing how you fit into all of that. These are very contradictory images.

Mr. Allen: But then again too a lot of us have different images that we do play with, talk with, use. I am using you right now.

Therapist: Uh huh. You have some real contradictory images of relationships, then.

Mr. Allen: You lost me. (laugh)

Therapist: We're talking about you and me [Yeah.] right now and how you see me. On the one hand you see me as a whipping post—a fan—something you can dump on. On the other hand, you want me to be a person—to be helpful to you.

Mr. Allen: But I see you as a person.

Therapist: But you also see me as a nonperson.

Mr. Allen: I see you as a nonperson because I have what you are as a professional person in my head. . . . I use you to get this out of me. I was never taught anything at home as to how to release my anger, and through all my life I have refused to let it build up in me. The reason why is because little things bother me. And I figure if I let the little things build up, then the big things build up, then all of a sudden I will be a screaming vicious person. But I don't want that to happen. I see you as someplace I can come once a week and say "Here, you take it!" I don't want this buildup, this overload, this override. I have to shovel it off on somebody. It's the same way as hitting a post, hitting a door.

Therapist: You see this as a place to come and dump your feelings.

Mr. Allen: Right, because I don't know anywhere to go. I mean, I call the volunteer AIDS groups and they send me a piece of meat with two eyes who sits there and doesn't talk at all. And my friends have their own situations.

Therapist: If I'm some person and this is some place where you can come dump your feelings, though, then I might as well be a piece of meat with two eyes who sits here and doesn't say anything.

Mr. Allen: No. Why do you say that?

Therapist: Because then I am not a person.

Mr. Allen: Yes, you are a person because you have feelings. You know what I am feeling or you know how I am feeling.

Therapist: What are you wanting from me?

Mr. Allen: I want from you to not give me the answers to the problems but to help me give myself the answers to why I let all this stuff not bother me so much.

Therapist: Or why you let it bother you?

Patient: Or why I let it bother me so much.

At the beginning of this vignette, the therapist introduced the idea of how the patient's interpersonal dynamics might hypothetically play out in the session (i.e., "How would that work in here? How would I use you?"). Such abstract, theoretical questions are usually not particularly helpful in providing patients with emotional insight into their patterns. Ms. Morris, however, corrected herself and asked a here-and-now question about how the patient might have already been feeling used by her (i.e., "Or how do you see me as using you?"). Even this question must be asked in the context of sufficient interplay between therapist and patient so that the maladaptive motif has had a chance to emerge.

Mr. Allen was able to convey that he saw his therapist as a whipping post—that she was there to allow him to ventilate his anger. From an interactional (as opposed to an intrapsychic) viewpoint, Mr. Allen's catharsis involves his expressing previously withheld feelings with the opportunity to see whether the feared outcome occurs (e.g., the therapist retaliates, he himself is overwhelmed).

The reader may be thinking about the applicability of the concept of *projective identification* here (Ogden, 1982). In object relations theory, projective identification assumes that an individual projects unacceptable feelings and representations of the self onto a recipient, and acts in such a way so as to induce this person to feel and behave in ways congruent with these disowned feelings and representations. In this way the intrapsychic process of projection becomes interpersonal (Cashdan, 1988). In this vignette the patient could be seen as projecting some of his "shit" at the therapist. ("Here, you take it!") It could be interpreted that Mr. Allen was acting in such a manner so as to induce Ms. Morris to experience herself as *shitty, abused,* or *overwhelmed,* thereby identifying with these aspects of Mr. Allen.

I prefer to take a more descriptive view of the interactional process, making the fewest inferences possible. One does not need to posit automatically that the patient projects affect or self-representations onto the therapist, only that the therapist is induced by the patient to behave and feel in a particular way. In some therapeutic interchanges the therapist *may* come to feel like the patient is feeling, but from a TLDP viewpoint this should not be automatically assumed.

Returning to the specific case at hand, Ms. Morris commented on the interpersonal process in typical TLDP fashion. By introducing the way Mr. Allen treated her like an object ("That makes me sound not human"), and focusing on their relationship in the here and now ("You're saying two different things about our relationship"), she was establishing herself as a presence in the room. She was trying to give both of them the experience of two human beings connecting, rather than her continuing to feel objectified. Furthermore, she was also trying to help Mr. Allen recognize how his pattern with her is replicated in other interpersonal relationships ("You have some real contradictory images of relationships, then").

Here we see the essence of the therapeutic situation in which the focus of the treatment (in this case, grief work) is superimposed on a dysfunctional interpersonal style. By continually challenging Mr. Allen's attempts at discounting her as a person ("If . . . this is some place where you can come and dump your feelings, though, then I might as well be a piece of meat with two eyes who sits here and doesn't say anything"), she undermines his CMP and paves the way for them to work as a team on his grief. The following vignette from the next (10th) session illustrates the confluence of working on the patient's underlying defensive pattern and his more immediate needs.

[VIDEOTAPE]

Mr. Allen: I mean, when you feel your immune system is down and your doctor tells you you need an iron supplement and all they have is vitamins, you get mad. You can't come out and start talking about it, because society backs away.

Therapist: You've had a lot of experiences in which you feel alone, very different, and that people will reject you. And do reject you, and that makes you angry.

Mr. Allen: Only when I talk about it publicly. If you are in a crowd and pass gas, people will move away. Society has taught us, "You have a disease. You smell bad." They are all told to move away because it's scary for them. It's frightening for them.

Therapist: But that's distressing for you.

Mr. Allen: Distressing because I feel a little bit of abandonment.

Therapist: Yes, sure, of course.

Mr. Allen: I mean, it's like you have it. "That's nice, but make sure you stay on that side of the room."

Therapist: I wonder if some of those same feelings about how other people might perceive you and how they might feel about you come up for you in here with me?

Mr. Allen: What is that? You lost me. (laughs)

Therapist: You know, this has happened before that I lose you when I raise questions about how the things you're talking about affect the two of us. What's it like when I ask you questions about our relationship?

Mr. Allen: How is it?

Therapist: Are you aware of any particular feelings?

Mr. Allen: Yeah. (pause) The only way I can put it is a crude way. And that is someone to dump on.

Therapist: Uh huh.

Mr. Allen: Right now I have nobody to dump my feelings—to dump my frustrations—to dump my anger.

Therapist: Do you have any thoughts about how I might feel about your seeing me as someone to dump on?

Mr. Allen: Can you go by that again?

Therapist: Do you have any thoughts about how I might feel?

Mr. Allen: I don't know how you feel because you're doing a job. I don't know how to separate you from a professional person doing your job and as a person listening to my conversation. I don't know how to divide or how to separate you. (laugh) I mean, it's like I want to feel that you are listening and helping me because you want to—what does the word *befriend* mean? To be a friend?—to befriend me or (shifts position) you are doing it because of a profession. Because you are to help me uncover my own problems or solve my own problems. Because I know you cannot give me answers. But you can unlock the door. You've got the key (chuckle), as they say.

Therapist: Maybe this helps to explain some of the confusion that you feel when I ask you about our relationship. That when I do raise those questions, then it's confusing because then I become a person.

Mr. Allen: (sadder and more slowly) It's confusing because you are someone who has come into my space, my life, that, ah, I have to (pause) talk and give out all my information because you can't find the key unless you have all the parts of the puzzle. But at the same time, how can I really get close to you, because I know that like Tommy, one day you'll be gone.

Therapist: (nods) Mm hmm.

Mr. Allen: So I don't know. (sadly) I don't want to keep reading the book. When I say the book, my life, and when I get to chapter 12 the person will put the book down because it was boring or that's as far as they wanted to go. There's no one else to talk to about stuff like this. I have probably told you more about my life than Jim.

Therapist: Your best friend. (crosses her arms in front of her chest) What I'm hearing you say is that because this will end, you have some questions about just how close we can be. And another part of that seems to be questioning how I would feel about you. And fears that I too will reject you—abandon you.

Mr. Allen: I don't fear rejection. What I fear is abandonment.

Over and over again in this segment, Ms. Morris brought the discussion back to their relationship. In doing so, she did not "move away" as the patient dreaded. The patient's fears about others' moving away were overdetermined by his personality style (which caused people, including the

HIV-group members, to reject him), by the deaths of those around him (including his partner), and by his sexual orientation and medical status (stigmatized by society).

Ms. Morris's question about how Mr. Allen thought she might feel about being "dumped on" elucidated his fears of abandonment should he get close to her. Mr. Allen's answer revealed his real-life dilemma about how his distancing was an attempt at protecting himself from being hurt, but at the cost of keeping him from obtaining the nurturance and understanding he so much wanted.

As Ms. Morris discussed the ending of the therapy and how that caused Mr. Allen concerns about how close he wanted to get to her, she became somewhat uncomfortable. In supervision, she was able to talk about her guilt about the time-limited nature of the therapy for this man who was confronting his own death. By exploring how her pity for Mr. Allen's prematurely mourning his own death would only serve to heighten his sense of hopelessness and helplessness and further contribute to his depression, Ms. Morris was able to maintain her availability to the patient during sessions and work on his achieving closeness with others.

In the 12th session, the patient said he had written his father a letter, telling him about his HIV-positive status. He had previously not told his father this news for fear his father would reply that it was what he deserved for being homosexual. Mr. Allen was surprised but relieved when his father took the news well and wished to be supportive.* This positive experience led to a discussion in therapy regarding intimacy and closeness with others in his life. By the end of therapy, Mr. Allen had a plan to live with a friend who was also HIV-positive, so they could "be there for each other."

The therapy ended as planned after 16 sessions. In the last session, Mr. Allen expressed a wish that if he became symptomatic from AIDS in the future, he could return for "some supportive therapy." He acknowledged that talking helped reduce his fears. He presented Ms. Morris with a book of meditations and also requested (and received) a hug as they parted. Ms. Morris assured the patient that the clinic was available to him in the future.

Two years later, Mr. Allen did reenter another brief therapy for nine ses-

*This patient's positive experience in telling his father does not appear to be an isolated occurrence. John Markowitz and colleagues (1992) related that in their interpersonal therapy with depressed HIV-positive outpatients, they originally failed to recognize that the patients' loneliness was not due simply to the stigmatization of the HIV diagnosis, but also to interpersonal issues (i.e., disputes). The investigators initially had made the assumption, along with their patients, that those infected would be rejected if they disclosed their HIV status to significant others. Only when the therapists began to see that withholding such medical information could be a manifestation of an interpersonal dispute did they work with patients around examining the availability of support. They found acceptance to be more accessible than had been assumed.

sions. By that time he had AIDS, with symptoms of decreased vision, weight loss, peripheral neuropathy, fatigue, and diarrhea. This therapy focused on dealing with his growing impairments and allowing him to discuss his plans for suicide if the quality of his life declined further. One year later he came back to therapy for seven visits for help with handling his becoming blind. At that time he was not judged to be clinically depressed, and appeared to be active with friends and church. He died 15 months after his last contact with the clinic.

The case of Mr. Allen illustrates the usefulness of *serial, intermittent, brief therapies.* His return to the clinic was never discouraged nor seen as a treatment failure. Since Mr. Allen experienced his initial time-limited therapy as helpful, it became a resource to which he returned over time for additional brief therapies. This view of the availability of short-term therapies over the individual's life span is consistent with the position of the therapist as family practitioner initially described in 1979 (Cummings & Vandenbos, 1979) and most recently by Nicholas Cummings (1995) in his primer for survival in the age of managed care.

Intermittent treatment of HIV/AIDS patients needs to be sensitive to the phase of the patient's illness (Devine, in press). Initial therapeutic concerns may center around ambivalence regarding antibody testing, learning one is positive, disclosures to others, and future plans. Later in the progression of the illness, as the patient develops physical symptoms and impairments, the focus may be on personal and work-related limitations and increasing dependence on others and the medical system. In the terminal stages of the illness, patients are concerned with decisions about the quality of life, the aggressiveness of medical treatments, and death and dying issues.

The reader may be wondering why we attempted a time-limited therapy at all with an underlying personality style usually considered to be impervious to brief therapy. We chose to stay attuned to changes within the therapy sessions in order to judge the viability of TLDP with this man, rather than deciding a priori that he could not benefit. As the TLDP therapy just described demonstrates, while we did not "cure" Mr. Allen of his narcissistic personality style, we were able to provide some inroads to his walled-off and distancing stance and permit him to do some grieving.

CHRONIC SITUATION PROMOTING A PATIENT'S CMP

While the patient's CMP is usually begun in childhood, fostered by faulty relationships with parents, sometimes a devastating situation occurs much later in life that can precipitate a fundamental change in the way the person relates to others.* The case of Mr. Pedotti illustrates such an occurrence. His medical illness was so chronic and incapacitating that it set in motion a pattern of disturbed interpersonal relationships which were not evidenced prior to his disabilities.

Mr. Pedotti, a short, thin, 62-year-old man, had had diabetes since the age of 20. At the time of his referral to the Brief Psychotherapy Program, he had had diabetic retinopathy and kidney failure and was receiving hemodialysis three times a week. Mr. Pedotti was referred by his primary care physician for help with depression, insomnia, and anxiety. Mr. Pedotti felt that he was dying and that his life was over. His physician had been treating him with antianxiety agents (lorazepam) for his chronic anxiety. The patient was initially seen in the psychiatry service medication clinic, where he was diagnosed as having an adjustment disorder secondary to his medical problems. He was started on trazodone for the insomnia and depression and his lorazepam was tapered. At that time he appeared haggard and moved slowly. His affect was restricted, and he was occasionally tearful.

Mr. Pedotti lived with his wife of 42 years. They had four healthy grown children. As a young man, Mr. Pedotti had been a professional boxer until the onset of his diabetes. He then worked for a short time as a manager of a small store, but finally he had to retire because of his medical problems.

Mr. Pedotti was referred for TLDP and was assigned to work with Claire Vann, a social work intern. Following a two-session assessment, he was offered 16 additional sessions of once-a-week therapy. He missed three of these appointments (once when his father died). The following is a summary of the sequential salient features of his therapy and their meaning within the TLDP format.

Session 1: Mr. Pedotti was accompanied by his wife in the waiting room. Immediately, Mrs. Pedotti began telling the therapist of her husband's difficulties. While his wife talked, Mr. Pedotti remained silent, looking sullen and dejected. Finally the therapist was able to extricate the patient from his wife, and he walked slowly to the therapy room. During his first visit, Mr. Pedotti described his history of medical problems and his sadness over how they restricted his activities. He said that his three brothers were all in good health, and he wondered whether he had inherited his condition from his father. Mr. Pedotti said that at times he would withdraw from others ("shun people"), not take care of his appearance, and question the reasons for his

---

*Portions of this section previously published as part of the chapter "Brief psychodynamically informed therapy for medically ill patients," by H. Levenson and R. E. Hales in *Medical-Psychiatric Practice Vol. II,* edited by A. Stoudemire and B. S. Fogel (1993), are included here with the permission of American Psychiatric Press.

"misfortune." During these periods, Mr. Pedotti said, his children typically responded by leaving him alone, and his wife assumed more of his responsibilities such as making his medical appointments.

Mr. Pedotti talked about having thoughts of death, but denied suicidal ideation or plans. He seemed to Ms. Vann to be more interested in help with his physical needs than with his emotional difficulties. During the first session, Mr. Pedotti was so physically distressed that he stood for part of it. Throughout the session, Mr. Pedotti waited for the therapist to ask questions; at times when she did not, he became anxious. He spoke softly and slowly, staring at the floor.

By allowing Mr. Pedotti to tell his own story, Ms. Vann observed and reacted to his passivity. Mr. Pedotti seemed comfortable letting his wife and the therapist take control. Ms. Vann's countertransferential reactions to the patient included feelings of uselessness ("Perhaps he just needs consultation around his medical condition"), emotional distance ("I felt somewhat bored during the session"), and pity. Ms. Vann suspected that Mr. Pedotti's passivity and powerlessness had much to do with his depression and anxiety, but was still unsure about the appropriateness and efficacy of TLDP, given Mr. Pedotti's preoccupation with his physical condition.

Session 2: Mr. Pedotti arrived promptly for his appointment, again accompanied by his wife. An important theme in this visit was his discussion of the way others responded to him. With Ms. Vann's empathic questioning, Mr. Pedotti elaborated on how his family members "leave me alone." Although Mr. Pedotti initially said that their distance "did not bother" him, the therapist was able to elicit that he interpreted their distance as evidence that they did not care about or understand what he was going through. He was afraid others would see him as "crazy" or not "trying." Mr. Pedotti expressed his wish that others would encourage him and show interest, and he recalled the days when, as a boxer, he was admired by others.

Following this session, Ms. Vann assessed that TLDP would be appropriate for Mr. Pedotti. He seemed willing to talk about his problems in interpersonal terms and not stay focused solely on his medical condition. Furthermore, and most important, the therapist was beginning to see how the patient's repetitive, maladaptive pattern was evidenced not only in his current relationships, but also in the here-and-now interaction with her. Mr. Pedotti turned to the therapist for constant direction and yet withdrew from interacting with her, in a way that discouraged her active collaboration. In fact, Ms. Vann felt useless and ready to withdraw from him—a pattern that Mr. Pedotti said happened with his wife and children. (It should be noted that patients' seeking direction from doctors and feeling passive in the face of medical illnesses are not unusual or pathological behaviors or feelings;

however, Mr. Pedotti gave evidence that this passive pattern occurred with significant others in his life and caused him to feel even more helpless, dependent, and isolated than is usually the case for patients with medical problems.) Mr. Pedotti, however, was not aware of how his own interpersonal behaviors (e.g., avoiding contact and isolating himself when depressed) promoted the very responses from others (e.g., inattention, infantilization) that made him feel worthless and abandoned.

After these two evaluation sessions, Ms. Vann delineated a working conceptualization of Mr. Pedotti's CMP, and derived the goals for treatment:

Acts of the self: Mr. Pedotti is a man who assumes a passive and sometimes depressive/withdrawn stance in the face of stressful circumstances to avoid being seen by others as crazy and as a failure. Part of this stance involves closing himself off emotionally (especially his anger), and part involves underfunctioning and giving his voice and power to others.

Expectations of others' reactions: Mr. Pedotti expects that others will show a lack of understanding, concern, and involvement with him. He believes others are no longer influenced by him and see him as useless or blameworthy—"a loser." He believes his family worries about his being a sick man; he expects they will take over his responsibilities when he does not feel well. He also expects that if he shows his feelings he will be judged crazy or as not trying.

Acts of others toward self: Mr. Pedotti's suppression of emotions and accompanying withdrawal lead to others' feeling a lack of connection. They respond by staying physically distant, communicating with him through his spokesperson (wife). This confirms Mr. Pedotti's fears that he cannot express his true feelings. His passivity is seen by others as a failure to try, and sometimes they blame him or become angry. Others pick up the responsibilities he drops and are not influenced by him.

Acts of the self toward the self (introject): Mr. Pedotti sees himself as a helpless, powerless victim. Since he views his strong emotions as a sign he is crazy, he suppresses them. He feels weak and considers himself useless and emasculated—just existing. He is disappointed in himself and treats himself like a loser, rather than the fighter he once was.

Goals:

(1) The new experience Mr. Pedotti needs in the context of the therapeutic relationship is to have more autonomy, control, and influence—to experience himself as a fighter again. Hopefully, Mr. Pedotti should have the experience of expressing his strong emotions to the therapist without being judged crazy. For the therapist, this means

   (a)   not taking control for him in sessions

   (b)   being directive *only* in examining process and encouraging affective expression

   (c)   responding positively to patient expressions of control and influence during sessions

   (d)   staying with his feelings

   (e)   not being frightened of Mr. Pedotti's strong emotions—especially anger.

(2) The new understanding Mr. Pedotti will hopefully achieve in the therapy is to see

   (a)   how his passive, distancing stance only serves to drives others away

   (b)   no matter how devastating his physical condition, he is still a worthwhile person with much to offer his loved ones.

From this formulation, Ms. Vann was able to anticipate transference–countertransference problems (e.g., the pull for the therapist to be overly solicitous or emotionally distant; the patient's heightened dependency needs as termination nears).

Sessions 3–6: Mr. Pedotti continued to come in with "no agenda," preferring that the therapist direct the session. Mr. Pedotti talked about how, as a boy, he and his brothers worked for migrant farm camps. His father praised him for being a strong worker who earned enough money to help his family buy a home. With the therapist's help, Mr. Pedotti was able to relate how his self-esteem had been tied to his physical abilities and how, now that he was so physically limited, he considered himself worthless.

Mr. Pedotti admitted that he did not communicate how depressed he was to his family. He preferred to withdraw to avoid revealing his "weakness." Although Mr. Pedotti said he could talk about his depression and anxiety in the sessions, the therapist observed that he showed little affective expression of his distress. As the therapist was able to get Mr. Pedotti to focus on his emotions within the sessions, he reported that he was feeling "better," but did not know why. He attributed it to his dialysis.

In the waiting room before the beginning of the fifth session, Mr. Pedotti's wife told Ms. Vann that her husband had to end the session early because of another commitment. The therapist replied, "It is up to your husband." However, *in the session*, Ms. Vann introduced the possibility of ending early. Then realizing how she had taken on this responsibility (paralleling the wife's role), the therapist asked the patient how he felt about her doing so. His reply, "Oh, fine," allowed patient and therapist to begin discussing his passive stance and its emotional costs and benefits. Ms. Vann also had the opportunity to self-disclose why she felt pulled to treat him as incapable.

In the sixth session, Mr. Pedotti was able to talk about how he suppressed his feelings even in the session, because he was afraid that Ms. Vann would "lock me up" in a psychiatric unit, "never to be released." Again, another opportunity presented itself in the here and now of the therapeutic relationship, this time for the therapist to support Mr. Pedotti's willingness to reveal himself. Ms. Vann pointed out to the patient how he had taken a risk in revealing his concerns to her in the session.

Sessions 7–10: In the middle portion of his brief therapy, Mr. Pedotti talked about his father's situation, which the therapist could see dramatically paralleled his own. Mr. Pedotti viewed his father as docile and powerless in a relationship in which his father's new wife insulated, controlled, and spoke for him. Mr. Pedotti found this to be more true when his father (who also had diabetes) was more physically compromised. Mr. Pedotti talked about anger toward this woman, but denied any similarities to his own situation. A discussion about anger ensued, in which it became clear that Mr. Pedotti feared expressing his anger because he expected it would be met with disapproval. However, the times he could recall having been angry, he thought that others listened to him and took him seriously. Mr. Pedotti was intrigued with this disparity between what he expected and what he experienced.

Ms. Vann suggested that in the past Mr. Pedotti may have behaved as though the worst would happen, and that perhaps he was just waiting to die. She contrasted this attitude with the patient's identity as a boxer and a fighter. The patient readily expanded the metaphor and expressed that his opponent, which he saw as his physical problem, was "very big" and he was at a loss to know how to fight it. In subsequent sessions, the therapist worked on reframing the "fight" as not against his disease but rather as against his emotionally and mentally "giving up." At the end of the eighth session, Mr. Pedotti talked about the possibility of getting a kidney transplant and he wondered whether one of his three brothers would donate a kidney.

Mr. Pedotti missed his next appointment due to the death of his father. In the 10th session, he talked about his anger toward both his father and his father's wife. "My father died years before his death." During this session, when the therapist drew parallels between his father's situation and his own, Mr. Pedotti was able to acknowledge how his own passivity and withdrawal were also rendering him almost dead. He spoke about wanting increased interaction with his family and for the first time expressed hope about receiving a transplant.

Sessions 11–15: During the last third of his therapy, Mr. Pedotti spent much of his time talking about his growing awareness of similarities between his father's emotional and social reaction to severe illness and his own. He described his desire to live as fully as long as possible rather than to withdraw into a premature emotional death.

During these last sessions, the focus repeatedly returned to the termination of the therapy and the relationship that had evolved between Mr. Pedotti and Ms. Vann. Mr. Pedotti discussed his desire to remain in psychotherapy and requested that it be continued. While his therapist acknowledged Mr. Pedotti's assertiveness, she told him that his present therapy could not continue, but that the decision about subsequent treatment was his to make. However, Ms. Vann also said she welcomed hearing his thoughts and feelings about their therapy's coming to a close.

Mr. Pedotti initially replied that he did not have the time to think about the ending of the therapy, because of difficulties he was having at the medical center getting a second opinion regarding a proposed cataract procedure. He described his treatment by various medical staff disparagingly: "Intern students who just leave me up in the air." His therapist (a trainee) used this opportunity to ask Mr. Pedotti about parallels between this recent experience and feelings of being left without her help and support. With some difficulty, Mr. Pedotti was able to discuss his anxiety, sadness, and even some anger about termination. Ms. Vann validated his feelings by stating that they were understandable given the circumstances (i.e., the closeness that had evolved between the two of them, and the help the patient had received from their work together), but she steadfastly maintained the termination date.

Although Ms. Vann was not totally sure that Mr. Pedotti would continue to make the gains he had during his therapy, she assessed that to extend the therapy would probably be more antitherapeutic than helpful. By sticking to the planned termination, the therapist hoped to convey the message to Mr. Pedotti that she thought of him as a "fighter" who was able to be victorious. In addition, termination provided an opportunity for Mr. Pedotti to understand his readiness to suppress negative affect, and to allow the expression of feelings about losing his relationship with his therapist.

By the end of the 15-session therapy, Mr. Pedotti seemed to find a purpose "in making a difference" to loved ones, especially his grandchildren. He reestablished intimate contacts with his immediate and extended family. He became more assertive with his wife about his own medical treatment. He became involved in more social activities. In sum, he was able to regain a sense of himself as a fighter who, rather than fighting a disease, was fighting the pull to give up and die.

Two months after his last therapy session, Mr. Pedotti had a successful kidney transplant. His mental status as recorded in his chart by his physician

1 month following his transplant is as follows: "Soft-spoken, friendly, good eye contact, mildly restricted affect, denies depression, goal directed, future oriented."

The treatments of both Mr. Allen and Mr. Pedotti were particularly difficult because of their interpersonal and medical complexity. I think the therapies turned out as well as they did in part because the therapists were operating within a methodological approach that helped them discern interventions consistent with the formulation. Working in the here and now with a circumscribed focus allowed the therapists to intervene without becoming overwhelmed or conveying their dismay to their patients. The systematic TLDP framework gave the therapists added perspective and confidence, which seemed to foster hope and promote progress in their patients (Frank, 1974).

Vanderbilt Therapeutic Strategies Scale

I. PSYCHODYNAMIC INTERVIEWING STYLE

1. **Therapist encourages the patient to experience and express affect in the session.**

1	2	3	4	5
not at all characteristic		characteristic		extremely characteristic

2. **Therapist encourages the patient's expression and/or exploration of feelings in relation to a significant other (including therapist).**

1	2	3	4	5
not at all characteristic		characteristic		extremely characteristic

3. **Therapist encourages the patient's expression and/or exploration of thoughts and beliefs in relation to a significant other (including therapist).**

1	2	3	4	5
not at all characteristic		characteristic		extremely characteristic

4. **Therapist actively attempts to engage the patient in a collaborative effort.**

1	2	3	4	5
not at all characteristic		characteristic		extremely characteristic

5. **Therapist responds to the patient in an accepting and understanding manner.**

1	2	3	4	5
not at all characteristic		characteristic		extremely characteristic

6. Therapist attempts to maintain a focused line of inquiry.

1	2	3	4	5
not at all characteristic		characteristic		extremely characteristic

7. Therapist inquires into the personal or unique meanings of the patient's words.

1	2	3	4	5
not at all characteristic		characteristic		extremely characteristic

8. Therapist responds to the patient's statements or descriptions by seeking concrete detail.

1	2	3	4	5
not at all characteristic		characteristic		extremely characteristic

9. Therapist attends to seemingly important statements or events.

1	2	3	4	5
not at all characteristic		characteristic		extremely characteristic

10. Therapist shows evidence of listening receptively.

1	2	3	4	5
not at all characteristic		characteristic		extremely characteristic

11. Therapist appears to maintain an optimal participant–observer stance.

1	2	3	4	5
not at all characteristic		characteristic		extremely characteristic

12. Therapist uses open-ended questions.

1	2	3	4	5
not at all characteristic		characteristic		extremely characteristic

II. TLDP SPECIFIC STRATEGIES

13. Therapist specifically addresses transactions in the patient–therapist relationship.

1	2	3	4	5
not at all characteristic		characteristic		extremely characteristic

14. **Therapist encourages the patient to explore feelings and thoughts about the therapist or the therapeutic relationship.**

1	2	3	4	5
not at all characteristic		characteristic		extremely characteristic

15. **Therapist encourages the patient to discuss how the therapist might feel or think about the patient.**

1	2	3	4	5
not at all characteristic		characteristic		extremely characteristic

16. **Therapist discusses own reactions to some aspect of the patient's behavior in relation to the therapist.**

1	2	3	4	5
not at all characteristic		characteristic		extremely characteristic

17. **Therapist attempts to explore patterns that might constitute a cyclical maladaptive pattern in the patient's interpersonal relationships.**

1	2	3	4	5
not at all characteristic		characteristic		extremely characteristic

18. **Therapist asks about the patient's introject (how the patient feels about and treats himself or herself).**

1	2	3	4	5
not at all characteristic		characteristic		extremely characteristic

19. **Therapist links a recurrent pattern of behavior or interpersonal conflict to transactions between the patient and therapist.**

1	2	3	4	5
not at all characteristic		characteristic		extremely characteristic

20. **Therapist addresses obstacles (e.g., silences, coming late, avoidance of meaningful topics) that might influence the therapeutic process.**

1	2	3	4	5
not at all characteristic		characteristic		extremely characteristic

21. **Therapist discusses an aspect of the time-limited nature of TLDP or termination.**

1	2	3	4	5
not at all characteristic		characteristic		extremely characteristic

22. **Therapist provides the opportunity for the patient to have a new experience of himself or herself and/or the therapist relevant to the patient's particular cyclical maladaptive pattern.**

1	2	3	4	5
not at all characteristic		characteristic		extremely characteristic

Manual for the Vanderbilt Therapeutic Strategies Scale

Stephen F. Butler and the Center for Psychotherapy Research Team
Vanderbilt University

THIS MANUAL is to accompany the Vanderbilt Therapeutic Strategies Scale. The scale is intended to be descriptive (i.e., what is being done) and, to some extent, evaluative (i.e., how *well* it is being done). An effort has been made to make the items quite specific, requiring a relatively low level of inference. The rater's task is to search for concrete evidence that a particular behavior or therapist action has occurred. If the therapist does not address the topic described in a given item (e.g., feelings), the rating of the particular segment should reflect this fact (i.e., "not at all characteristic"). This should not be considered condemning of the therapist, since it is recognized that he or she may ask about feelings in the next segment. It may be best for the rater to consider the Therapeutic Strategies Scale as rating "segments" rather than "therapists." The goal is to describe the segment as accurately and reliably as possible.

Some items, intended to reflect the *quality* of the therapeutic interaction, cannot be made as specific as other items. These items are indicated by an asterisk (*). The rater must try to capture the quality of the therapist's performance. It is understood that these ratings often involve the rater's personal reaction to the session, rather than the identification of specific events, actions, or behaviors on the part of the therapist. A therapist's ability to respond to a patient with acceptance and understanding, for example, may be reflected in all of his or her actions.

Each item in the Scale is rated on a scale from 1 (not at all characteristic) to 5 (extremely characteristic). Half-point ratings are permissible. Because specific evidence is often needed to rate an item higher than 1, it is expected that the lowest scores will be used. Similarly, the highest ratings should also be used. A 5 should not take on the "mystical" significance of a 10 in Olympic gymnastics, where only one or two people in the world are expected to perform perfectly. Thus, although a given segment may generally receive low or high scores, the entire range of scores should be expected to be used across segments and therapists.

Rating guidelines are provided for each item. When considering these guidelines, some general points should be kept in mind. First, the ability of any therapist to carry out a given strategy or intervention is inherently limited by the quality of the patient's participation. The Therapeutic Strategies Scale is designed to assess *therapist* performance, but it must be recognized that this cannot be realistically (or theoretically) independent of the patient's contribution to the process. Despite this difficult problem, the Scale assumes that, in most cases, there ought to be evidence of therapists' efforts to initiate a therapeutic process. Thus, it is the therapist's task to *ask* about feelings, for instance, or about the patient–therapist relationship. One cannot blame a difficult patient alone for a poor process if the therapist offered few opportunities for the patient to engage in a productive process. Another point to consider is that what often separates the skillful therapist from an unskilled one are efforts to follow through with a particular line of questioning. Thus, if a therapist asks what a patient is feeling right now, and the patient answers, "Nothing," the therapist can either take that response at face value, or follow it up. This does *not* mean that the therapist challenges or cajoles the patient. But the skillful therapist does not necessarily drop the topic. Some tactful exploration of the patient's experience may be warranted. Such a follow-up might be, "What happens when I ask you about feelings?" In this instance the follow-up might reveal that the patient does not understand what the therapist means, or the patient may suspect that the therapist is not really interested, etc. Skillful follow-up should be distinguished from undesirable "overdoing it." To achieve a high rating on a given item, the therapist should be genuinely *trying* to implement a strategy without giving up too soon (after too little effort). Along these lines is the situation where a therapist is clearly attempting to implement a specified strategy, but does so in a *manner* that is overbearing, authoritarian, rigid, etc. When this occurs, the rating should be high for the specific strategy, but low on those items dealing specifically with the therapist's manner. A final, general rating problem might arise when the *patient initiates* a discussion of an issue or topic assessed by a particular item, or when the patient engages in extensive discussion with limited therapist involvement. In these cases the rating should reflect the degree to which the therapist *facilitates* the exploration of the topic in question. For present purposes, facilitation refers to more than a passive acceptance on the part of the therapist. The therapist must actively encourage, prompt, and work with the patient. If the therapist's input works to prematurely close discussion/exploration, of a topic raised by a patient then a 1 is scored on the relevant item.

The following item descriptions are intended as guides in making reliable distinctions between therapist behaviors. When possible, rules have been specified to assist in making the rating. The complex nature of ratings on the Therapeutic Strategies Scale requires that the rater use his or her judgment based on the guidelines provided.

PSYCHODYNAMIC INTERVIEWING STYLE

1. *Therapist encourages the patient to experience and express affect in the session.* If the therapist makes no inquiries into the patient's affective experience during the rated segment, score a 1 on this item. If the topic of feelings is approached but it is done tentatively or unclearly, score 2 or 3. Higher ratings of 4 or 5 reflect clear efforts on the therapist's part to foster discussion and sharing of feelings. This includes efforts to follow up on initial efforts to explore feelings ("When I asked you how that made you feel, you changed the subject; what happens when I ask about feelings?"). The highest score of 5 is warranted *only* if the clear purpose of the therapist's efforts is to focus on feelings that are occurring in the *here and now*. It is possible for the therapist to get a high score even if the patient never shares feelings, if the therapist makes clear efforts to facilitate discussion and/or experience of feelings.

2. *Therapist encourages the patient's expression and/or exploration of feelings in relation to a significant other (including therapist).* This item presupposes the first item (i.e., a high score on item 2 must be accompanied by a high score on item 1). The kinds of comments or questions by the therapist would be the same as in item 1; however, the feelings in question must be explicitly related to another person. Again, the highest score of 5 is reserved for instances where the focus is on feelings in the *here and now*. Thus, questions about a patient's feelings over failing an exam would not be rated on this item, but discussion involving feelings about parental response to the failure

would be rated here. Also feelings about the therapist are rated here as well as under the TLDP Specific Strategies items (13–22).

3. *Therapist encourages the patient's expression and exploration of thoughts and beliefs in relation to a significant other (including therapist).* This item reflects the importance of understanding the patient's perspective, especially with regard to other people. Instances involving thoughts and beliefs about the therapist are also rated under the TLDP Specific Strategies section (items 13–22). Lower ratings, such as 2 or 3, indicate some mention of thoughts and beliefs but with limited exploration/elaboration of these. For ratings higher than a 3 the exploration/elaboration of the thoughts and beliefs should be *specific*. That is, the therapist should be attempting to get the patient to go beyond his or her initial description of thoughts and beliefs about other people by seeking specific information about the nature of the thoughts and beliefs, the situations in which these occur, with whom, etc. Extensive exploration or elaboration of thoughts and beliefs geared toward the identification of automatic or unconscious assumptions about other people deserve a 4. Sustained and focused efforts to explore and elaborate such thoughts and beliefs warrants a 5. (Note: See also item 13).

*4. *Therapist actively attempts to engage the patient in a collaborative effort.* This item is intended to be a measure of the quality of the therapeutic interaction. Specifically, lower scores, 1 and 2, suggest that the therapist is actively undermining a collaborative alliance or failing to address serious problems in the collaborative atmosphere of their interaction. A rating of 3 is made when the therapist is neither undermining the process nor actively attempting to enhance the collaboration. Higher ratings, 4 and 5, are made when there are specific actions on the part of the therapist to create a collaborative atmosphere. There should be a sense that the therapist and patient will work together, a "we-ness" that is implied by the therapist's behavior. One example might be when a therapist checks with the patient in a manner which conveys that the patient is the "expert" regarding the proper "fit" of interpretations, conclusions, goals, etc. The distinction between a 4 and 5 rests on the rater's judgment regarding the extent of the therapist's efforts to ensure collaboration.

*5. *Therapist responds to the patient in an accepting and understanding manner.* This item is also a rating of the quality of the therapeutic interaction. Therapist behaviors/attitudes which might indicate an absence of acceptance and understanding include: a judgmental attitude, condescension, rudeness, disapproval, guilt-induction, exasperation, or annoyance. A rating of 1 will necessitate a clear example of inappropriate attitude on the part of the therapist. A 2 would indicate that the rater detects some, perhaps subtle, evidence of the therapist's disrespect. Ratings of 3 and 4 are considered the ordinary range of "unremarkable" therapy. A rating of 5 is reserved for examples of exceptional acceptance/understanding on the part of the therapist. An example of this might occur when a patient is putting himself or herself down for some "terrible or disgusting" event (e.g., recounting an experience of "reckless" or "irresponsible" sex, giving vent to sadistic urges, etc.). A rating of 5 would be made if the therapist seems genuinely nonjudgmental and gently explores the patient's thoughts, feelings, alternatives for dealing with future situations, etc.

6. Therapist attempts to maintain a focused line of inquiry. This item is intended to rate the degree to which the therapist attempts to explore and elaborate topics/issues in a focused and organized manner. If the therapist introduces topics that are tangential or unrelated to the therapeutic process or in other ways actively interrupt the process, this warrants a low score such as 1 or 2. If the therapist simply follows the patient's lead, then a 3 is in order. Specific and active attempts to create a focused session deserve the highest scores. Such attempts might involve asking how a present topic relates to earlier topics, enlisting the patient's aid in identifying and understanding connections between topics, or making summary statements suggesting how topics that are different on the surface might be related. If the therapist's attempts to focus the session are authoritarian and controlling, the rating should be high; the *manner* of focusing is rated on other items (e.g., items 4, 5, 10, or 11).

7. *Therapist inquires into the personal or unique meanings of the patient's words.* This item is restricted to events where the therapist *explicitly* asks the patient what is meant by a particular word or phrase and explores the personal meaning of words used to describe experiences. Lower ratings of 2 or 3 reflect very general inquiries into personal meanings with little or no follow-up so that the meaning remains vague. Higher ratings of 4 or 5 reflect both specific inquiries into personal meanings (i.e., frequency) and/or the exploration of the personal meaning, possibly relating the meaning to important beliefs, feelings, themes, or patterns.

8. *Therapist responds to the patient's statements or descriptions by seeking concrete detail.* This item is intended to measure the extent to which the therapist seeks concrete detail. In order to obtain a rating above a 1, the therapist should ask the patient to elaborate on a statement, belief, description, etc. Ratings of 2 reflect vague or occasional efforts on the therapist's part to seek detail. Examples of such statements might be, "Can you be more specific?" or "What do you mean by that?" Lower ratings on this item would also be given in instances where the therapist asks *only* for details of "facts" such as: "Where were you living?" or "What year was that?" "What movie did you see?" Ratings of 3 reflect an unremarkable or ordinary amount of detail seeking on

the part of the therapist. This might be where the therapist asks for detail, but there is little follow-up, so that the patient's experience is not made concrete or precise. Higher ratings of 4 require explicit requests for concrete specifics, especially of the patient's subjective experiences. The highest rating of 5 is given when concrete, *behavioral* detail is sought. The goal here might be to create a visual image in the therapist's mind of what happened and the patient's response to what happened. If the patient says, "My boss doesn't like me," the therapist might respond, "What does your boss say or do that leads you to believe that?" Or if a patient tried to arrange a date but "everything went wrong," the therapist might ask, "What exactly did you say when you asked her out?" As always, the highest ratings are given when such attempts are followed through.

*9. *Therapist attends to seemingly important statements or events.* Ratings should be 1 or 2 if the rater feels that significant events or statements are routinely ignored by the therapist or if a particularly obvious event (e.g., crying, an extremely abrupt change of topic) is ignored. Clearly, no therapist can take advantage of *all* opportunities. Failure to capitalize on apparent chances does not automatically warrant low scores. Ratings for this item should be made with respect to the therapeutic process at the moment. If the session seems to be going nowhere or the patient seems resistant and the therapist remains passive, neglecting all opportunities, a 1 is scored. A rating of 3 is given to a segment of discourse where the therapist is following the patient's lead and there is no evidence of either missing important events or taking pains to explore an event. (Note: In the videotaped sessions, many therapists mechanically mention the patient's reaction to the camera. By itself, such an effort only warrants a 3. A lower or higher rating would be warranted depending on how this handled.) A rating of 4 is made when the therapist attempts to explore an important issue or event. Particularly in-depth exploration of an event warrants a 5, especially if the therapist attempts to relate the event to the patient's problematic character style. Sometimes when a therapist attempts to explore important issues, the patient will deny that the issue is important. For the highest ratings, the therapist should not be put off by a patient's initial denial that the event might be significant. In the case of such denial that an event is important, the skillful therapist may choose to explore the significance of the denial itself. Such a strategy would receive a high rating here even though the initial topic is not pursued.

*10. *Therapist shows evidence of listening receptively.* Listening implies an active receptivity to what the patient is trying to communicate. Ratings of 1 or 2 reflect the presence of actions that interfere with receptive listening, such as: interrupting the patient; avoiding what the patient seems to be trying to say; contradicting the patient; taking the lead away from the patient by forcing one's own agenda; belaboring points which seem to be missing the mark; talking too much; responding to issues in a selective manner that constricts the patient's opportunity for expression; appearing uninterested, yawning, fidgeting, looking away, etc. A rating of 3 means that the therapist seems to be following the patient in a "usual" or unremarkable manner. This rating might be used when the therapist is listening very passively, so that it is impossible to tell whether or not the therapist hears and understands the patient. On this item, an extremely passive therapist should get no higher than a 3. Ratings of 4 or 5 reflect active attempts to clarify what the patient is trying to communicate, asking for details and specifics (see items 7, 8, and 9) in such a way that it is clear that the therapist is hearing and attempting to understand the patient's communications. High ratings should also reflect ongoing attempts to check with the patient that what the therapist has heard is what the patient meant to communicate (self-correction: for example, a therapist may say, "What I hear you saying is . . .").

*11. *Therapist appears to maintain an optimal participant–observer stance.* Low ratings of 1 and 2 are made when the therapist's participation in the relationship seemingly lacks awareness of how his or her own behavior is affecting the patient. When this happens, the rater may begin to feel that the therapist is in "collusion" with the patient, or the therapist may appear too distant and/or too involved. Examples of being too distant include those segments where the therapist seems uninvolved, cold, remote, or detached. This may manifest itself as a low activity level (see also item 10), seeming indifference (see also item 5), or an overly intellectualized style. Examples of being too involved include those segments in which the therapist becomes embroiled in power struggles with the patient, responds in a complementary fashion to hostile or provocative communications, or overreacts to the patient's distress by becoming upset, excessively reassuring, etc. A segment is rated 3 if the therapist's involvement seems more or less appropriate, but there is no effort to utilize observations of their interaction. Higher ratings of 4 and 5 are given to those segments in which the therapist effectively moves between participating in the relationship and observing it. Thus, very high ratings will almost always involve direct comments on the relationship, with the highest ratings reserved for comments that relate to the *here and now* (see Specific Strategies section). Thus, the therapist might say something like, "We seem to be arguing just now; I wonder how that developed," or "You mentioned how you hate it when your husband scolds you, and I was wondering if my comment just now felt like scolding."

*12. *Therapist uses open-ended questions.* Ratings of this item are intended to measure the extent to which the therapist's mode of inquiry is primarily characterized by open-ended questions. Segments where the therapist rarely asks questions, but tends to "interpret" or make "pronouncements" are rated 1. A score of 2 indicates that there is some effort to ask questions, but a tendency to make "pronouncements," rather than inquiries, is in evidence. A score of 3 suggests that the therapist usually asks questions but occasionally seems to make pronouncements that negatively influence patients' ability or willingness to communicate their experience. A situation that is sometimes observed is a kind of compromise between a pronouncement and a question, where an observation or interpretation ends with a questioning tone ("So, you're feeling detached?"). While such questions can be used skillfully, these are not considered open-ended questions, because they tend to pull for a yes/no type of response. The rater must decide whether this style of questioning is overdone and limits the patient's expression (score a 1), or whether such a convention is used sparingly (score a 3 or 4). A score of 4 indicates that the predominant mode of inquiry is open-ended questions, but there are also questions that seemingly restrict the patient's "response set." This is often seen when a therapist seems to give the patient a multiple choice test ("Are you angry or sad?"). The highest score of 5 is given when the therapist's predominant mode of inquiry is open-ended questions, and he or she only rarely asks restrictive questions. It should be noted that for some patients it is quite appropriate to provide alternatives and/or vocabulary for describing their experience when doing so is a new and unfamiliar practice for them. Nevertheless, the skillful therapist minimizes this, and, when such questions are asked, the skillful therapist goes further to check out the extent to which the words used convey the patient's experience accurately.

TLDP-SPECIFIC STRATEGIES

13. *Therapist specifically addresses transactions in the patient–therapist relationship.* More so than other items, this item is a *frequency* item. This means that if there is no discussion of the patient–therapist relationship, then rate a 1. If there is some brief mention of the relationship *on the part of the therapist* but no follow-up by either patient or therapist, rate a 2. A moderate amount of discussion about the relationship yields a 3, and so forth through 4 and 5. This is not a quality item. Its main purpose is to reflect the degree to which the discussion in the rated segment is focused on the patient–therapist relationship. This will happen not at all, a little, some, much, or very much.

14. *Therapist encourages the patient to explore feelings and thoughts about the therapist or the therapeutic relationship.* This item rates the extent to which the therapist attempts to explore the patient's feelings, thoughts, fantasies, and resistances that occur with respect to the therapist or the therapeutic rela-

tionship. If the therapist does not inquire into the patient's experience of the therapist or the therapeutic situation, then score a 1. Tentative or limited explorations of the patient's experience of these warrants a 2 or 3 rating. Higher ratings of 4 or 5 require the presence of extensive inquiry and follow-through, evidencing unambiguous intent on the part of the therapist to understand the patient's experience of the therapist or therapeutic situation. This item specifically requires ratings of the degree of the therapist's effort in this direction. A therapist who seems to be "overdoing it" might get a high rating on this item but lower ratings on such items as 10 or 11.

15. *Therapist encourages the patient to discuss how the therapist might feel or think about the patient.* This item deals with the extent to which the therapist attempts to understand "What might be the patient's experience of my intentions, attitudes, or feelings about him or her?" If there are no inquiries regarding the patient's thoughts about how the therapist might be responding to the patient, then score a 1. Tentative or limited explorations into the patient's hypotheses about the therapist's response to him or her warrant a 2 or 3. Extensive exploration and follow-through of this line of inquiry should receive the higher scores of 4 and 5. Again, this item reflects only the therapist's focus on elaborating the patient's view of the therapist (concerns about "overdoing it," etc., are rated elsewhere; see items 10 and 11).

16. *Therapist uses own reactions to some aspect of the patient's behavior to clarify communications or guide exploration of possible distortions in the patient's perceptions of others' reactions, intentions, etc.* If there is no discussion of the therapist's personal reactions or if the personal reactions are simply self-disclosure, then score a 1. Rating this item beyond 1 requires some evidence that the therapist is using his or her own reactions to (a) clarify communication ("You seem to have heard what I said as criticism, while that was not my intention") or (b) to guide discussion of the patient's maladaptive patterns ("Just now I noticed I was trying to justify myself. Do you find that others try to justify themselves to you?"). Moderately skillful use of this strategy, 2 or 3, may involve slightly cumbersome, unclear, or tentative discussions of personal reactions. It is also possible that, while attempting this strategy, a novice therapist may appear to be blaming the patient. The *effort* should be rated on this item; the *"blaming"* should then be recorded on item 5. The higher rating of 4 should be made when the therapist uses personal reactions in an appropriate way. The highest rating of 5 is made when there is an attempt by the therapist to link his own reaction to the patient's patterns in other interpersonal settings (i.e., CMP) during the segment.

17. *Therapist seeks to explore patterns that might constitute a cyclical maladaptive pattern in the patient's interpersonal relationships.* A rating of 1 is warranted if the therapist makes no attempts at pattern seeking. This might occur when

the therapist seems to be trying to "support" the patient, give the patient "feedback" or "advice," or the therapist may simply be engaged in listening quietly. A rating of 2 might be indicated when the therapist makes some comments or asks questions that suggest vague or tentative efforts to elaborate and explore general patterns in the patient's interactions. For example, the therapist may suggest, "You have difficulty trusting men," but this theme is then dropped. For a rating higher than 2, there must be evidence that the therapist attempts to "put something together." A 3 indicates that the therapist actively pursues generalizations of the patient's interpersonal material and may link different relationships (not necessarily with the therapist; see item 19) that share a common pattern. To rate higher than a 3, there should be some evidence that the therapist is suggesting a *sequencing of events in a causally connected manner.* Thus, the rater should look for instances where the therapist says something like, "It seems that when you do X, other people tend to do Y." A 4 is indicated if the therapist's efforts to identify a pattern *appear* to utilize the categories stipulated by the CMP procedure (i.e., acts of self, expectations of others, acts of others, introject). The highest rating of 5 is reserved for those segments where the therapist *clearly* uses CMP categories and the cyclic framework to explore or elaborate a theme. Thus, if a patient describes something that could be an "act of self," a high rating would be made if the therapist responds with something like, "How do you expect other people will respond when you do that?" A high rating need not, however, involve an entire CMP. It makes no difference whether the patterns discussed involve the therapist (see item 19).

18. *Therapist asks about the patient's introject (how the patient feels about and treats himself or herself).* A 1 rating is made when the therapist makes no specific inquiries into the patient's experience of him or herself. Any inquiry regarding how the patient feels about, thinks about, or treats himself or herself warrants a rating higher than 1. A borderline example might be, "How do you feel when you do that?" An inquiry that focuses on how the person feels toward someone else ("I feel furious with her") is not an example of introject. If, on the other hand, the focus is on how the patient feels about him or herself ("I was ashamed of myself for actually doing that"), then this item is rated (Note: A better question would be, "How do you feel *about yourself* when you do that?"). Lower ratings of 2 or 3 indicate that a relevant inquiry has been made but there is little or no attempt to follow up, get more detail, or relate the introject to a larger pattern (i.e., CMP). Attempts to follow up, clarify, or relate the introject to interpersonal patterns warrant higher ratings of 4 or 5. (Note: In the latter case see also item 17.)

19. *Therapist links a recurrent pattern of behavior or interpersonal conflict to transactions between the patient and therapist.* The segment is rated 1 if there is no linkage in either direction (i.e., in therapy → other relationships, or other

relationships → in therapy). Score a 2 if the linkage is vague or tentatively offered, seemingly implied by the discussion, or otherwise unclear. A score of 3 is given when the therapist makes a clear linking interpretation but there is no follow-up discussion or elaboration. Scores of 4 and 5 differentiate degrees of follow-up and discussion. A moderate amount of discussion and elaboration merits a 4. More extensive discussion, especially discussion that relates the link to clearly CMP material, rates a 5. Note that the discussion of a link must be *explicit* to rate higher than a 2, and the link can be made in either direction. When a linkage is rated, also note the rating on item 13.

20. *Therapist addresses obstacles (e.g., silences, coming late, avoidance of meaningful topics) that might influence the therapeutic process.* The decision for this item is whether or not the therapist addresses a resistance or obstacle to the therapeutic process. In general, such obstacles *are* the content material of psychotherapy and include any activity on the part of the patient that impedes a productive process for the duration of the session. Thus, an obstacle can be the patient's inability to think of something to say, inability to trust the therapist, coming late, etc. Rating this item does not involve decisions regarding the appropriateness, timing, or manner evidenced in this strategy. If the therapist does not address any impediment or potential impediment to an open, collaborative, productive process, then score 1. If the therapist makes mention of some obstacle in passing but does not explore it, score a 2. An example might be when a therapist notes that the patient is 15 minutes late but immediately goes on to discuss other content; or if the patient cannot think of anything to say, and the therapist provides a topic, "Well, let's talk about your mother." A 3 involves more than mention in passing of an obstacle, but the elaboration is vague, tentative, or quickly dropped. A rating of 4 is made when the therapist attempts to explore possible motives, insecurities, feelings, or other meanings of the obstacle. A rating of 5 is made when the obstacle seems to have been adequately discussed and understood. Even if the patient is resistant, the therapist may deserve a 5 by exploring the patient's difficulties in discussing the obstacle (e.g., "It seems to be hard for us to discuss your missing last session without canceling. What are your thoughts about this kind of discussion?").

21. *Therapist discusses an aspect of the time-limited nature of TLDP or termination.* For a rating to be made on this item, explicit discussion of separation from or ending with the therapist must be observed. If there is no discussion of these issues during the rated segment, then score a 1. Or if the patient casually mentions the number of sessions left, and the therapist immediately steers the conversation in other directions, score this as a 1. If the topic is mentioned by the therapist, but no follow-up or elaboration is attempted, score a 2. If the therapist were to mention that there are only X number of sessions left, or say "We're about in the middle of our therapy" but no effort is

made to elaborate on feelings, reactions, etc., likewise score a 2. A 3 is scored if the topic of termination is discussed to some extent, but the therapist seems vague, tentative, or unclear. Higher scores of 4 and 5 differentiate degrees of exploration and elaboration on patient's reactions to termination or the idea of termination. As usual, the degree to which the therapist follows through on this difficult topic is important. Since many patients deny the importance of termination, a therapist who seems unable to pursue the topic may receive a score of 3 or 4. If the therapist proceeds to question the patient's reactions to *other* endings, deaths, etc., this might warrant a 4 or 5.

*†22. *Therapist provides the opportunity for the patient to have a new experience of himself or herself and/or the therapist relevant to the patient's particular cyclical maladaptive pattern.* This item is intended to measure the quality of the therapist's interventions that are designed to undermine the patient's CMP. The therapist should not concentrate on a forced or unauthentic reaction designed to be *opposite* to that usually expected from others (e.g., to be effusive if others are aloof), but rather to emphasize those specific behaviors from his or her therapeutic stance that would be most therapeutic for a particular patient (i.e., those behaviors or attitudes that would most counteract the patient's cyclical maladaptive pattern). Therapist behaviors/attitudes that might warrant a 1 would be those indicating active collusion with the patient's CMP by responding in a complementary fashion to the pushes and pulls from the patient. For example, a therapist praises a patient for certain behaviors when that patient's CMP involves her feeling she has to please to be accepted. A rating of 2 is made if the therapist does not make use of opportunities to relate in a new manner, but does *not* collude in a reenactment. For example, with a patient working on issues about being ignored, the therapist listens to clinical material, but does not follow up on the patient's not mentioning the therapist's lateness. A rating of 3 indicates inclusion of a new experience. For example, when a patient with an irresponsible style informs the therapist he will be missing next week's session, the therapist chooses to focus on the patient's letting him/her know in advance rather than on the lack of attendance. Higher ratings of 4 and 5 are given to those segments where the therapist is able to seize the opportunity to expand or deepen experiences that are designed to undermine the patient's CMP. Here the therapist makes clear and/or repeated efforts to promote such experiential learning (for example, facilitating new behaviors that the patient sees as "risky").

---

*Item reflects the *quality* of the interaction
†Item written by H. Levenson
Reprinted with permission of S. F. Butler and H. H. Strupp

References

Adler, G., & Beckett, A. (1989). Psychotherapy of the patient with an HIV infection. *Psychosomatics, 30,* 203–208.

Alexander, F., & French, T. M. (1946). *Psychoanalytic therapy: Principles and applications.* New York: Ronald Press.

Altman, N. (1993). Psychoanalysis and the urban poor. *Psychoanalytic Dialogues, 3,* 29–50.

American Psychiatric Association (1994). *Diagnostic and statistical manual of mental disorders: DSM IV.* Washington, DC: American Psychiatric Press.

Anchin, J. C., & Kiesler, D. J. (Eds.). (1982). *Handbook of interpersonal psychotherapy.* New York: Pergamon Press.

Anderson, S. C., & Mandell, D. L. (1989). The use of self-disclosure by professional social workers. *Social Casework, 70,* 259–267.

Ankuta, G. Y., & Abeles, N. (1993). Client satisfaction, clinical significance, and meaningful change in psychotherapy. *Professional Psychology: Research and Practice, 24,* 70–74.

Aron, L. (1990). One-person and two-person psychologies and the method of psychoanalysis. *Psychoanalytic Psychology, 7,* 475–495.

Aron, L. (1991). The patient's experience of the analyst's subjectivity. *Psychoanalytic Dialogues, 11,* 29–51.

Bartholomew, K., & Horowitz, L. M. (1991). Attachment styles among young adults: A test of a four-category model. *Journal of Personality and Social Psychology, 61,* 226–244.

Bauer, G. P., & Kobos, J. C. (1987). *Brief therapy: Short-term psychodynamic intervention.* Northvale, NJ: Jason Aronson.

Beck, A. T., Rush, A. J., Shaw, B. F., & Emery, G. (1979). *Cognitive therapy of depression.* New York: Guilford.

Beebe, B., & Lachman, F. (1988). The contribution of mother–infant mutual influence to the origins of self and object representations. *Psychoanalytic Psychology, 5,* 305–357.

Bein, E. (1994, August). Stages of meaningful change and clinical significance in time-limited dynamic psychotherapy. In M. B. Gurtman (Chair), *Inventory of Interpersonal Problems: Clinical and research applications.* Symposium conducted at the American Psychological Association convention, Los Angeles.

Bein, E. (1995). *A long-term follow-up study on veterans receiving time-limited dynamic psychotherapy.* Unpublished doctoral dissertation, Pacific Graduate School of Psychology, Palo Alto, CA.

Bein, E., Levenson, H., & Overstreet, D. (1994, June). Outcome and follow-up data from the VAST project. In H. Levenson (Chair), *Outcome and follow-up data in brief dynamic therapy: Caveat emptor, caveat vendor.* Symposium conducted at the annual international meeting of the Society for Psychotherapy Research, York, England.

Beitman, B. D., & Klerman, G. L. (Eds.) (1991). *Integrating pharmacotherapy and psychotherapy.* Washington, DC: American Psychiatric Press.

Beitman, B. D., & Maxim, P. (1984). A survey of psychiatric practice: Implications for residency training. *Journal of Psychiatric Education, 8,* 149–153.

Benjamin, L. S. (1993). *Interpersonal diagnosis and treatment of personality disorders.* New York: Guilford.

Bennett, M. J. (1983). Focal psychotherapy: Terminable and interminable. *American Journal of Psychotherapy, 37,* 365–375.

Bennett, M. J. (1994). Can competing psychotherapists be managed? *Managed Care Quarterly, 2,* 29–35.

Berne, E. (1964). *Games people play.* New York: Grove.

Bertalanffy, L. von (1969). *General systems theory: Essays on its foundation and development* (rev. ed.). New York: Braziller.

Bibring, E. (1954). Psychoanalysis and the dynamic psychotherapies. *Journal of the American Psychoanalytic Association, 2,* 745–770.

Binder, J. L. (1993). Is it time to improve psychotherapy training? *Clinical Psychology Review, 13,* 301–318.

Binder, J. L., Henry, W. P., & Strupp, H. H. (1987). An appraisal of selection criteria for dynamic psychotherapies and implications for setting time limits. *Psychiatry, 50,* 154–166.

Bloom, B. (1992). *Planned short-term psychotherapy: A clinical handbook.* Boston: Allyn and Bacon.

Boesky, D. (1990). The psychoanalytic process and its components. *Psychoanalytic Quarterly, 59,* 550–584.

Bolter, K. (1987). *Differences in therapy-related values and attitudes between short-term and long-term therapists.* Unpublished doctoral dissertation, California School of Professional Psychology, Berkeley.

Bolter, K., Levenson, H., & Alvarez, W. (1990). Differences in values between short-term and long-term therapists. *Professional Psychology: Research and Practice, 4,* 285–290.

Bongar, B., Markey, L. A., & Peterson, L. G. (1991). Views on the difficult and dreaded patient: A preliminary investigation. *Medical Psychotherapy, 4,* 9–16.

Bowlby, J. (1969). *Attachment and loss. Vol. 1, Attachment.* New York: Basic Books.

Bowlby, J. (1973). *Attachment and loss. Vol. 2, Separation, anxiety, and anger.* New York: Basic Books.

Bradmiller, L. J. (1978). Self-disclosure in the helping relationship. *Social Work Research and Abstracts, 14,* 28–35.

Bransford, J. D., Franks, J. J., Vye, N. H., & Sherwood, R. D. (1989). New approaches to instruction: Because wisdom can't be told. In S. Vosniadou & A. Ortony (Eds.), *Similarity and analogical reasoning.* New York: Cambridge University Press.

Brehm, S. S. (1966). *A theory of psychological reactance.* New York: Academic Press.

Brown, J. E., & Slee, P. T. (1986). Paradoxical strategies: The ethics of intervention. *Professional Psychology: Research and Practice, 10,* 487–491.

Brown, S. (1985). *Treating the alcoholic: A developmental model of recovery.* New York: Wiley.

Budman, S. H., & Armstrong, E. (1992). Training for managed care settings: How to make it happen. *Psychotherapy, 29,* 416–421.

Budman, S. H., & Gurman, A. S. (1983). The practice of brief therapy. *Professional Psychology: Research and Practice, 14,* 277–292.

Budman, S. H., & Gurman, A. S. (1988). *Theory and practice of brief psychotherapy.* New York: Guilford.

Budman, S. H., & Stone, J. (1983). Advances in brief psychotherapy: A review of recent literature. *Hospital and Community Psychiatry, 34,* 939–946.

Burke, W. (1992). Countertransference disclosure and the asymmetry/mutuality dilemma. *Psychoanalytic Dialogues, 2,* 241–271.

Burlingame, G. M., & Fuhriman, A. (1987). Conceptualizing short-term treatment: A comparative review. *Counseling Psychologist, 15,* 557–595.

Burlingame, G. M., Fuhriman, A., Paul, S., & Ogles, B. (1989). Implementing a time-limited therapy program: Differential effects of training and experience. *Psychotherapy, 26,* 303–313.

Butler, S. F., & Binder, J. L. (1987). Cyclical psychodynamics and the triangle of insight: An integration. *Psychiatry, 50,* 218–231.

Butler, S. F., & the Center for Psychotherapy Research Team (1986). *Working manual for the Vanderbilt Therapeutic Strategies Scale.* Unpublished manuscript. Vanderbilt University, Nashville, TN.

Butler, S. F., Flasher, L. V., & Strupp, H. H. (1993). Countertransference and qualities of the psychotherapist. In N. E. Miller, L. Luborsky, J. P. Barber, & J. P. Docherty (Eds.), *Psychodynamic treatment research: A handbook for clinical practice.* New York: Basic Books.

Butler, S. F., Lane, T. W., & Strupp, H. H. (1988, June). *Patterns of therapeutic skill acquisition as a result of training in time-limited dynamic psychotherpy.* Paper presented at the annual meeting of the Society for Psychotherapy Research, Santa Fe, NM.

Butler, S. F., & Strupp, H. H. (1989, June). *Issues in training therapists to competency: The Vanderbilt experience.* Paper presented at the annual meeting of the Society for Psychotherapy Research, Toronto.

Butler, S. F., & Strupp, H. H. (1991). Psychodynamic psychotherapy. In M. Hersen, A. Kazdin, & A. Bellack (Eds.), *The clinical psychology handbook* (2nd ed.). New York: Pergamon.

Butler, S. F., Strupp, H. H., & Binder, J. L. (1993). Time-limited dynamic psychotherapy. In S. Budman, M. Hoyt, & S. Friedman (Eds.), *The first session in brief therapy.* New York: Guilford.

Butler, S. F., Strupp, H. H., & Lane, T. W. (1987, June). *The Time-Limited Dynamic Psychotherapy Therapeutic Strategies Scale: Development of an adherence measure.* Paper presented to the international meeting of the Society for Psychotherapy Research, Ulm, West Germany.

Cashdan, S. (1988). *Object relations theory.* New York: Norton.

Chiles, J. A., Carlin, A. S., Benjamin, G. A., & Beitman, B. D. (1991). A physician, a nonmedical psychotherapist, and a patient: The pharmacotherapy-psychotherapy triangle. In B. D. Beitman & G. L. Klerman (Eds.), *Integrating pharmacotherapy and psychotherapy.* Washington, DC: American Psychiatric Press.

Clarkin, J. F., Frances, A. F., Taintor, Z., & Warburg, M. (1980). Training in brief therapy: Survey of psychiatric residency programs. *American Journal of Psychiatry, 137,* 978–979.

Cooper, S. H. (1987). Changes in psychoanalytic ideas: Transference interpretations. *Journal of the American Psychoanalytic Association, 35,* 77–98.

Crits-Christoph, P., & Barber, J. P. (Eds.). (1991). *Handbook of short-term dynamic psychotherapy.* New York: Basic Books.

Crits-Christoph, P., Cooper, A., & Luborsky, L. (1988). The accuracy of therapists' interpretations and the outcome of dynamic psychotherapy. *Journal of Consulting and Clinical Psychology, 56,* 490–495.

Cummings, N. A. (1986). The dismantling of our health system. *American Psychologist, 41,* 426–431.

Cummings, N. A. (1995). Impact of managed care on employment and training: A primer for survival. *Professional Psychology: Research and Practice, 26*, 10–15.

Cummings, N. A., & Vandenbos, G. R. (1979). The general practice of psychology. *Professional Psychology, 10*, 430–440.

Curtis, J. M. (1981). Indications and contraindications in the use of therapist's self-disclosure. *Psychological Reports, 29*, 449–507.

Davanloo, H. (Ed.). (1978). *Basic principles and techniques in short-term dynamic psychotherapy.* New York: Spectrum.

Davanloo, H. (1980). A method of short-term dynamic psychotherapy. In H. Davanloo (Ed.), *Short-term dynamic psychotherapy.* New Jersey: Jason Aronson.

Davidovitz, D. (1995). *Prevalence and training in brief therapy: A national survey of psychiatrists, psychologists, and social workers.* Unpublished doctoral dissertation, Wright Institute, Berkeley, CA.

Derogatis, L. R. (1983). *SCL-90R administration, scoring and procedures manual-II for the revised version.* Baltimore, MD: Clinical Psychometric Research.

Devine, J. (in press). Psychotherapeutic techniques in HIV disease. In J. W. Dilley & R. Marks (Eds.), *Facing the future.* San Francisco: UCSF AIDS Project.

Dietzel, C. S., & Abeles, N. (1975). Client–therapist complementarity and therapeutic outcome. *Journal of Counseling Psychology, 22*, 264–272.

Eagle, M. N. (1984). *Recent developments in psychoanalysis: A critical evaluation.* New York: McGraw-Hill.

Eaton, T. T., Abeles, N., & Gutfreund, M. J. (1988). Therapeutic alliance and outcome: Impact of treatment length and pretreatment symptomatology. *Psychotherapy: Theory, Research and Practice, 25*, 536–542.

Emde, R. N. (1991). Positive emotions for psychoanalytic theory: Surprises from infancy research and new directions. *Journal of the American Psychoanalytic Association, 39*, 5–44.

Fenichel, O. (1941). *Problems of psychoanalytic technique.* New York: Psychoanalytic Quarterly.

Flegenheimer, W. V. (1982). *Techniques of brief psychotherapy.* New Jersey: Jason Aronson.

Foreman, S. A., & Marmar, C. R. (1985). Therapist actions that address initially poor therapeutic alliances in psychotherapy. *American Journal of Psychiatry, 142*, 922–926.

Fortune, A. E. (1987). Client and social worker reactions to termination. *Clinical Social Work Journal, 15*, 159–171.

Frank, J. D. (1974). *Persuasion and healing.* New York: Schocken.

Freud, S. [1904] (1953). Freud's psycho-analytic method. In E. Jones (Ed.), *Collected papers: Early papers* (Vol. 1, pp. 264–271). London: Hogarth.

Freud, S. [1915] (1957). The unconscious. In J. Strachey (Trans. and Ed.),

The standard edition of the complete psychological works of Sigmund Freud (Vol. 14). London: Hogarth.

Gabbard, G. O. (1993). An overview of countertransference with borderline patients. *Journal of Psychotherapy Practice and Research, 2,* 7–18.

Garfield, S. L. (1989). *The practice of brief psychotherapy.* Elmsford, NY: Pergamon.

Gaston, L. (1990). The concept of the alliance and its role in psychotherapy: Theoretical and empirical considerations. *Psychotherapy: Theory, Research and Practice, 27,* 143–153.

Gendlin, E. T. (1991). On emotion in therapy. In J. D. Safran & L. S. Greenberg (Eds.), *Emotion, psychotherapy, and change.* New York: Guilford.

Gill, M. M. (1979). The analysis of the transference. *Journal of the American Psychoanalytic Association, 27,* 263–288.

Gill, M. M. (1982). *Analysis of transference: Vol I. Theory and technique.* New York: International Universities Press.

Gill, M. M. (1993). Interaction and interpretation. *Psychoanalytic Dialogues, 3,* 111–122.

Greenberg, J. R. (1986). The problem of analytic neutrality. *Contemporary Psychoanalysis, 22,* 76–86.

Greenberg, J. R. (1991). Countertransference and reality. *Psychoanalytic Dialogues, 1,* 52–73.

Greenberg, J. R., & Mitchell, S. A. (1983). *Object relations in psychoanalytic theory.* Cambridge, MA: Harvard University Press.

Guidano, V. F. (1991). Affective change events in a cognitive therapy system approach. In J. D. Safran & L. S. Greenberg (Eds.), *Emotion, psychotherapy, and change.* New York: Guilford.

Haley, J. (1976). *Problem solving therapy.* San Francisco: Jossey-Bass.

Harrist, R. S., Quintana, S. M., Strupp, H. H., Henry, W. P. (1994). Internalization of interpersonal process in time-limited dynamic psychotherapy. *Psychotherapy, 31,* 49–57.

Hartmann, K. (1994). *Case formulation and countertransference in time-limited dynamic psychotherapy.* Unpublished doctoral dissertation, Pacific Graduate School of Psychology, Palo Alto, CA.

Hartmann, K., & Levenson, H. (1995, June). *Case formulation in TLDP.* Presentation at the annual meeting of the Society for Psychotherapy Research, Vancouver, British Columbia.

Henry, W., Strupp, H., Schacht, T. E., & Gaston, L. (1994). Psychodynamic approaches. In A. Bergin & S. Garfield (Eds.), *The handbook of psychotherapy and behavior change* (4th ed.). New York: Wiley.

Henry, W. P., Schacht, T. E., Strupp, H. H., Butler, S. F., & Binder, J. L. (1993a). Effects of training in time-limited dynamic psychotherapy: Mediators of therapists' responses to training. *Journal of Consulting and Clinical Psychology, 61*, 441–447.

Henry, W. P., Strupp, H. H., Butler, S. F., Schacht, T. E., & Binder, J. L. (1993b). Effects of training in time-limited dynamic psychotherapy: Changes in therapist behavior. *Journal of Consulting and Clinical Psychology, 61*, 434–440.

Hill, C. E., Helms, J. E., Tichenor, V., Spiegel, S. B., O'Grady, K. E., & Perry, E. S. (1988). Effects of therapist response modes in brief psychotherapy. *Journal of Counseling Psychology, 35*, 222–233.

Hill, C. E., Mahalik, J. R., & Thompson, B. J. (1989). Therapist self-disclosure. *Psychotherapy, 26*, 290–295.

Hirsch, I. (1992). An interpersonal perspective: The analyst's unwitting participation in the patient's change. *Psychoanalytic Psychology, 9*, 299–312.

Hoffman, I. Z. (1992). Some practical implications of a social-constructivist view of the psychoanalytic situation. *Psychoanalytic Dialogues, 2*, 287–304.

Horowitz, L. M., Rosenberg, S. E., Baer, B. A., Ureno, G., & Vallasenor, V. S. (1988). Inventory of Interpersonal Problems: Psychometric properties and clinical applications. *Journal of Consulting and Clinical Psychology, 56*, 885–892.

Horowitz, M. (1976). *Stress response syndromes.* New York: Basic Books.

Horowitz, M. (1987). *States of mind: Analysis of change in psychotherapy* (2nd ed.). New York: Plenum.

Horowitz, M. (1988). *Introduction to psychodynamics: A new synthesis.* New York: Basic Books.

Horowitz, M., Marmar, C., Krupnick, J., Wilner, N., Kaltreider, N., & Wallerstein, R. (1984). *Personality styles and brief psychotherapy.* New York: Basic Books.

Howard, K. I., Kopta, S. M., Krause, M. S., & Orlinsky, D. E. (1986). The dose–effect relationship in psychotherapy. *American Psychologist, 41*, 159–164.

Hoyt, M. F. (1985). Therapist resistances to short-term dynamic psychotherapy. *Journal of the American Academy of Psychoanalysis, 13*, 93–112.

Hoyt, M. F., & Austad, C. S. (1992). Psychotherapy in a staff model health organization: Providing and assuring quality care in the future. *Psychotherapy, 29*, 119–129.

Johnson, D. H., & Gelso, C. J. (1980). The effectiveness of time limits in counseling and psychotherapy: A critical review. *Counseling Psychology, 9*, 70–83.

Johnson, D. W., & Noonan, M. P. (1972). Effects of acceptance and reciprocation of self-disclosure. *Journal of Counseling Psychology, 19*, 411–416.

Kadden, R. M., Cooney, N. L., Getter, H., & Litt, M. D. (1989). Matching alcoholics to coping skills or interactional therapies: Posttreatment results. *Journal of Consulting and Clinical Psychology, 57*, 698–704.

Kagan, J. (1989). Temperamental contributions to social behavior. *American Psychologist, 44,* 668–674.

Kelly, G. (1955). *Psychology of personal constructs.* New York: Norton.

Kelly, K. V. (1992). Parallel treatment: Therapy with one clinician and medication with another. *Hospital and Community Psychiatry, 43,* 778–780.

Khatzian, E. J. (1988). The primary care therapist and patient needs in substance abuse treatment. *American Journal of Drug and Alcohol Abuse, 14,* 159–67.

Kiesler, D. J. (1982). Confronting the client–therapist relationship in psychotherapy. In J. C. Anchin & D. J. Kiesler (Eds.), *Handbook of interpersonal psychotherapy.* New York: Pergamon.

Kiesler, D. J. (1988). *Therapeutic metacommuniation: Therapist impact disclosure as feedback in psychotherapy.* Palo Alto, CA: Consulting Psychologists Press.

Kisch, J. (1991). The need for psychopharmacological collaboration in managed mental health care. In C. S. Austad & W. H. Berman (Eds.), *Psychotherapy in managed health care.* Washington, DC: American Psychological Association.

Kohlenberg, R. J., & Tsai, M. (1991). *FAP: Functional analytic psychotherapy.* New York: Plenum.

Kopta, S. M., Howard, K. I., Lowry, J. L., & Beutler, L. E. (1994). Patterns of symptomatic recovery in psychotherapy. *Journal of Clinical and Consulting Psychology, 62,* 1009–1016.

Koss, M., & Shiang, J. (1993). Research on brief psychotherapy. In A. Bergin & S. Garfield (Eds.), *Handbook of psychotherapy and behavior change* (4th ed.). New York: Wiley.

Krystal, H. (1988). *Integration and self-healing: Affect, trauma, alexithymia.* Hillsdale, NJ: Analytic Press.

La Salvia, T. (1993). Enhancing addiction treatment through psychoeducational groups. *Journal of Substance Abuse Treatment, 10,* 439–444.

Lambert, M. J. (1983). Introduction to assessment of psychotherapy outcome: Historical perspective and current issues. In M. J. Lambert, E. R. Christensen, & S. S. DeJulio (Eds.), *The assessment of psychotherapy outcome.* New York: Wiley-Interscience.

Lambert, M. J., & Bergin, A. E. (1994). Effectiveness of psychotherapy. In A. E. Bergin & S. L. Garfield (Eds.), *Handbook of psychotherapy and behavior change. (4th ed.).* New York: Wiley.

Levenson, H., & Bein, E. (1993, June). VA Short-term Psychotherapy Research Project: Outcome. In D. A. Shapiro (Chair), *Long-term outcome of brief dynamic psychotherapy.* Symposium conducted at the annual international meeting of the Society for Psychotherapy Research, Pittsburgh.

Levenson, H., & Bolter, K. (1988, August). Short-term Psychotherapy Values and Attitudes: Changes with Training. In H. Levenson (Chair), *Issues in training and teaching brief therapy.* Symposium conducted at the convention of the American Psychological Association, Atlanta.

Levenson, H., & Butler, S. F. (1994). Brief dynamic individual psychotherapy. In R. E. Hales, S. C. Yudofsky, & J. A. Talbott (Eds.), *The American Psychiatric Press textbook of psychiatry.* Washington, DC: American Psychiatric Press.

Levenson, H., & Davidovitz, D. (1995, August). *Prevalence of and training in brief therapy: Results of a national survey of psychiatrists, psychologists, and social workers.* Presentation at the annual convention of the American Psychological Association, New York.

Levenson, H., & Hales, R. E. (1993). Brief psychodynamically informed therapy for medically ill patients. In A. Stoudemire and B. S. Fogel (Eds.), *Medical-psychiatric practice, vol. 2.* Washington, DC: American Psychiatric Press.

Levenson, H., Speed, J., & Budman, S. H. (1995). Therapist's experience, training, and skill in brief therapy: A bicoastal survey. *American Journal of Psychotherapy, 49,* 95–117.

Levinson, H. L. (1977). Termination in psychotherapy: Some salient issues. *Social Casework, 58,* 480–489.

Litt, M. D., Barbor, T. F., Delboca, F. K., Kadden, R. M., & Cooney, N. L. (1992). Types of alcoholics II: Application of an empirically derived typology to treatment matching. *Archives of General Psychiatry, 49,* 609–614.

Lorr, M., McNair, D. M., Michaux, W. W., & Raskin, A. (1962). Frequency of treatment and change in psychotherapy. *Journal of Abnormal and Social Psychology, 64,* 281–292.

Luborsky, L. (1984). *Principles of psychoanalytic psychotherapy: A manual for supportive-expressive treatment.* New York: Basic Books.

Luborsky, L., & Crits-Christoph, P. (1990). *Understanding transference: The core conflictual relationship theme method.* New York: Basic Books.

Luborsky, L., McLellan, A. T., Woody, G. E., et al. (1985). Therapist success and its determinants. *Archives of General Psychiatry, 42,* 602–611.

MacKenzie, K. R. (1988). Recent developments in brief psychotherapy. *Hospital and Community Psychiatry, 39,* 742–752.

MacKenzie, K. R. (1991). Principles of brief intensive psychotherapy. *Psychiatric Annals, 21,* 398–422.

Malan, D. H. (1963). *A study of brief psychotherapy.* New York: Plenum.

Malan, D. H. (1976). *The frontier of brief psychotherapy.* New York: Plenum.

Malan, D. H. (1979). *Individual psychotherapy and the science of psychodynamics.* London: Butterworth.

Mann, J. (1973). *Time-limited psychotherapy.* Cambridge, MA: Harvard University Press.

Markowitz, J., Klerman, G., & Perry, S. (1992). Interpersonal psychotherapy of depressed HIV positive outpatients. *Hospital and Community Psychiatry, 43,* 885–890.

Marmar, C. R., Gaston, L., Gallagher, D., et al. (1989). Alliance and outcome in late-life depression. *Journal of Nervous and Mental Disorders, 177,* 464–472.

Martin, E. S., & Schurtman, R. (1985). Termination anxiety as it affects the therapist. *Psychotherapy, 22,* 92–96.

Marx, S. A., & Gelso, C. J. (1987). Termination of individual counseling in a university counseling center. *Journal of Counseling Psychology, 34,* 3–9.

McCarthy, P. R., & Betz, N. E. (1978). Differential effects of self-disclosing versus self-involved counselor statements. *Journal of Counseling Psychology, 25,* 251–256.

McCullough, L., Farber, B. A., Winston, A., Porter, F., Pollack, J., Vingiano, W., Laikin, M., & Trujillo, M. (1991). The relationship of patient–therapist interaction to outcome in brief psychotherapy. *Psychotherapy, 28,* 525–532.

Menninger, K. (1958). *Theory of psychoanalytic technique.* New York: Basic Books.

Merikangas, K. R., & Weissman, N. M. (1986). Epidemiology of DSM-III Axis II personality disorders. In A. J. Frances & R. E. Hales (Eds.), *Psychiatry update: American Psychiatric Association annual review* (Vol. 5). Washington, DC: American Psychiatric Press.

Messer, S. B., & Warren, S. (1995). *Models of brief psychodynamic therapy: A comparative approach.* New York: Guilford.

Minuchin, S. (1974). *Families and family therapy.* Cambridge, MA: Harvard University Press.

Mitchell, S. (1988). *Relational concepts in psychoanalysis: An integration.* Cambridge, MA: Harvard University Press.

Mitchell, S. (1994). Something old, something new: Commentary on Steven Stern's "needed relationships." *Psychoanalytic Dialogues, 4,* 363–369.

Neff, W. L., Lambert, M. J., Lunnen, K. M., Budman, S. H., & Levenson, H. (1994, Nov.). *Therapists' attitudes toward short-term therapy: Changes with training.* Paper presented at the meeting of the National Employee Assistance Program Association, Boston.

Neill, J. R. (1979). The difficult patient: Identification and response. *Journal of Clinical Psychiatry, 40,* 209–212.

Ogden, T. (1982). *Projective identification and psychotherapeutic technique.* New Jersey: Jason Aronson.

O'Hanlon, W. H., & Weiner-Davis, M. (1988). *In search of solutions: A new direction in psychotherapy.* New York: Norton.

O'Malley, S. S., Foley, S. H., Watkins, S. D., Imber, S. B., Sotsky, S. M., & Elkins, I. (1988). Therapist competence and patient outcome in interpersonal psychotherapy of depression. *Journal of Consulting and Clinical Psychology, 56*, 496–501.

Orlinsky, D. E., & Howard, K. I. (1986). Process and outcome in psychotherapy. In S. L. Garfield & A. E. Bergin (Eds.), *Handbook of psychotherapy and behavior change (3rd ed.).* New York: Wiley.

Overstreet, D. L. (1993). *Patient contribution to differential outcome in time-limited dynamic psychotherapy: An empirical analysis.* Unpublished doctoral dissertation, Wright Institute, Berkeley, CA.

Palombo, J. (1987). Spontaneous self-disclosures in psychotherapy. *Clinical Social Work Journal, 15*, 107–120.

Patterson, V., Levene, H., & Breger, L. (1977). A one year follow-up of two forms of brief psychotherapy. *American Journal of Psychotherapy, 31*, 76–82.

Peake, T. H., Bordin, C. M., & Archer, R. P. (1988). *Brief psychotherapies: Changing frames of mind.* Beverly Hills, CA: Sage.

Pekarik, G., & Wierzbicki, M. (1986). The relationship between clients' expected and actual treatment duration. *Psychotherapy, 23*, 532–534.

Perry, S., Cooper, A. M., & Michels, R. (1987). The psychodynamic formulation: Its purpose, structure, and clinical application. *American Journal of Psychiatry, 144*, 543–551.

Perry, S. W., & Markowitz, J. (1986). Psychiatric interventions for AIDS-spectrum disorders. *Hospital and Community Psychiatry, 37*, 1001–1006.

Phillips, E. L. (1985). *Psychotherapy revised: New frontiers in research and practice.* Hillsdale, NJ: Erlbaum.

Phillips, E. L. (1987). The ubiquitous decay curve: Delivery similarities in psychotherapy, medicine and addiction. *Professional Psychology: Research and Practice, 18*, 650–652.

Pilkonis, P. A., & Frank, E. (1988). Personality pathology in recurrent depression: Nature, prevalence and relationship to treatment response. *American Journal of Psychiatry, 145*, 435–441.

Piper, W. E., Azim, H. F. A., Joyce, A. S., & McCallum, M. (1991). Transference interpretations, therapeutic alliance, and outcome in short-term individual psychotherapy. *Archives of General Psychiatry, 48*, 946–953.

Piper, W. E., Debbane, E. G., Bienvenu, J. P., & Garant, J. (1984). A comparative study of four forms of psychotherapy. *Journal of Consulting and Clinical Psychology, 52*, 268–279.

Piper, W. E., Joyce, A. S., McCallum, M., & Azim, H. F. A. (1993). Concentration and correspondence of transference interpretations in short-term psychotherapy. *Journal of Consulting and Clinical Psychology, 61*, 586–595.

Popper, K. R., & Eccles, J. C. (1977). *The self and its brain.* New York: Springer.

Pumpian-Mindlin, E. (1953). Consideration in the selection of patients for short-term therapy. *American Journal of Psychotherapy, 7,* 641–652.

Quintana, S. M., & Meara, N. M. (1990). Internalization of the therapeutic relationship in short term psychotherapy. *Journal of Counseling Psychology, 37,* 123–130.

Rau, F. (1989, February). *Length and stay in therapy: Myths and reality.* Paper presented at the annual convention of the California State Psychological Association, San Francisco.

Reder, P., & Tyson, R. L. (1980). Patient dropout from individual psychotherapy: A review and discussion. *Bulletin of the Menninger Clinic, 44,* 229–252.

Renik, O. (1993). Countertransference enactment and the psychoanalytic process. In M. J. Horowitz, O. F. Kernberg, & E. M. Weinshel (Eds.), *Psychic structure and psychic change: Essays in honor of Robert S. Wallerstein, M.D.* Madison, CT: International Universities Press.

Rosenthal, R. (1976). *Experimenter effects in behavioral research.* New York: Halsted Press.

Rounsaville, B. J., O'Malley, S., Foley, S., & Weissman, M. M. (1988). Role of manual-guided training in the conduct and efficacy of interpersonal psychotherapy for depression. *Journal of Consulting and Clinical Psychology, 56,* 681–688.

Safran, J. D. (1984). Assessing the cognitive–interpersonal cycle. *Cognitive Therapy and Research, 87,* 333–348.

Safran, J. D. (1990). Towards a refinement of cognitive therapy in light of interpersonal theory: II. Practice. *Clinical Psychology Review, 10,* 107–121.

Safran, J. D., & Greenberg, L. S. (1991). Affective change processes: Synthesis and critical analysis. In J. D. Safran & L. S. Greenberg (Eds.), *Emotion, psychotherapy, and change.* New York: Guilford.

Safran, J. D., & Segal, Z. V. (1990). *Interpersonal process in cognitive therapy.* New York: Basic Books.

Sampson, H., & Weiss, J. (1986). Testing hypotheses: The approach of the Mount Zion Psychotherapy Research Group. In L. S. Greenberg & N. M. Pinsof (Eds.), *The psychotherapeutic process: A research handbook.* New York: Guilford.

Sandler, J. (1976). Countertransference and role-responsiveness. *International Review of Psycho-Analysis, 3,* 43–47.

Sansone, R. A., Fine, M. A., & Dennis, A. B. (1991). Treatment impressions and termination experiences with borderline patients. *American Journal of Psychotherapy, 45,* 173–180.

Schacht, T. E. (1991). Can psychotherapy education advance psychotherapy integration? A view from the cognitive psychology of expertise. *Journal of Psychotherapy Integration, 1,* 305–319.

Schacht, T. E., Binder, J. L., & Strupp, H. H. (1984). The dynamic focus. In H. H. Strupp & J. L. Binder, *Psychotherapy in a new key: A guide to time-limited dynamic psychotherapy.* New York: Basic Books.

Schneider, W. J., & Pinkerton, R. S. (1986). Short-term psychotherapy and graduate training in psychology. *Professional Psychology: Research and Practice,* 17, 574–579.

Shea, M. T., Widiger, T., & Klein, M. H. (1992). Comorbidity of personality disorders and depression: Implications for treatment. *Journal of Consulting and Clinical Psychology,* 60, 857–868.

Sifneos, P. E. (1972). *Short-term psychotherapy and emotional crisis.* Cambridge, MA: Harvard University Press.

Sifneos, P. E. (1973). The prevalence of "alexithymic" characteristics in psychosomatic patients. *Journal of Psychotherapy and Psychosomatics,* 22, 255–262.

Sifneos, P. E. (1979/1987). *Short-term dynamic psychotherapy: Evaluation and technique.* New York: Plenum.

Silberschatz, G., Fetter, P., & Curtis, J. (1986). How do interpretations influence the process of psychotherapy? *Journal of Consulting and Clinical Psychology,* 54, 646–652.

Sledge, W. H., Moras, K., Hartley, D., & Levine, M. (1990). Effect of time-limited psychotherapy on patient dropout rates. *American Journal of Psychiatry,* 147, 1341–1347.

Sovner, R. (1991). A psychopharmacology service model. In C. S. Austad & W. H. Berman (Eds.), *Psychotherapy in managed health care.* Washington, DC: American Psychological Association.

Speed, J. (1992). *Therapists' practice, training, and skill in brief therapy: A survey of California and Massachusetts psychologists.* Unpublished doctoral dissertation, Wright Institute, Berkeley, CA.

Steenbarger, B. N. (1994). Duration and outcome in psychotherapy: An integrative review. *Professional Psychology: Research and Practice,* 25, 111–119.

Stern, S. (1993). Managed care, brief therapy, and therapeutic integrity. *Psychotherapy,* 30, 162–175.

Stern, S. (1994). Needed relationships and repeated relationships: An integrated relational perspective. *Psychoanalytic Dialogues,* 4, 317–345.

Strachey, J. (1934). The nature of the therapeutic action of psychoanalysis. *International Journal of Psychoanalysis,* 15, 127–159.

Straker, M. (1968). Brief psychotherapy in an outpatient clinic: Evolution and evaluation. *American Journal of Psychiatry,* 124, 1219–1226.

Strupp, H. H. (1955a). An objective comparison of Rogerian and psychoanalytic techniques. *Journal of Consulting Psychology,* 19, 1–7.

Strupp, H. H. (1955b). The effect of the psychotherapist's personal analysis upon his techniques. *Journal of Consulting Psychology,* 19, 197–204.

Strupp, H. H. (1955c). Psychotherapeutic technique, professional affiliation, and experience level. *Journal of Consulting Psychology, 19,* 97–102.

Strupp, H. H. (1957). A multidimensional system for analyzing psychotherapeutic techniques. *Psychiatry, 20,* 293–306.

Strupp, H. H. (1958). The psychotherapist's contribution to the treatment process: An experimental investigation. *Behavioral Science, 3,* 43–67.

Strupp, H. H. (1960). *Psychotherapists in action: Explorations of the therapist's contribution to the treatment process.* New York: Grune & Stratton.

Strupp, H. H. (1993). The Vanderbilt psychotherapy studies: Synopsis. *Journal of Consulting and Clinical Psychology, 61,* 431–433.

Strupp, H. H. (1980a). Success and failure in time-limited psychotherapy: A systematic comparison of two cases (Comparison 1). *Archives of General Psychiatry, 37,* 595–603.

Strupp, H. H. (1980b). Success and failure in time-limited psychotherapy: A systematic comparison of two cases (Comparison 2). *Archives of General Psychiatry, 37,* 708–716.

Strupp, H. H. (1980c). Success an failure in time-limited psychotherapy: With special refrence to the performance of a lay counselor (Comparison 3). *Archives of General Psychiatry, 37,* 831–841.

Strupp, H. H. (1980d). Success and failure in time-limited psychotherapy: Further evidence (Comparison 4). *Archives of General Psychiatry, 37,* 947–954.

Strupp, H. H., & Binder, J. L. (1984). *Psychotherapy in a new key.* New York: Basic Books.

Strupp, H. H., & Hadley, S. W. (1979). Specific versus nonspecific factors in psychotherapy: A controlled study of outcome. *Archives of General Psychiatry, 36,* 1125–1136.

Sullivan, H. S. (1953). *The interpersonal theory of psychiatry.* New York: Norton.

Talmon, M. (1990). *Single-session therapy: Maximizing the effect of the first (and often only) therapeutic encounter.* San Francisco: Jossey-Bass.

Taylor, G. J., Bagby, R. M., & Parker, J. D. A. (1991). The alexithymia construct. *Psychosomatics, 32,* 153–163.

Thackrey, M., Butler, S. F., & Strupp, H. H. (1985, June). *Measurement of patient capacity for dynamic process.* Paper presented at the meeting of the Society for Psychotherapy Research, Evanston, IL.

Thompson, L. W., Gallagher, D., & Czirr, R. (1988). Personality disorder and outcome in the treatment of late-life depression. *Journal of Geriatric Psychiatry, 21,* 133–146.

Truax, C. B., & Carkhuff, R. R. (1965). Client and therapist transparency in the psychotherapeutic encounter. *Journal of Counseling Psychology, 12,* 3–8.

Ursano, R. J., & Dressler, D. M. (1977). Brief versus long-term psychotherapy: Clinician attitudes and organizational design. *Comprehensive Psychiatry, 18,* 55–60.

Walter, J., & Peller, J. (1992). *Becoming solution focused in brief therapy.* New York: Brunner/Mazel.

Watzlawick, P. (1967). *Pragmatics of human communication.* New York: Norton.

Weakland, J., Fisch, R., & Watzlawick, P. (1974). Brief therapy: Focused problem resolution. *Family Process, 13,* 141–168.

Weddington, W. W., & Cavenar, J. O. (1979). Termination initiated by the therapist: A countertransference storm. *American Journal of Psychiatry, 136,* 1302–1305.

Weiss, J. (1993). *How psychotherapy works.* New York: Guilford.

Weiss, J., Sampson, H., and the Mount Zion Psychotherapy Research Group (1986). *The psychoanalytic process: Theory, clinical observation and empirical research.* New York: Guilford.

Weissman, M. M., & Klerman, G. L. (1991). Interpersonal psychotherapy for depression. In B. D. Beitman & G. Klerman (Eds.), *Integrating pharmacotherapy and psychotherapy.* Washington, DC: American Psychological Association.

Wilkinson, S. M., & Gabbard, G. O. (1993). Therapeutic self-disclosure with borderline patients. *Journal of Psychotherapy Practice and Research, 2,* 282–295.

Winokur, M., & Dasberg, H. (1983). Teaching and learning short-term dynamic psychotherapy. *Bulletin of the Menninger Clinic, 47,* 36–52.

Wolberg, L. R. (1965). The techniques of short-term psychotherapy. In L. R. Wolberg (Ed.), *Short-term psychotherapy.* New York: Grune & Stratton.

Wolf, E. (1986). Discrepancies between analysand and analyst in experiencing the analysis. In A. Goldberg (Ed.), *Progress in self psychology II.* New York: Guilford.

Wolstein, B. (1983). The pluralism of perspectives on counter-transference. *Contemporary Psychoanalysis, 19,* 506–521.

Zetzel, E. (1956). Current concept of transference. *International Journal of Psychoanalysis, 37,* 369–376.

Zweben, J. (1993). Recovery-oriented psychotherapy: A model for addiction treatment. *Psychotherapy, 30,* 259–268.

Index